IFIP Advances in Information and Communication Technology

493

Editor-in-Chief

Kai Rannenberg, Goethe University Frankfurt, Germany

Editorial Board

IFIP – The International Federation for Information Processing

IFIP was founded in 1960 under the auspices of UNESCO, following the first World Computer Congress held in Paris the previous year. A federation for societies working in information processing, IFIP's aim is two-fold: to support information processing in the countries of its members and to encourage technology transfer to developing nations. As its mission statement clearly states:

> IFIP is the global non-profit federation of societies of ICT professionals that aims at achieving a worldwide professional and socially responsible development and application of information and communication technologies.

IFIP is a non-profit-making organization, run almost solely by 2500 volunteers. It operates through a number of technical committees and working groups, which organize events and publications. IFIP's events range from large international open conferences to working conferences and local seminars.

The flagship event is the IFIP World Computer Congress, at which both invited and contributed papers are presented. Contributed papers are rigorously refereed and the rejection rate is high.

As with the Congress, participation in the open conferences is open to all and papers may be invited or submitted. Again, submitted papers are stringently refereed.

The working conferences are structured differently. They are usually run by a working group and attendance is generally smaller and occasionally by invitation only. Their purpose is to create an atmosphere conducive to innovation and development. Refereeing is also rigorous and papers are subjected to extensive group discussion.

Publications arising from IFIP events vary. The papers presented at the IFIP World Computer Congress and at open conferences are published as conference proceedings, while the results of the working conferences are often published as collections of selected and edited papers.

IFIP distinguishes three types of institutional membership: Country Representative Members, Members at Large, and Associate Members. The type of organization that can apply for membership is a wide variety and includes national or international societies of individual computer scientists/ICT professionals, associations or federations of such societies, government institutions/government related organizations, national or international research institutes or consortia, universities, academies of sciences, companies, national or international associations or federations of companies.

More information about this series at http://www.springer.com/series/6102

Torsten Brinda · Nicholas Mavengere
Ilkka Haukijärvi · Cathy Lewin
Don Passey (Eds.)

Stakeholders and Information Technology in Education

IFIP TC 3 International Conference, SaITE 2016
Guimarães, Portugal, July 5–8, 2016
Revised Selected Papers

 Springer

Editors
Torsten Brinda
University of Duisburg-Essen
Essen
Germany

Cathy Lewin
Manchester Metropolitan University
Manchester
UK

Nicholas Mavengere
University of Tampere
Tampere
Finland

Don Passey
Lancaster University
Lancaster
UK

Ilkka Haukijärvi
Tampere University of Applied Sciences
Tampere
Finland

ISSN 1868-4238   ISSN 1868-422X (electronic)
IFIP Advances in Information and Communication Technology
ISBN 978-3-319-54686-5   ISBN 978-3-319-54687-2   (eBook)
DOI 10.1007/978-3-319-54687-2

Library of Congress Control Number: 2017933867

Printed on acid-free paper

This Springer imprint is published by Springer Nature
The registered company is Springer International Publishing AG
The registered company address is: Gewerbestrasse 11, 6330 Cham, Switzerland

Preface

IFIP SaITE 2016 was held in Guimarães, Portugal, during July 5–8, 2016. The conference focused on the topic of "Stakeholders and Information Technology in Education". Open to researchers, policy makers, educators, and practitioners, the conference invited presentations on current projects and findings relating to how information technology (IT) in education was being adopted and used by different stakeholders, such as students, teachers, parents, or advisers, for example.

The conference involved 65 participants (including three who joined remotely), from across four continents (Europe, Asia-Pacific, Africa, and America). Those involved came from 22 countries, including Australia, Cyprus, Finland, France, Germany, India, Ireland, Japan, New Zealand, Norway, Slovenia, South Africa, Spain, Switzerland, the UK, and the USA.

Participant submissions covered the five key themes of the conference:

- Linking formal and informal education
- Researching transformation of applications of technologies in educational contexts
- Exploring implications of computer science education
- Preparing a new generation of computer professionals
- Strategic use and professional development in policy and management

Submissions of full papers, short papers, symposia, and system presentations were reviewed by the international Program Committee members and additional reviewers. For presentation, this was done on the basis of the quality of the submission, its relevance and potential contribution to the field, and its potential to benefit others. In total, 48 submissions were involved in a double-blind peer-review process. On average, each paper received 3.5 reviews through this two-stage process, where authors had a chance to revise their papers on the basis of the conference and reviewer feedback. Subsequently, 15 full papers and two short papers were selected for inclusion in this book.

The book is structured into four topical parts:

- The first part focuses on "Developing Practices and Involving Stakeholders in the Field of Computer Studies." In this part, you will find contributions on methodical implementation, introduction to programming, and on competency modeling in the field of computing education. Passey, Hawkins, and Clift report on fathers and male guardians becoming involved in their children's education in primary schools through computing practices; Matsuzawa, Tanaka, and Sakai identify advantages of using block-based visual language for introductory programming; Micheuz explores the challenges that Austrian secondary schools face in implementing computing; Kramer, Tobinski, and Brinda model competences in object-oriented programming; and Holvikivi, Lakkala, and Muukkonen report on outcomes of collaborative practices introduced in undergraduate computing courses.

- The second part addresses "Key Stakeholder Practices in Teacher Training". The focus of this part is the use of MOOCs in teacher training and the design of introductory student teacher education in computer science. Langseth and Haugsbakken discuss the introduction and outcomes of a blended bMOOC in Norwegian teacher training education; Bakki, Cherkaoui, Oubahssi, and George consider enhancement of learner motivation through appropriate pedagogical scenario development in cMOOCs; and Overland explores identities of and subsequent challenges for student teachers in computing.
- The third part deals with "Developments in Educational Management". The contributions in this section focus on the one hand on the digital transformation of educational institutions, and on the other hand on developments in this field over the past 20 years. Breiter explores the challenges of datafication for future educational management; Gajewski considers whether IT tools can address problems of e-cheating; Hernández-Bolaños and Rodríguez-Díaz report how business process management can lead to e-governance in a university; Correia considers the growth of entrepreneurialism in higher education and enterprise preparation of educational technologists; and Osorio and Nieves identify research maturity of IT in educational management from 20 years of conference proceedings.
- The fourth and final part is about "Information and Communication Technologies for Social and National Development". A symposium on this topic was held at the conference. The contributions give insight into this area through various studies, including a number across Africa. Mavengere and Ruohonen explore the role of digital pedagogies in developing collaboration and learning quality; Koivu, Ruohonen, Mavengere, Hederman, and Grimson report on information and ICT skill training needs for health professionals in South Africa; Pankomera and Greunen identify challenges and ways forward for ICT development in the education system in Malawi; and Ogunbase and Raisamo report how a West African Digital University might address needs for increased levels of higher education.

We hope you will enjoy reading this book. We particularly thank the authors for making new insights accessible to us all in this field.

February 2017

Torsten Brinda
Nicholas Mavengere
Ilkka Haukijärvi
Cathy Lewin
Don Passey

Organization

International Program Committee Chairs

Don Passey	Lancaster University, UK
Cathy Lewin	Manchester Metropolitan University, UK

International Program Committee Members

Christine Bescherer	Ludwig University of Education, Germany
Sindre Roesvik	Giske Kommune, Norway
João Álvaro Carvalho	University of Minho, Guimarães, Portugal
Ana Carvalho	University of Coimbra, Portugal
Torsten Brinda	University of Duisburg-Essen, Germany
Nicholas Mavengere	University of Tampere, Finland
Ilkka Haukijärvi	Tampere University of Applied Sciences, Finland

Additional Reviewers

Rakesh Mohan Bhatt	HNB Garhwal University, India
Andrej Brodnik	University of Ljubljana, Slovenia
Maiga Chang	School of Computing and Information Systems, Edmonton, Canada
Sue Cranmer	Lancaster University, UK
Valentina Dagienė	Vilnius University, Lithuania
Birgit Eickelmann	University of Paderborn, Germany
Monique Grandbastien	LORIA, Université de Lorraine, France
Pieter Hogenbirk	Odino, The Netherlands
Jaana Holvikivi	Metropolia University of Applied Sciences, Finland
Anthony Jones	University of Melbourne, Australia
Steve Kennewell	Cardiff Metropolitan University, UK
Tong-Ming Lim	Sunway University, Malaysia
Gioko Maina	Aga Khan Academy, Mombasa, Kenya
Peter Micheuz	Alpen Adria University of Klagenfurt, Austria
Wolfgang Müller	University of Education Weingarten, Germany
Margaret Niess	Oregon State University, USA
Kleopatra Nikolopoulou	University of Athens, Greece
Keryn Pratt	University of Otago, New Zealand
Clark Quinn	Quinnovation, USA
Christine Redman	The University of Melbourne, Australia
Ralf Romeike	University of Erlangen-Nuremberg, Germany
Mikko Ruohonen	University of Tampere, Finland
Eric Sanchez	University of Fribourg, Switzerland

Sigrid Schubert   University of Siegen, Germany
Andreas Schwill   University of Potsdam, Germany
Arthur Tatnall   Victoria University, Australia
Márta Turcsányi-Szabó   Media & Educational Informatics, Hungary
Mary Webb   King's College London, UK
Michael Weigend   Holzkamp Gesamtschule, Germany

Local Organizing Committee Chair

João Álvaro Carvalho   University of Minho, Guimarães, Portugal

Local Organizing Committee Members

Ana Carvalho   University of Coimbra, Portugal
António Castro   University of Minho, Guimarães, Portugal
Leonor Lima Torres   University of Minho, Guimarães, Portugal

Contents

**Information and Communication Technologies for Social and National
Development**

Computer Studies - Developing Practices and Involving Stakeholders

Fathers and Male Guardians Are Important Stakeholders in Children's Education: Do *Lego* Building and *Scratch*-like Programming Activities Hold a Key to Involving Them More?

Don Passey[1(✉)], Gavin Hawkins[2], and Darren Clift[2]

[1] Department of Educational Research, Centre for Technology Enhanced Learning,
Lancaster University, Lancashire, UK
d.passey@lancaster.ac.uk
[2] Learning Technologies, Directorate of Education, Wolverhampton City Council,
Wolverhampton, UK
{ghawkins,dclift}@cloudw.co.uk

Abstract. Previous research indicates positive influences on engagement, expectation and outcomes of learning when fathers and male guardians support and work with their children. In primary school settings, fathers and male guardians are less frequently seen to be involved in educational, school-based discussions and activities. The research reported in this paper indicates how a contemporary project is positively supporting father and male guardian involvement with their children, using technologies (*Lego Technics Mindstorms* and *Scratch*-like programming) as an important medium, where building and programming enable shared and collaborative learning. The findings highlight important ways in which this project is enabling this shared activity learning, through intergenerational learning practices. Clear implications for wider national and international development are raised. Recommendations are offered.

Keywords: Fathers/male guardians · Learning with children · Collaborative activities · Intergenerational learning · Primary school development

1 Introduction

This paper explores the role of activities that support learning, where parents and guardians can work with their children through collaborative endeavour using technologies. Technology can play an important part in such activities; it can provide a medium where children and their parents and guardians can work together, where they can share how they are working as well as working collaboratively on the outcomes of their working. This paper focuses on collaborative endeavours using technologies at primary school level (where children are between 5 and 11 years of age). In this school sector, it is recognised in a number of countries that parents associate with their children's schools often; but mothers and female guardians are more frequently seen by schools coming in

T. Brinda et al. (Eds.): SaITE 2016, IFIP AICT 493, pp. 3–15, 2016.
DOI: 10.1007/978-3-319-54687-2_1

to work with their children, talking to their children immediately after school, and coming into school to discuss their progress. In a study in the United States (US), for example, Rimm-Kaufmann and Zang [1] found that in a sample of parents and guardians from a low-income population, about half of the fathers or male guardians had no contact with the teachers of their children in nursery schools, and only one in ten fathers or male guardians communicated with their child's infant school.

In this paper, we look at a project that has been run in three primary schools in a local authority in England; the project has sought to bring fathers and male guardians into school to work with their children, using technologies as a medium through which shared and collaborative learning can occur. In the project described, a case study has been used to look at activities in two different sites, and identifies outcomes arising. The findings indicate that this form of activity should be considered for wider practice, both to support the current curriculum that is stipulated in England, but also to potentially support engagement and learning between fathers and male guardians and their children more widely internationally.

2   Roles of Parents and Guardians (Particularly Males) in Children's Learning

Parents and guardians contribute to their children's learning, as recognised and measured in a number of past research studies. For example, as Bransford, Brown and Cocking [2] stated in their wide review of school-based learning and effective learning practices in the US: "Parents are especially good at helping their children make connections" (p. 153). The authors suggested that parents and guardians are not only in a position to support their children, but may have important insights and personal knowledge that allow their children to see how to make learning connections, with other contexts and other ideas and knowledge. Desforges and Abouchaar [3], from their review of research findings in this field stated that: "parental involvement in the form of 'at-home good parenting' has a significant positive effect on children's achievement" (p. 4). They concluded that: "In the primary age range the impact caused by different levels of parental involvement is much bigger than differences associated with variations in the quality of schools" (pp. 4–5). In a later review of research on this topic, Harris and Goodall stated [4] that:

> "Parental engagement is a powerful lever for raising achievement in schools. Where parents and teachers work together to improve learning, the gains in achievement are significant. Parents have the greatest influence on the achievement of young people through supporting their learning in the home rather than supporting activities in the school. It is their support of learning within the home environment that makes the maximum difference to achievement." (p. 5)

These authors pointed to the need for forms of interactions between parents and children's learning to be as direct as possible if impact is to arise. In this context, in enabling direct interaction, technologies have a clear and already recognised part to play. But educational engagement of children that will affect their resultant outcomes must go beyond merely having access to technologies, or selecting resources, or using resources that are designed in particular ways, or depending on teachers choosing pedagogies to match learning approaches (as argued and discussed in McFarlane [5], for example). Key influences that bring about wider engagement and enhanced outcomes are socially driven – for example, parents encouraging children by taking note of their work and positively praising them, being present in environments where children's work is seen to be valued, asking questions about their work, or discussing with other children who take interest in their work and take pleasure in their findings (as discussed in government policy documents in England by the independent inspection service Ofsted [6], and by the government education department DfES [7]). In terms of supporting engagement that is educationally effective, parents and guardians can interact socially, while technologies support these social drivers through specific affordances that link and enhance these interactions. In the United Kingdom (UK), the potential for technologies to enhance home-based activities for learners and their parents and guardians has been highlighted by research over a number of years. Early studies explored the potential of the Internet and networking infrastructure, initially linking homes and schools, then using mobile technologies to allow interactions and resources to move via mobile technologies (laptops and palmtops) between schools and homes (described in Passey *et al.* [8, 9]; Kirkwood [10]; Passey [11–13]).

In terms of measuring the impact of home-based engagement on children's learning, Somekh *et al.* [14] explored differences in national test results in 28 schools in England, all supported with high levels of information and communication technologies (ICT), over a 4-year period, comparing them to a group and to national test averages. The researchers reported that while the Test Bed primary schools "were performing less well than matched comparator schools on a range of key performance measures: Key Stage 2 [age 7 to 11 years] English, mathematics, science and the APS [average points score] per institution" (p. 8), that by the end of the project, the shift over the 4-year period from 2002 to 2006 was, for mathematics, 64% to 75% compared to 74% to 73% for the comparator schools.

Watson and Watson [15], in 2011, reported that technologically-based resources can afford choice and self-pacing for learners, indicating that resources can provide opportunities for children to work in locations remote from classrooms and schools. However, the role of parenting itself is clear from the results of other studies. Kiernan and Mensah [16] studied 5,462 children, who were assessed at age 5 years, and with mothers interviewed at periodic intervals. They found that: "children from poor families and those with lower levels of family resources who experienced more positive parenting were more likely to do well in school" (pp. 327–328). Using technologies to support engagement with children's learning needs, therefore, to support and work with effective practices of parent and guardian engagement as well as offering activities that can provide learning support.

Existing research evidence indicates that enhancing parental and guardian engagement in learning practices can enable children to gain from parents' and guardians' interests. They can see and use role models of their parents' and guardians' practices, enabling children to more positively develop their own longer-term practices. As a Big Lottery Fund report [17] on out-of-school-hours learning states with regard to community-linked projects, these: "can help young people to develop their skills, and increase parental involvement" (p. 46). But, as Byron [18] and Plowman, McPake and

Stephen [19]) have pointed out, there is a need to consider the developing social needs and shifting social relationships of young people over time. How technologies support parental engagement and interactions for home and out-of-hours learning contexts of 5 year old children and of 12 year old children should consider their potentially different stages of social development and social relationships with parents and guardians.

In terms of fathers and male guardians, rather than parents and guardians as a whole, Cullen, Cullen, Band, Davis and Lindsay [20], in a study investigating Parent Support Advisor (PSA) pilots in 15 local authorities (LAs) in England indicated limited involvement with fathers in support of their children's learning and learning engagement in homes (as well as limitations in terms of planning for such involvement). Previous studies have shown that father and male guardian interest, high but reasonable expectations of their children, and direct involvement with their children's learning, are all associated with higher levels of test results, better progress in school and more positive attitudes towards future education (see Goldman [21]). The ways that fathers and male guardians can influence their children's learning (and how in some studies this can affect boys rather than girls, and vice versa) is discussed in greater depth in a review by the Fatherhood Institute [22]. However, other studies have pointed to the fact that low levels of father and male guardian involvement (especially during school time) may be linked to working practices, if fathers and male guardians have commitments at those certain times of the day (Peters, Seeds, Goldstein and Coleman [23]).

3   The *Lego* Build and *Scratch*-like Programming Project

While Furlong and Davies [24] analysed the different ways that parents and guardians could work with their children, this activity has taken a project-based approach within the school setting. Project-based activities have been deployed in primary schools to support interactions between parents and guardians and their children, although the range of these activities that involve uses of technologies, as shown by a recent review [25], is much more limited than are the levels of many other forms of resources accessible to learners. The project that is the focus of the research reported in this paper was developed and run by Wolverhampton City Council in 2015 and 2016. Run in a number of schools, the project lasts for 3 to 5 weeks, with each weekly session being some one-and-a-half to two hours in length. The schools identified already had an interest in parental engagement and had previously undertaken programmes focused on improving parental understanding and involvement in basic skills (phonetic understanding, reading with their children, calculation processes, etc.). The senior leadership teams, within the schools concerned, saw the potential to extend existing programmes to include elements of computer science and also offer 21st century skills to parents and guardians.

The schools are within economically deprived areas of the city, with high levels of unemployment, low levels of adult academic achievement and high mobility (including an above average intake from 'New Arrivals' and families with 'English as an Additional Language'). A significant driver for the schools concerned was to ensure that the programme could be accessed by families newly arrived in England and in turn increase access to the school and to educational skills for those families.

In one school (School A), four weekly sessions each 2 hours in length, involved fathers and male guardians with their children:

- Building a robot in week 1. *Lego Technics (Mindstorms)* was used for building the robot, as no explanation was needed for children when they started to use this technology.
- Programming the robot in week 2. *Scratch*-like programs were used for the programming.
- Creating a course and programming the robot to navigate it in week 3.
- Racing their robots on a track, observed by other children and teachers in the school, with time to discuss what they had done in week 4.

In another school (School B), the project ran over 3 weeks, each session being one-and-three-quarter hours in length. The focus and the expected outcomes of each of these sessions are shown in Table 1.

Table 1. Project content and expected outcomes in School B.

Week	Content	Expected outcomes
1	Introductions Initial outline of the project Children and parents/guardians work on the initial build of the basic robot • Build guides are provided • Photograph the process at each stage • Staff to provide support and advice	Parents/guardians and children work together to build the initial robot • Following instructions • Solving any problems or issues • Talking and evaluating their models • Recording of the process
2	Programming Using the model built last week, begin to experiment with the programming application Key commands should be • Directions • Distances • Loop statements • Develop single commands into algorithms	This session will involve lots of trial and error as each pairing develop instructions intended to control their robot Particular outcomes should be • Fewest commands • Shortest routes • Algorithms which loop • Saved sequences Each pair will be encouraged to film their robot's final program
3	'Top Gear Pointless Challenge' A series of challenges will be set up in order to program and control the model around a specific course Navigating around the course will require accurate algorithms and 'points' will be awarded and deducted for speed and accuracy	Apply previous learning in order to solve a range of challenges • Problem solving skills • Speaking and listening skills • Accurate computer programming and measuring of time, distance and speed

The technologies involved in the project were *LEGO Education Mindstorms EV3* and the associated *LEGO Education app*. The *EV3* equipment allows for a program-mable module to be built into a range of models designed to undertake specific tasks.

It was decided to use *LEGO* products as the assembly techniques of *LEGO* are relatively simple and the equipment is designed to involve two people within the build and programming processes. Furthermore, full instructions are provided by *LEGO Education* which encourage discussion and problem-solving during both the build and programming stages of the activity.

Table 2. Project content and expected outcomes in extension project.

Session	Content	Expected outcomes
1	**Robotics** Introductions Initial outline of project Children and parents work on the initial build of the basic robot: • Build guides are provided • Photographing the process at each stage • Staff to provide support and advice	Parents and children work together to build the initial robot Following instructions: • Solving any problems or issues • Talking about and evaluating their models • Recording of the process
2	**Robotics - Programming** Using the model built last week, begin to experiment with the programming application. Key commands should be: • Directions • Distances • Loop statements • Develop single commands into algorithms	This session will involve lots of trial and error as each pairing develops instructions intended to control their robot. Particular outcomes should be: • Fewest commands • Shortest routes • Algorithms which loop • Saved sequences Each pair will be encouraged to film their robot's final program
3	**Robotics - "Top Gear Pointless Challenge"** A series of challenges will be set up in order to programme and control the model around a specific course. Navigating around the course will require accurate algorithms and "points" will be awarded and deducted for speed and accuracy	Apply previous learning in order to solve a range of challenges: • Problem solving skills • Speaking and listening skills • Accurate computer programming and measuring of time, distance and speed
4	**3D Design - Sketch Up** Use of *Google Sketch Up* to produce a 3D design in preparation for a 3D model. The design could be for something at home or a modification to their robot or an artefact relating to a school topic or project	3D design and online modelling skills: • Precise measurements • Visualising models • Problem solving and speaking and listening skills • Software skills (rotation, reflection, perspective, etc.)
5	**3D Printing - Makerbots** Using the activity from last week, the designs will be 3D printed in order that the children can take them home. Designs will need to be evaluated in order that they can be printed, e.g. all points must meet, no free-standing parts, etc.	The 3D printers will accurately print the model as designed so each pair will need to spend time discussing the integrity of their model to ensure that the printer can build up the model in layers: • Visualisation skills • Problem solving • Editing and correcting issues as they arise during the process • Personal resilience

The Learning Technologies Team provided both the equipment and the iPads needed to undertake the tasks and were very much seen as facilitators during the project; helping with the build process and also offering initial and ongoing support during the programming process, although due to the nature of the icon-driven app, very little initial training was required.

Two new projects are planned to be delivered during the late spring and early summer of 2016, with a slightly amended model, designed to extend further some of the skills associated with three-dimensional (3D) design and printing. The project content and expected outcomes are shown in Table 2.

4 Methodological Approaches and Methods

The research adopted a case study approach. As Yin [26] says, "case studies are the preferred method when (a) "how" or "why" questions are being posed, (b) the investigator has little control over events, and (c) the focus is on a contemporary phenomenon within a real-life context" (p. 2). This was exactly the situation the researchers confronted: they wanted to know how this project might be working and why it might be successful or adopted elsewhere; they did not want to intervene within the project activities as it was felt that these should be directed by the children working with their parent or guardian; and the project was contemporary in nature within a real-life school activity context.

The research questions that were identified at the outset were:

- How is this project working for children and their parents or guardians?
- What factors might suggest it could be adopted successfully elsewhere?
- How did children work with their parents or guardians?
- How did the activity fit within a school-based context?

Within this case study, three sites were involved, but the methods deployed to gather evidence in each case were similar. Evidence was gathered through:

- Documentary records of the project run in each case.
- Reflections by project staff involved in each case.
- Discussions with teachers, parents and guardians and children in each case.
- Observations in one case.
- Video reflections from both parents and children.

5 Findings from a Multiple Case Study

In School A, four fathers and male guardians were involved in the four-week activity; in three cases, the fathers and male guardians worked with their sons, and in one case with a daughter. The four fathers and guardians came from different cultural and employment backgrounds. One father was from the Middle East with an engineering background, and three fathers and guardians were from the local area (with White British cultural backgrounds). The children were of different ages; the son of the Middle Eastern father was 7 years of age, while the other children were 10 years of age.

The staff running the project, reflecting on the outcomes from across the four weeks, reported that in week 1, fathers and male guardians tended to lead on the build activity, discussing this with their children. In week 2, however, children tended to lead on the programming, while in week 3 both parties tended to be involved equally. Discussion generally between children and their fathers or guardians was found to be on task throughout these sessions.

Observation of the activity in week 4 showed that fathers and male guardians and children were working positively together. Early in the session, fathers and male guardians marked out the track that would be used for the race. The children tended to start on the programming, taking particular care with the programming needed to move the robots forward particular distances and to move them in different directions – using estimations from their previous trial experiences, both in terms of distance of travel and of angles of change of direction, using trial and error to amend and revise these details in other cases, and adjusting their robots until their movements were matched to their requirements. The ways in which the children and parents or guardians worked together differed in some respects. In one case, the father/guardian looked at instructions for the programming, while the child did the programming. In another case, the father/guardian did the programming, and in this latter case, the child had showed the father/guardian how to do the programming the previous week. He stated that he had no previous experience with programming until he encountered it in this project; additionally, he indicated that he enjoyed the opportunity to engage with this form of activity, however.

Discussions with the fathers and male guardians highlighted how the form of the activity had engaged them positively in working with their children and in coming into the school. One father described how he remembered using *Big Track* in the past, when he was at school. He remembered that buttons needed to be pushed a number of times to direct a robot to move it forward a certain distance. He indicated how he had used this past experience in the current context, and how he had started to apply his experience to the programming he had undertaken the previous week. Other fathers also indicated how their previous experiences and interests had affected their engagement with this project. One parent said that he enjoyed activities that involved building, so had come along as his son also enjoyed this form of activity. Another father indicated how he had a long history of building, using *Meccano* and *Lego*. He said that this, coupled with a personal invitation from a teacher, had influenced his decision to come along. Another father indicated how he felt the activity would enable him to spend time working together with his child. Evidence from these fathers and male guardians indicated that these parents were more willing to participate in these school activities, and they referred to the project as a catalyst.

Since this initial project was completed, two further cohorts of parents and children in this school requested to be involved and they formed cohorts for revised projects (outlined in Table 2 above). The school also identified funding to establish a LEGO Innovation Centre, which will be used both within curriculum time to support lesson-based activities, but will also be available for 'family learning' and extra-curricular activities. An additional by-product will be the availability for use of the Centre for staff professional development (within the school and more widely, sub-regionally).

In a second school, School B, five children were involved; three fathers and male guardians worked with their children (one girl and two boys), while two mothers and female guardians worked with their children (one boy and one girl). As in the case of School A, teachers had specifically targeted these parents and guardians, as they were seen less in the school than other parents and guardians.

In this school, the project staff observed a high level of engagement of both parents and guardians and children. Again, children and their parents or guardians tended to work collaboratively by using their respective strengths and previous experiences. Overall, it was recognised that those who were strong builders were not the strong programmers. Interestingly, the strong builders tended to be the parents and guardians, while the strong programmers tended to be the children. Clearly this pairing provided an ideal grouping for shared and collaborative endeavour. It was also reported that in this school (School B) the pairs had managed to get further with the programming, while children were less successful and less quick in School A. It was felt that part of the reason for this might have been due to changing to use of *iPads* in School B, allowing Bluetooth connectivity to be used to support more rapid testing of the effects of revised programming. With *Bluetooth*, the effects of programming could be seen more quickly. Trial and error, therefore, could be used more effectively, with less time happening between each successive trial.

Since the project, the school (School B) has gained from increased involvement from the parents and guardians. This is explained by school staff, both in terms of increased confidence when talking with staff in school, and in terms of greater comfort arising from their beliefs that the school values their involvement in their children's education. In addition, the school has seen the benefit of 'family learning' activities and is planning further projects and sourcing funding to develop a Family Learning Centre with associated resources and staffing.

6   Discussion

This project meets some the requirements of the current national curriculum for computing in England [27]. Indeed, the role of computing in developing creativity and problem-solving skills is not only highlighted as needs within that national curriculum, but is also highlighted by *Lego* as outcomes that can arise when children use these technologies [28].

However, this project goes beyond meeting the needs of a national curriculum, or even the needs for supporting the development of creativity and problem solving. It does this by adding an important social dimension – enabling fathers and guardians to work with their children in ways that both parties are contributing to a collaborative endeavour. It is not necessarily possible for the children or their fathers and guardians to know exactly which elements they contributed to the final solution; but they can be proud of the fact that they have both contributed, perhaps children more on the programming side and fathers and guardians more on the build side.

From a school point of view, parents and guardians they see less in the school are encouraged through this activity to attend, and to work with their children. This builds their relationships and options for further participation.

An essential bi-product of the project has been the recognition of the importance of educational skills beyond those traditionally associated with parents and children working together (reading, learning spelling-lists, phonic practice, traditional homework activities, etc.). This is important as it heightens the awareness of the 'softer skills' of problem-solving, collaboration and discussion, rather than just the completion of a task set by the child's teacher. It follows, therefore, that parents and children increasingly see the value of such skills and are more often able to apply them to their more traditional homework activities.

Clearly, there is a requirement for schools to make an initial investment in equipment and staff training; however, it is clear that the initial financial investment can reap significant returns, both from an engagement perspective but also from an increase in attainment within the computing curriculum. Clearly, additional research will need to focus on broader attainment measures.

7   Conclusions, Implications and Recommendations

In terms of the research questions highlighted at the outset:

- How is this project working for children and their parents or guardians? Evidence indicates that this was a successful project: children worked positively and were engaged with their parents or guardians; they discussed and worked together to develop a collaborative outcome; they all achieved success in building and programming; they developed skills that met the needs of the national curriculum; and they developed practices that they could adopt elsewhere, including at home.
- What factors might suggest it could be adopted successfully elsewhere? The children and parents and guardians in these schools came from what can be considered to be 'ordinary' backgrounds. If this activity works in this context, then it may well work in other contexts. Parents and guardians who were targeted did come into school, they worked with their children, sharing their skills and understanding, and contributed positively to the outcomes.
- How did children work with their parents or guardians? Children worked positively and were engaged with their parents or guardians; they discussed and worked together to develop a collaborative outcome; they contributed particularly in terms of programming; they developed skills in this respect that met the needs of the national curriculum; and they used creative and problem-solving skills to address challenges that they met.
- How did the activity fit within a school-based context? In terms of the school-based context, this project worked positively. Parents and guardians were encouraged to come into school, and the school could look to develop participation with these parents and guardians beyond this activity.

There are clear implications:

- Schools need to recruit cohorts and could, in some circumstances, target particular ethnic groups, age groups, socio-economic groups, etc.
- Schools need to invest in both equipment and staff time (or use a local support team with sufficient resources to deliver the projects – as in the case of the Learning Technologies Team in Wolverhampton).

Recommendations for policy, practice and research are:

- For policy, evidence of the impact of parental engagement on children's learning is clearly argued; therefore, funding should be made available for schools to initiate such schemes.
- Greater importance should be placed on the 'softer skills' of collaboration, problem-solving and resilience within curricular contexts.
- There should be formal accreditation for both children and parents who complete such projects and also for schools who are willing to commit to a culture of family learning.
- For practice, there should be greater opportunities for parents to become involved in their children's learning within the school day, for example, with mathematics, reading, science days or lessons, where parents are encouraged to work alongside their children. Too often parents only attend school during curriculum time for celebration events rather than to be involved in the processes leading to that celebration.
- Programmes focusing on skills deemed to be essential for employment within shortage areas within localities, for example, engineering and computing skills, should be developed further.
- For research, there should be opportunities for a wider research agenda to investigate regional variations, for example, across the UK and Europe, focusing more specifically on attainment outcomes.
- Opportunities focusing on the contribution of softer skills to academic outcomes.
- Future employment opportunities for parents undertaking this form of project and other family learning experiences.
- The impact of *LEGO Educational* and *Scratch*-like activities within a national curriculum context.

Acknowledgements. The authors would like to thank: the children, parents and staff of Eastfield and Bantock Primary Schools for their enthusiasm and willingness to be involved; LEGO Education UK for providing advice, support and additional resources; and Wolverhampton City Council's East Park Action Group for funding the project reported here and for providing administrative support.

References

1. Rimm-Kaufmann, S.E., Zhang, Y.B.: Father-school communication in preschool and kindergarten. Sch. Psychol. Rev. **34**(3), 287–308 (2005)
2. Bransford, J.D., Brown, A.L., Cocking, R.R. (eds.): How People Learn: Brain, Mind, Experience, and School. National Academy Press, Washington, DC (2000)

3. Desforges, C., Abouchaar, A.: The impact of parental involvement, parental support and family education on pupil achievement and adjustment: a literature review. Report Number 433. Department of Education and Skills, London (2003)
4. Harris, A., Goodall, J.: Engaging parents in raising achievement: do parents know they matter? Research Report DCSF-RW004. DCSF, London (2007)
5. McFarlane, A.: Learners, learning and new technologies. Educ. Media Int. **40**(3), 219–227 (2003)
6. Office for Standards in Education: Family learning: a survey of current practice. Ofsted, London (2000)
7. Her Majesty's Government Green Paper: Every Child Matters. The Stationery Office, Norwich (2003)
8. Passey, D., Forsyth, K., Hutchison, D., Scott, A., Williams, N.: Superhighways Evaluation - Group D - Home-School Links: Final Report. NCET, Coventry (1997)
9. Passey, D., Forsyth, K., Hutchison, D., Scott, A., Williams, N.: Summary: group D - home-school links. In: Scrimshaw, P. (ed.) Preparing for the Information Age: Synoptic Report of the Education Departments' Superhighways Initiative. DfEE, London, WO, Cardiff, DENI, Belfast, The Scottish Office, Edinburgh (1997)
10. Kirkwood, A.: Learning at home with information and communication technologies. Distance Educ. **21**(2), 248–259 (2000)
11. Passey, D.: Developing home-school ICT uses: challenging values and thinking. In: Connected Thinking: Report of a Seminar Organised by the Society of Education Officers. Society of Education Officers, London (2000)
12. Passey, D.: Developing home-school links: implications for learners, learning, and learning support. In: Taylor, H., Hogenbirk, P. (eds.) Information and Communication Technologies in Education: the School of the Future. Kluwer Academic Publishers, Boston (2000)
13. Passey, D.: Developing teaching strategies for distance (out-of-school) learning in primary and secondary schools. Educ. Multimedia Int. **37**(1), 45–57 (2000)
14. Somekh, B., Underwood, J., Convery, A., Dillon, G., Jarvis, J., Lewin, C., Mavers, D., Saxon, D., Sing, S., Steadman, S., Twining, P., Woodrow, D.: Evaluation of the ICT Test Bed project Final Report June 2007. Becta, Coventry (2007)
15. Watson, S.L., Watson, W.R.: The role of technology and computer-based instruction in a disadvantaged alternative school's culture of learning. Comput. Sch. **28**(1), 39–55 (2011)
16. Kiernan, K.E., Mensah, F.K.: Poverty, family resources and children's early educational attainment: the mediating role of parenting. Br. Educ. Res. J. **37**(2), 317–336 (2011)
17. Big Lottery Fund: Building the future of learning: A guide to sustaining out of hours learning. Big Lottery, London (n.d.)
18. Department for Children, Schools and Families: Safer Children in a Digital World: The Report of the Byron Review. DCSF, London (2008)
19. Plowman, L., McPake, J., Stephen, C.: Just picking it up? Young children learning with technology at home. Camb. J. Educ. **38**(3), 303–319 (2008)
20. Cullen, S.M., Cullen, M.A., Band, S., Davis, L., Lindsay, G.: Supporting fathers to engage with their children's learning and education: an under-developed aspect of the parent support adviser pilot. Br. Educ. Res. J. **37**(3), 485–500 (2011)
21. Goldman, R.: Fathers' Involvement in their Children's Education. National Family and Parenting Institute, London (2005)
22. The Fatherhood Institute: Fathers' impact on their children's learning and achievement. Fatherhood Institute, Abergavenny (2010)
23. Peters, M., Seeds, K., Goldstein, A., Coleman, N.: Parental Involvement in Children's Education. Research Report DCSF RR034. DCSF, London (2008)

24. Furlong, A., Davies, C.: Young people, new technologies and learning at home: taking context seriously. Oxf. Rev. Educ. **38**(1), 45–62 (2011)
25. Passey, D.: Inclusive technology enhanced learning: Overcoming Cognitive, Physical, Emotional and Geographic Challenges. Routledge, New York, NY (2013)
26. Yin, R.K.: Case Study Research: Design and Methods, 4th edn. Sage, Thousand Oaks (2009)
27. DFE: Statutory guidance – National curriculum in England: computing programmes of study. DFE, London (2013). https://www.gov.uk/government/publications/national-curriculum-in-england-computing-programmes-of-study/national-curriculum-in-england-computing-programmes-of-study. Accessed 5 Jan 2015
28. Gauntlett, D., Ackermann, E., Whitebread, D., Wolbers, T., Weckstrom, C., Thomsen, B.S.: The Future of Learning. Lego Learning Institute, n.p. (n.d.)

Measuring an Impact of Block-Based Language in Introductory Programming

Yoshiaki Matsuzawa[1(✉)], Yoshiki Tanaka[2], and Sanshiro Sakai[2]

[1] Aoyama Gakuin Univeristy, 5-10-1 Fuchinobe, Sagamiahra, Kanagawa, Japan
matsuzawa@si.aoyama.ac.jp
[2] Shizuoka University, 3-5-1 Johoku, Hamamatsu, Shizuoka, Japan

Abstract. The use of block-based visual language in introductory programming is a popular method in education. However, there is little research which provides evidence showing advantages of block-based language. This paper presents the results of learning data analysis with fine grain logs recorded by students' development environment where the students can select their language in block-based or Java. A total of 400+ students' logs collected each of four years were analyzed. The results show that migration from Block to Java can be consistently seen each year, although the whole block-editing rate was influenced by the method of the instructor's introduction. Though block-editing did not affect working time and Lines of Code (LOC), it could reduce the compile error correction time, whereas using Java requires approximately 20% of compile error correction time for students. We concluded that block-based language worked to encourage students to focus high-level algorithm creation, as well as it provides an advantage to understanding text-based language.

Keywords: Programming education · Block-based language · Learning analytics · Working time analysis · Compile error analysis

1 Introduction

The body of introductory programming is not to develop an understanding of the grammar of particular programming languages, but it should develop the problem-solving skills with computing that is called "computational thinking" [1]. The similar concept has been proposed by the United Nations Educational, Scientific and Cultural Organization (UNESCO), as "designing a task-oriented algorithm" [2]. Both statements include common sense. One is to focus on the thinking and creation of algorithms. Another is that computing is not only dependent upon the use of actual computers, but logical modeling for the required problem-solving.

A use of visual language, especially "building-block approach" [3] is the most popular way to form the learning environment for the purpose of education. Many block-based languages for education have been proposed over more than

© IFIP International Federation for Information Processing 2016
Published by Springer International Publishing AG 2016. All Rights Reserved
T. Brinda et al. (Eds.): SaITE 2016, IFIP AICT 493, pp. 16–25, 2016.
DOI: 10.1007/978-3-319-54687-2_2

two decades, and yet developers continue by trial and error to improve the language using modern software technology. The first workshop specifically block-based language focused was held in the last year (Blocks and Beyond in Visual Languages and Human-Centric Computing (VL/HCC 2015) [4]). The workshop was able to collect a remarkable number of submissions, the participants discussed the design of the next generation of block-based language, including the topic of how to design the tools as a bridge to text-based language (e.g. [5,6]).

However, as the workshop stated "Despite their popularity, there has been remarkably little research on the usability, effectiveness, or generalizability of affordances from these environments" [4], there is little research which provides evidence showing advantages of block-based language. Practitioners using visual programming languages believe that the visual programming approach is an effective way in developing computational thinking because learners can focus on their problem-solving tasks [7]. The block-based language should be used as scaffolding to text-based language. However, the belief is not verified, and the percentage of degree is not clear yet.

Hence, we tried learning data analysis with fine grain logs recorded by students' development environment. We conducted the introductory education using the tools we developed, where the learners can switch their language between visual-block language (Block) and one for a text-based language (Java) by bidirectional translation technology. The data analysis was conducted mainly using the data of time students spent. These include amount of total working time, the time using block-editor, the time of compile error correction. The tile representation of each student shows gradual migration to Java on their own schedule, and reducing compile error correction time shows the success by focusing on high-level algorithm creation.

2   Related Work

There have been many reports of using block languages for introductory programming education [8,9], as well as reports on the development of new block languages [10–14]. Researchers agree that block-based languages feel familiar to beginners, however they are not a standard for use in introductory programming. Not a few researchers/practitioners claim disadvantages of block-based language, particularly that block-based language is different from common practical languages used in industry, so that students have difficulty in moving to text-based programming after their introductory programming course.

Hence, which text-based or block-based language we should use in introductory programming is still an unsolved theme in this field. Lewis et al., conducted direct comparison using Scratch and Logo [15], however, their results were very limited to illustrate the advantage of block-based language. Matsuzawa et al. demonstrated gradual migration from block-based to text-based language using a bidirectional translation system [16]. Although the limitation of the study is that they showed only trajectory of their working time, they demonstrated the capability of transition to text-based language from block-based language.

From the viewpoint of tool proposition, a rich number of tools have been proposed on migration from block-based languages or text-based languages, and it is still growing. Pasternak [17] proposed offering the ability to translate a program written in Block to a program written in Java. Google Blockly [14] can be translated into multiple languages (e.g., into Java-script or Python) from its block representation. In 2012, Dann et al. tackled the problem of figuring out how students can transfer their knowledge of Alice3 (a block-based language) to Java programming, and they reported that experience with a block language behaved as a helpful scaffolding for students learning to program in Java [18].

The present research projects are attempts to raise the "ceiling of programming" up to practical programming levels. One approach is to raise the ceiling of block-based language. Harvey et al. [19] proposed a functionality they called BYOB ("Build Your Own Block") in Scratch. This functionality expands the descriptive capabilities of the block language. The purpose of the project is to support a block language suitable for a wide range of users, from beginners to professionals. The developers of Scratch and Squeak are currently working on a GP project [6]. GP will be the first block-based language written by itself, where learners can explore the entire software system by the level of learners' interest. It means the tool will provide an open-ended, no ceiling environment, where either text-based or block-based is merely one of the representations.

Another approach is to promote migration from block-based to text-based language by making educational scaffolding on the tools. The most popular approach is considered to develop language translation systems. Warth et al. proposed a bidirectional translation system, "TileScript", between a block language and JavaScript [20], although that research verified only that the technical requirements could be met to implement the prototype system. Matsuzawa et al. demonstrated a mutual translation between Block and Java [16]. Similar attempts are growing a variety of languages. BlockPy [5] is designed for education in Python. PencilCode [21] is specially designed for migration to text-based language using modern Javascript technology.

Improvement of the editing environment of text-based language is another approach. One distinction of the BBC micro:bit project described above is providing an intermediate layer of editing system called TouchDevelop, which provides some scaffolding for text editing and, is designed for the migration to text-based language. Homer et al. proposes Tiled Grace, which is a tiled representation of Grace and, was an originally designed text-based language for education [22]. Kolling et al., who is the founder of GreenFoot, proposes the "Frame-Based Editing" [23] where the "frame" is added to support novices with Java.

3   Method

3.1   Tool: Bidirectional Translation System

We conducted empirical studies in our introductory programming class over the span of four years. The goal of the study was to evaluate the impact of

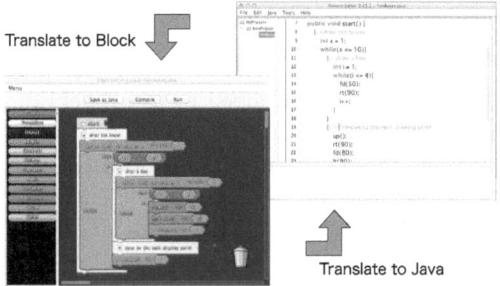

Fig. 1. Bidirectional translation system between Block and Java.

introducing block-based language. In each year, we used a bidirectional transla-tion system between Block and Java proposed in the previous study [16]. The resulting environment has two interfaces, one for the (visual) Block language and one for the textual Java language, as well as a system for bidirectional translation between the two languages. Figure 1 shows the user interface for the environment. All the students in our class were given the opportunity to select the language they used to solve their programming assignments.

3.2 Research Question

In the previous study, Matsuzawa et al. demonstrated that learners would choose to use Block first, which will act as scaffolding for learning programming, and then learners will gradually migrate to Java on their own schedule. We expanded the research to explore the further impact of the environment. The original two research questions for this paper are as follows:

RQ1 Can the gradual migration nature be seen consistently every year, even if some variables change (students, teachers, method of teaching, or tool func-tionality)?

RQ2 Does the tool (BlockEditor) successfully encourage students to focus their algorithm creation by removing compile error correction opportunity? If so, how much wasted time can we save?

3.3 Educational Environment Descriptions

The introductory programming course was designed for art students, rather than for computer science students. Therefore, the objective of the course was to develop an understanding of task-oriented programming. The objective was inde-pendent from any programming language, although Java language was used in the actual environment. Approximately 100 students participated in this course each year; two lecturers and six teaching assistants conducted the class.

Because of RQ1, we conducted an action research. Actions taken each year in our experimental course were listed as follows:

1st year (2012) The first year we started to use BlockEditor with the Block-Java translation system.

2nd year (2013) Major improvements in BlockEditor were made, especially the functionality of the variable scope indicator and the design of the block for method creation. The improvement was made using the method calling navigation system MeRV [24].

3rd year (2014) Main lecturer changed from the author of Block Editor to a teacher who was from outside the research. The lecturer used Java using sample codes, whereas the former lecturer used Block for explanation.

4th year (2015) Compulsory assignments using Block was reduced from 4 times to once. The opportunity for everyone to use Block was reduced.

3.4   Metrics

All the students' activities in the development environment were recorded by PPV (Programming Process Visualizer) [25], and the logs used to calculate metrics to analyze the learning process. We calculated five kinds of metrics as follows for both RQ1 and RQ2.

Working Time (WoT) The working time for each assignment. It was calculated by summing up the time and excluding periods of longer than 5 min with no user operation in the development environment.

Block Editing Working Time Ratio (BWT%) The ratio of working time to block out of the total working time. We can assume students used Java outside of BWT.

$$BWT\% = \frac{BWT(WorkingTimewithBlock)}{WoT} \tag{1}$$

Compile Error Correction Time (ECT) Compile Error Correction time calculated by activity logs for each compilation error occurrence. Further description will be provided below.

Compile Error Correction Time Ratio (ECT%) The ratio of compile error correction time out of the total working time.

$$ECT\% = \frac{ECT}{WoT} \tag{2}$$

Lines of Code (LOC) Lines of Code for finally submitted assignment.

The technical description of the calculation method for ECT was provided by this paper [26]. The difference in time between the error occurred and resolved, will be calculated in a general case. However, sometimes multiple errors occur or are resolved at the same time. For such cases, the system calculates by the amount of time spent in error collection by the number of errors. An assumption of the method is the difficulty of corrections is equal in every case.

Table 1. Descriptive statistics for the calculated metrics.

Year	#student	#task	BWT%	WoT	ECT	ECT%	LOC
2012	102	36	36.7(17.5)	47.9(15.8)	6.8(2.9)	14.3(4.7)	57.9(14.4)
2013	96	38	45.9(23.3)	51.7(25.3)	5.3(2.6)	12.2(4.6)	66.3(36.6)
2014	106	34	29.6(21.8)	44.6(14.4)	5.9(3.5)	14.6(5.9)	65.5(59.1)
2015	100	48	19.2(23.7)	43.4(15.5)	5.8(3.0)	15.1(5.5)	65.7(49.2)
Total	404	156	32.7(23.7)	46.8(18.4)	6.0(3.1)	14.1(5.3)	63.8(43.4)

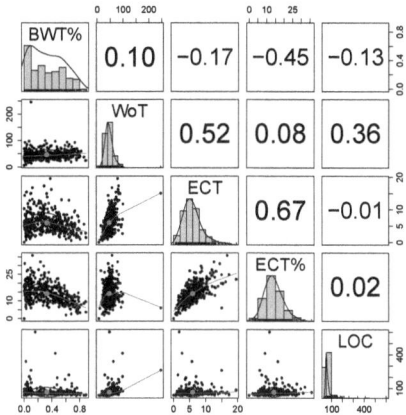

Fig. 2. Correlation table between 5 metrics

4   Results

4.1   Results of Statistics

Descriptive statistics for all calculated metrics are summarized in Table 1. For each metric, the number shows the average of the value, and the number in parenthesis shows the standard deviation of the distribution. The unit of value for BWT% and ECT% is the percentage amount per hundred, for WoT and ECT is minutes, for LOC is the number of lines, respectively. The average of BWT% was 32.7 for all year, although the data for each year indicates the variations in value. The total average of ECT% was 14.1. If we assume that block can swipe ECT, and the fact of BWT%, we estimate the ECT% using Java as approximately 20%.

We calculated Pearson Correlation for all combinations of the 5 metrics, the results are shown in Fig. 2. The most significant result is BET% has a negative correlation with ECT%, which clearly indicates the Block-editing was able to reduce the compile error correction time. The results also indicate Block-editing did not affect working time and LOC, which means that the quality of the outcome by Block-editing is equivalent to the outcome by text-editing.

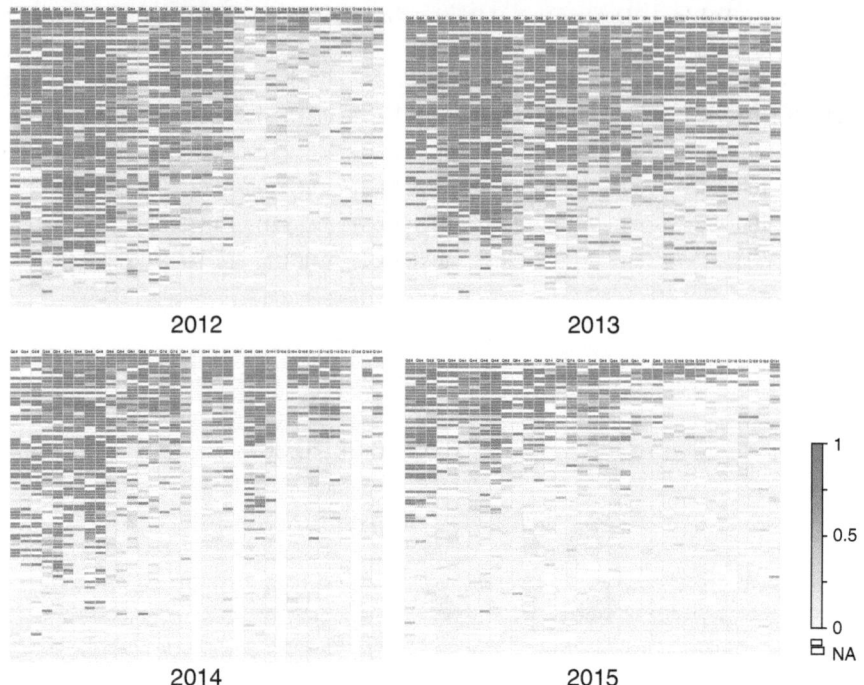

Fig. 3. Grid representation of BWT% (Block Editing Rate) for each student.

4.2 Grid Representations

We created a grid representation of the rate of BlockEditor using (BET%) to illustrate the nature of the seamless migration from Block to Java. The representation is shown in Fig. 3. Each column represents one task assigned to students, arranged in chronological order from left to right. Each row represents one student; the rows are sorted by course-average BET% with higher rows indicating higher average use. Each cell represents the value of BET% for a particular student completing a particular task. High-intensity color indicates a high BET%, and low-intensity indicates an BET% of 0 (i.e., using only Java). We selected 36 tasks which were mostly common for all four years, however three of the tasks selected were lacking in 2014. The tasks can be seen as vertical white belts in 2014.

We can observe that the seamless migration both overall (by the number of students who used Java in the class) and at the individual level for all 4 years were consistent. A sudden drop of the whole rate could be seen in the middle of 2012; however, it improved to a milder migration in 2013. As the class content involved introducing method/function, the improvement was caused by the action of improvement of tool functionality, as we described in Sect. 3.3. Although the pattern of gradation of migration can be seen each year, the entire density is different; 2014 and 2015 are low-density. The density corresponds to the average ratio of the year as shown in Table 1. In the classes of 2014 and 2015, we could

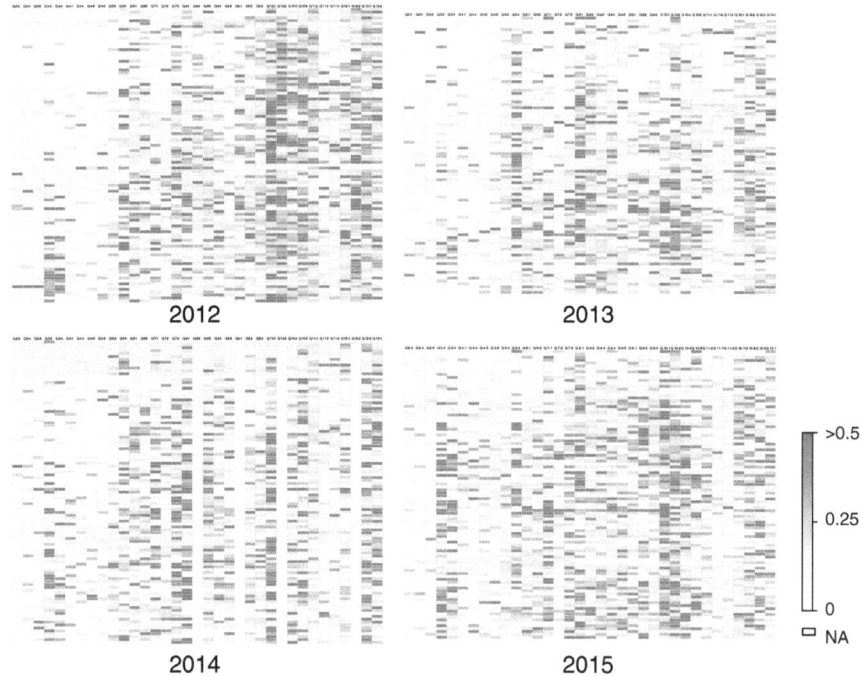

Fig. 4. Grid representation of ECT% (Compile Error Correction Rate) for each student.

not observe any other difference with the exception of the actions described in Sect. 3.3; the cause of the difference is influenced by the method of the instruction by the teacher, and opportunities to use Block.

We created another grid representation using Compile Error Correction Time Rate (ECT%). The representation is shown in Fig. 4. When we compare Figs. 3 and 4, we can observe that inverted illustration. This means the Block reduces the compile error correction rate, the result corresponds with the result of statistic correlation (Fig. 2) and our intuitive sense. Cells with high ratio focus on the latter part of the class (right-side on charts), because more advanced grammar content (e.g. Method/Function, collection) was introduced. Another significant result we can observe is that the factor of task was bigger than the BET% in the past. For example, the latter part of 2012 clearly illustrates that density of ECT% shows no difference between the high BET% group and the low BET% group.

5   Discussion

RQ1 asked "Can the gradual migration nature be seen consistently each year, even with some variable changes?". The results were generally positive: we can consistently see the migration nature. These results reinforced evidence that a block language can successfully act as scaffolding for students learning text-based programming. However, the factor of the method of instruction, especially which language is used in the explanation in the lecture affects the selection of language. The impact can be calculated by comparing the lowest 19% of BET% (2015) to the highest 46% (2013). The result indicate that not only the tools, but also the educational design including the use of tools is important.

RQ2 asked "Does Block encourage students to focus their algorithm creation by removing compile error correction opportunity?". Both statistics and micro-analysis using grid representations indicate that Block clearly eliminates compile error correction time. The result itself is not surprising; however, it is not a small thing that the research revealed the amount (approx. 20%) of overhead which was wasted for compile error correction. We can eliminate 20% of overhead by Block, also can reduce to 10% in mixture usage. Additional observation shows that some students select Block-editing after being plagued with compile error correction. Hence, we concluded that block-based language worked to encourage students to focus on high-level algorithm creation.

The lack of direct evidence of the learners' understanding is still a limitation and requires further consideration. We believe that the results could reinforce existing evidence to encourage teachers who use a block language in introductory programming education.

Acknowledgments. This work was supported by JSPS KAKENHI Grant Numbers JP25730203, JP26280129.

References

1. Wing, J.: Computational thinking. Commun. ACM **49**(3), 33–35 (2006)
2. UNESCO: ICT Curriculum for School/Program of Teacher Development (2002). http://unesdoc.unesco.org/images/0012/001295/129538e.pdf
3. Maloney, J., Burd, L., Kafai, Y., Rusk, N., Silverman, B., Resnick, M.: Scratch: a sneak preview. In: Proceedings Second International Conference on Creating Connecting and Collaborating Through Computing, pp. 104–109 (2004)
4. Turbak, F. (Chair): Blocks and beyond: lessons and directions for first program-ming environments. http://cs.wellesley.edu/~blocks-and-beyond/. Accessed 3 Feb 2016
5. Bart, A., Tilevich, E., Shaffer, C., Kafura, D.: Position paper: from interest to usefulness with blockpy, a block-based, educational environment. In: Blocks and Beyond Workshop (Blocks and Beyond), pp. 87–89 (2015)
6. Monig, J., Ohshima, Y., Maloney, J.: Blocks at your fingertips: blurring the line between blocks and text in GP. In: Blocks and Beyond Workshop (Blocks and Beyond), pp. 51–53 (2015)
7. Fal, M., Cagiltay, N.: How scratch programming may enrich engineering education. In: 2nd International Engineering Education Conference (IEEC 2012), pp. 107–113 (2012)
8. Lewis, C.: What do students learn about programming from game, music video, and storytelling projects? In: Proceedings of the 43rd ACM Technical Symposium on Computer Science Education (SIGCSE 2012), pp. 643–648 (2012)
9. Ozoran, D., Cagiltay, N., Topalli, D.: Using scratch in introduction to program-ming course for engineering students. In: 2nd International Engineering Education Conference (IEEC 2012), pp. 125–132 (2012)

10. Ingalls, D., Kaehler, T., Maloney, J., Wallace, S., Kay, A.: Back to the future: the story of squeak, a practical smalltalk writtern in itself. In: Proceedings of ACM OOPSLA 1997, p. 318 (1997)
11. Scratch Team Lifelong Kindergarten Group MIT Media Lab: Scratch - imagine.program.share-. http://scratch.mit.edu/
12. Cooper, S., Dann, W., Pausch, R.: Teaching objects-first in introductory computer science. In: Proceedings of the 34th SIGCSE Technical Symposium on Computer Science Education, SIGCSE 2003, pp. 191–195. ACM, New York (2003)
13. Cheung, J.C., Ngai, G., Chan, S.C., Lau, W.W.: Filling the gap in programming instruction: a text-enhanced graphical programming environment for junior high students. In: SIGCSE 2009 Proceedings of the 40th ACM Technical Symposium on Computer Science Education, New York, NY, USA (2009)
14. Google Inc.: Blockly: a visual programming editor. http://code.google.com/p/blockly/. Accessed 17 Mar 2013
15. Lewis, C.: How programming environment shapes perception, learning and goals: logo vs. scratch. In: Proceedings of the 41st ACM Technical Symposium on Computer Science Education (SIGCSE 2010), pp. 346–350 (2010)
16. Matsuzawa, Y., Ohata, T., Sugiura, M., Sakai, S.: Language migration in non-cs introductory programming through mutual language translation environment. In: Proceedings of the 46th ACM Technical Symposium on Computer Science Education, SIGCSE 2015, pp. 185–190 (2015)
17. Pasternak, E.: Visual programming pedagogies and integrating current visual programming language features. Master's thesis, Carnegie Mellon University Robotics Institute Master's Degree (2009)
18. Dann, W., Cosgrove, D., Slater, D., Culyba, D., Cooper, S.: Mediated transfer: Alice 3 to java. In: Proceedings of the 43rd ACM Technical Symposium on Computer Science Education, SIGCSE 2012, pp. 141–146 (2012)
19. Harvey, B., Monig, J.: Bringing no ceiling to scratch: can one language serve kids and computer scientists? In: Constructionism 2010, Paris (2010)
20. Warth, A., Yamamiya, T., Ohshima, Y., Scott, W.: Toward a more scalable end-user scripting language. In: Proceedings Second International Conference on Creating Connecting and Collaborating Through Computing, pp. 172–178 (2008)
21. Bau, D., Bau, D.A., Dawson, M., Pickens, C.S.: Pencil code: block code for a text world. In: Proceedings of the 14th International Conference on Interaction Design and Children, pp. 445–448 (2015)
22. Homer, M., Noble, J.: Combining tiled and textual views of code. In: 2014 Second IEEE Working Conference on Software Visualization (VISSOFT), pp. 1–10 (2014)
23. Kölling, M., Brown, N.C.C., Altadmri, A.: Frame-based editing: easing the transition from blocks to text-based programming. In: Proceedings of the Workshop in Primary and Secondary Computing Education, WiPSCE 2015, pp. 29–38 (2015)
24. Ohata, T., Matsuzawa, Y., Sakai, S.: Merv: a scaffold to promote creating 2D map of method call structure in block-based programming language. In: IFIP TC3 2015, pp. 352–362 (2015)
25. Matsuzawa, Y., Okada, K., Sakai., S.: Programming process visualizer: a proposal of the tool for students to observe their programming process. In: Innovation and Technology in Computer Science Education (ITiCSE 2013), pp. 46–51 (2013)
26. Hirao, M., Matsuzawa, Y., Sakai, S.: Compile error collection viewer: visualization of learning curve for compile error correction. In: IFIP TC3 2015, pp. 310–309 (2015)

Curriculum Issues, Competence Models and Informatics Education in Austrian Secondary Schools: Challenges Now and Ahead

Peter Micheuz[✉]

Alpen-Adria-Universität, Institut Für Informatikdidaktik, Klagenfurt, Austria
peter.micheuz@aau.at

Abstract. At the core of this paper lies an overview of recent developments of Austrian curricula issues in the field of digital education. It puts this important part of educational governance into a broader perspective, comprising considerations about the nature of curricula. The coexistence and interdependency between competence models, national curricula and educational standards are elaborated, together with exemplary in-depth aspects of secondary digital education. After critical reflections about the continuing lack of a coherent and compulsory digital education at lower secondary level, recent amendments of Austrian informatics curricula for upper secondary level are presented and reviewed.

Keywords: Informatics · Curriculum · Digital · Competence · Educational standards

1 Introduction

The Austrian school system encompasses elementary level (grades 1 to 4 from the age of 6 years on), lower secondary level (grades 5 to 8), and upper secondary level (grades 9–12/13). Lower secondary level is divided into two types of obligatory schools, namely New Middle School (NMS) and academic secondary schools (AHS), upper secondary level is divided into AHS (grades 9–12) and vocational schools (BHS, grades 9–13).

Since the late 1980s, informatics education in Austrian schools has shown an inconsistent picture especially at lower secondary level. Despite ambitious local, regional and national interventions and initiatives, it lacks still cohesion, consistency and a sequenced structure. Recently, the situation has changed insofar as a framework for digital competences and informatics education has been developed. It should serve as a quasi-educational standard. Schools and teachers are expected to achieve these standards of ICT related knowledge and skills in a cross curricular way.

Upper secondary level provides all students from grade 9 on with obligatory and elective formal IT/informatics lessons which depends on the particular type of school (AHS or BHS). Since more than 30 years nationwide IT/informatics curricula defined a defacto standard for the respective disciplines with different denotations and among other subjects. Since the last decade, a general shift to competence and outcome

T. Brinda et al. (Eds.): SaITE 2016, IFIP AICT 493, pp. 26–36, 2016.
DOI: 10.1007/978-3-319-54687-2_3

orientation also affected IT/informatics curricula. Based on educational standards and competence models curricula have been renewed and revised.

This paper can be seen as a mixture of a current country report underpinned with some reflections on putting curricula issues into a wider context. Obviously (real) informatics education for all starts with grade 9, resulting from a poor curricular support at lower secondary level. There are efforts to provide digital competences for all students at lower secondary, but the competence model still lacks accountability and necessary curricula for the particular grades and age-groups.

In contrast to vocational schools at upper secondary level where IT-related education is obligatory, informatics at the AHS is, from grade 10 on, an elective subject with assumed but not yet validated decreasing enrollments.

After looking at curricula in a general context, this paper outlines the current situation in Austria about ongoing curricula issues within existing frameworks and competence models in the age group 10 to 18/19 years.

2   Curriculum Issues in a Broader Context

A curriculum can be seen as a contract between society, politics and schools/teachers about the way of organizing and providing sequences of learning experiences aimed at producing desired learning outcomes. The curriculum reflects the kind of society to which we aspire [1]. Another definition describes the curriculum as all planned learnings for which the school is responsible and all the experiences learners have under the guidance of the school. Curriculum is the totality of learning experiences provided to students so that they can attain general skills and knowledge at a variety of learning sites [2]. Put in the simplest way, a curriculum is a course or plan for learning [3].

Fig. 1. Poster at Aga Khan Academy Mombasa, Kenya, 2011.

A poster of Kenya's Institute of Education, which I photographed in front of the Aga Khan Academy in Mombasa during the IFIP conference "ICT and Informatics in a Globalized World of Education" in August 2011, demonstrates the importance of curricula issues especially in Kenya at that time. Moreover, it indicates that a curriculum is more than just written paper. As shown in the poster, a curriculum implies other educational areas, including the "core functions" as carrying out orientation for stakeholders, providing curriculum materials, teachers' training, media programmes and evaluation issues.

Curriculum issues and curriculum reforms cannot be judged without looking at the educational system, educational governance and the socio-cultural background, and as mirrored in the model, its range of influence.

For some years, in many countries curricula are interwoven with competence models and educational standards. Not least due to the disappointing results of international comparative studies such as TIMMS and PISA about 15 years ago, educational experts in many countries brought up the idea and concept of outcome orientation and educational standards.

3   Competence Models and Educational Standards

Educational standards can be regarded as precise and binding expectations in terms of competence attainment of the learners. The trigger and rationale for competence orientation not only in Austria, but in other European countries as well, was the need for comparing education systems. The EQF (European Qualification Framework [4]), published in 2008, put this idea into a relevant and influential document. Acting as a translation device to make national qualifications more readable across Europe, it has the potential to relate different countries' national qualifications systems. Although the EQF is voluntary and the member countries are not obliged to cross reference their frameworks, Austria's vocational school system has been strongly influenced by it and adopted its ideas from its release in 2008 on.

In 2011 the Federal Ministry of Education, Arts and Culture released competence models and defined educational standards for all subjects. Exemplarily, the competence model for Applied Informatics in the BHS is shown in Table 2.

Based on this competence model, new curricula have been developed. They represent more or less educational standards which consist of detailed descriptors as chunks of learning objectives. Each of these descriptors is assigned to one blank cell in Table 1. These new curricula are formulated with strict competence orientation [5]. Additionally, the syllabi (list of descriptors) from grade 10 onwards are split into modules for every semester. Accordingly, assessment takes place on a semester basis. Students get

Table 1. Competence model for Applied Informatics for vocational schools

		Action Dimension			
		Understanding	Applying	Analyzing	Developing
Content Dimension	Informatics Systems				
	Publication and Communication				
	Spreeadsheets				
	Databases				
	Informationtechnologie, Human and Society				
	Algorithms and Datastructures				

semester reports with qualifications and rights which were previously reserved to year-end reports [6].

Due to an Austrian common agreement on competence orientation among education experts, not only vocational schools had to switch from input-oriented educational plans to an outcome-oriented approach, but also lower secondary and upper non-vocational education as provided by NMS and AHS. As a consequence, two competence models have been developed.

Finally, the framework for Digital Competence and Basic Informatics Education (left table in Table 2) for lower secondary level has been published in 2011 [7]. It consists of four main categories and four content areas and 70 "I can ..." descriptors. Many sample tasks have been developed to illustrate and concretize the expected objectives and competencies within the Austrian project "DIGIKOMP" and the campaign "No child without digital competence" [8, 9]. It is worth mentioning that this competence model for lower secondary education, in contrast to other traditional subjects, has been developed without referring to an existing respective national core curriculum.

Table 2. Competence Models for General Secondary Education (grades 5–12)

Left table:

	Content	Levels of Competences		
		Knowing Understanding	Applying Designing	Reflecting Evaluating
Media Reflexion Related Topics	**Information Technology, Human and Society**			
	Impact of IT in Society			
	Responsibility in Using IT			
	Privacy and Data Security			
	Developments and Vocational Perspectives			
Digital Media Knowledge	**Informatics Systems**			
	Technical Components and their Use			
	Design and Use of Personal Information Systems			
	Data Exchange in Networks			
	Human-Machine Interface			
Use and Production of Digital Media	**Software Applications**			
	Documentation, Publication und Presentation			
	Calculation and Visualization			
	Search, Selection and Organisation of Information			
	Communication and Cooperation			
Principles and Computational Thinking	**Informatics Concepts**			
	Representation of Information			
	Structuring of Data			
	Automatization of Instructions			
	Coordination and Controlling of Processes			

Right table:

	Content	Levels of Competences		
		Knowing Understanding	Applying Designing	Reflecting Evaluating
Media Reflexion Related Topics	**Information Technology, Human and Society**			
	Impact of IT in Society			
	Responsibility in Using IT			
	Privacy and Data Security			
	History of Computing			
	Vocational Perspectives			I can reflect my responsibility when using IT systems in terms of quality and quantity. I can evaluate and recommend various measures to protect data and IT systems.
Digital Media Knowledge	**Informatics Systems**			
	Technical Basics and Functionalities			
	Operating Systems and Software			
	Networks			
	Human Computer Interaction			
Use and Creation of Digital Products	**Applied Informatics**			
	Production of Digital Artefacts			
	Calculation Models and Visualization			
	Search, Selection and Organisation of Information			I can design calculation models for solving problems. I can analyse data with specific software. I can visualize data appropriately.
	Communication and Cooperation			
Principles and Software Development	**Practical Informatics**			
	Concepts of Information Processing			
	Algorithms, Data Structures and Programming			
	Data Models and Databases			
	Intelligent Systems	I can explain important technical terms and concepts in the context of tables. I can describe, explain and sketch database models and relations between tables.		

One function of this model is to provide schools with guidance for implementing educational objectives. These can serve as a road map for policy makers, teachers, pupils and parents as well. A second is to form a basis for assessing educational outcomes in terms of widely accepted objectives [9, 13]. The competence model and its objectives can also provide an orientation for individual diagnosis and supplementary support measures.

Although there has been a broad agreement and commitment for "No child without digital competences" among many stakeholders, the challenge still remains to turn these designed ideas in the form of a competence model into a set of teaching practices. This will require much effort in terms of pre- and in-service training and the readiness of schools and teachers to achieve this goal.

One current approach, especially in the NMS, is a planning grid where teachers in all disciplines are invited to carry out selected and prepared tasks. By now, more than 200 sample tasks and assignments have been developed by teachers. They are published under a CC license on an official website [9]. Each task provides a range of variable learning objectives of the competence model. It is up to the teachers to find good progression pathways to cover as many learning objectives as possible.

Among many experts in Austria there is a concern that this cross curricular approach without a sequenced curriculum for the grades 5–8 and without a respective subject in its own right cannot be successful. A commissioned evaluation conducted by the Austrian educational institute BIFIE [10] could give an answer.

In the past and currently, still many schools in Austria offer formal IT and informatics lessons on an elective level and based on autonomous curricula. Together with a half-hearted implementation of DIGIKOMP (for lower secondary education) this leads necessarily to an undesirable patchwork and thus to an institutionalized digital gap between schools and pupils at an age of 14 years.

One key challenge in Austria's educational system is definitely to be clear about the necessity of a systematic and curricular-based implementation of digital competence for all pupils at lower secondary level.

4   Curricula for Upper (General) Secondary Education

4.1   Curriculum for the Obligatory Subject Informatics in the 9th Grade

Secondary academic schools (AHS, Gymnasium) provide a broad general secondary education at pre-university level for grades 5–12. Since the late 1980s, informatics has been compulsory in grade 9 and elective in the grades 10–12. Due to a major reform of the school leaving certification process (Matura) in 2015, there is a need for new competence oriented curricula, based on the existing competence model for upper secondary level (right grid in Table 1). Its similarity with the competence model for lower secondary level is obvious and intended. There are only a few changes in denotations which indicate the shift from digital competence (IT literacy) and ICT at lower secondary level to informatics at secondary level. This model consists of four categories, each further divided into four independent areas. Eighty descriptors in the form of "I can …" statements describe the competences, providing more detailed information about the objectives and the corresponding topics and serving as the basis for the new competence oriented informatics curriculum in the 9th grade. This should provide teachers and students with a comprehensive and clear picture of informatics.

The competence oriented curriculum for grade 9 which is an amalgam of the old curriculum of 2003 [11] and the competence model in Fig. 1, is in review for approval and will be enacted from the school year 2016/2017 on. Its subject matters and competencies (Table 3.) mirror the competence model in Table 2. Considering the fact that there are only two hours of lessons per week, it covers a very wide range of contents.

For many pupils aged 15 years this is the first contact with formal informatics lessons. Therefore, it may be questioned if the broad content including many objectives of this curriculum is overloaded.

Table 3. Contents of the curriculum in grade 9

Informatics, Human and Society
- Students describe the importance of computer science in society, evaluate its impact on individuals and society and examine exemplarily the advantages and disadvantages of digitalization
- They take measures and apply legal principles related to data security, privacy and copyright issues
- They describe and evaluate the development of computer science
- They know professions related to Informatics and applications of Informatics in various occupational areas
Informatics Systems
- Students describe and explain the structure of digital devices
- They explain the functionality of informatics systems
- They explain the basics of operating systems and handle graphical user interface and utilities
- They describe the basics of networked computers
Applied Informatics
- Students use standard software for communication and documentation as well as for the creation, publication and multimedia presentations of their own works
- They apply standard software for calculating and visualizing
- They know the basics of information management and use suitable software for the organization of their learning
- They can explore sources of information, systemize, structure, evaluate, process digital content and apply different representations of information
Practical Informatics
- Students explain terms and basic concepts of Informatics and put them into context
- They understand, design and represent algorithms and implement them in a programming language
- They explain basic principles of automata, data structures and programs
- They use data bases and design simple data models

Each intended curriculum is at first sight a theoretical plan which has to be implemented and achieved in practice. A pilot study about the contents taught in four elected schools has been conducted in the school year 2013/2014 and yielded interesting insights. The data were collected after an informed consent of the schools from the central database of an Austrian wide digital class register. Most academic secondary schools have outsourced the documentation of taught contents. Teachers have to record the subject matter they teach each week. Therefore, this central database provides a rich source of data which can be compared to the specification of content in the respective curriculum.

The word cloud (Fig. 2) gives an impression of the subject matter covered (or at least recorded as covered) by informatics teachers. It is striking that there is very little programming or databases. Standard software widely dominates the content. Although the sample of data is very small and needs to be extended to yield valid results, the assumption that informatics in grade 9 is mainly application driven has been confirmed.

Fig. 2. Contents taught in informatics lessons in grade 9 of four Austrian schools.

At this point it is opportune to point at different views on curriculum levels. The intended curriculum is content specific by the state, district or school to be addressed in a particular course or at a particular grade level. The implemented curriculum is content actually delivered by the teacher, and the attained curriculum is actually learned by the students [12].

Table 4 illustrates the long way from the intended curriculum to its way into the brains of the learners where effective curricula with the status "attained" leave something magic called "competence".

Table 4. Typology of curriculum representations [17]

INTENDED	Ideal	Vision (rationale or basic philosophy underlying a curriculum)
	Formal/Written	Intentions as specified in curriculum documents/ materials
IMPLEMENTED	Perceived	Curriculum as interpreted by its users (especially teachers)
	Operational	Actual process of teaching and learning (curriculum-in-action)
ATTAINED	Experiential	Learning experiences as perceived by learners
	Learned	Resulting learning outcomes of learners

The analyzed empirical data in the word cloud in Fig. 2 can be unambiguously assigned to the implemented and perceived curriculum. It shows how the teacher in grade 9 interprets the curriculum, but it does not tell us anything about the attained curriculum and the learning outcomes of the students.

These measurable learning outcomes are at the core of the idea of competence orientation. This is represented by the top dimension "consequences" of the Darmstadt Model, whereas the operational and experimental stage can be subsumed under the "decision area", the "battle zone" in the class where the curriculum meets the students in concrete lessons.

4.2   Informatics from Grade 10 to 12 as an Elective Subject

Influenced by the Austrian vocational education system, all curricula including the elective subject informatics for grades 10–12 in the AHS (Gymnasium) have undergone revisions. After an evaluation process the revised informatics curriculum will be implemented from the school year 2017/2018 on in grade 10, affecting the teaching and learning plans for all students who will choose this subject then.

A newly designed competence oriented oral final examination (so-called Matura) has been implemented and were conducted for the first time at the end of 2014/15 [13]. Oddly, these competence oriented exams took place before the new competence based curricula had been enacted. Despite these obvious formal deficiencies ("old curriculum and new Matura"), a nationwide cursory evaluation of the oral Informatics Matura yielded no obvious problems. Apparently, the competence model [11] sufficed as a reasonable basis and the old curriculum which has been implemented in 2003 is without constraints. It comprises eleven different topics, without any further specifications when and to what depth to teach the following broad topics:

Basic principles of information processing, concepts of operating systems, construction and operation of networks, databases, learning and work organization, concepts of programming, artificial intelligence, expansion of theoretical and technical foundations of computer science, basic algorithms and data structures, computer science, society and the world of work and legal issues.

Teachers are currently responsible for the selection and sequencing of these topics in combination with appropriate software tools. Together with the competence model, these topics serve as the basis for the oral Matura.

Readjusting curricula for the sake of alignment with the new Matura is just one reason for the recently revised informatics curriculum. The other one is a further reform ahead, namely "Modularization" in analogy to the reform in the BHS. This means also for the AHS that all syllabi including informatics from grade 10 onwards have to be split into modules for every semester, and assessment will take place on a semester basis similar to the practice at university level.

The replacement of the old curriculum with the significantly new one has been accomplished recently and waits for approval. Its implications for teachers and students will be substantial. The freedom of planning lessons for three years with broad topics will be replaced by six semesters with preset learning objectives and self-contained modules. Table 5 shows the proposed distribution of content areas. The numbers in brackets indicate the number of descriptors which put the learning objectives into more concrete terms.

Table 5. Distribution of content areas on a semester basis.

Grade Semester	Social Informatics	Technical Informatics	Applied Informatics	Practical Informatics	Legend
Grade 12 Sem 2	Integration of topics and content, repetition				**Social Informatics** Relevance of IT (RIT), Privacy/Data security (PDS), History of IT (HIS), Vocational Perspectives (VOC))
Grade 12 Sem 1	L1 RIT (2) L2 PDS (6) L2 HIS (1)	L4 SYS (1) L2 OSS (2) L1 HMI (1)	L1 COM (1)	L2 CON (3) L4 ADP (6) L1 INS (3)	**Informatics Systems** Structure and Function of IT-Systems (SYS), Operating Systems and Software (OSS), Networks (NET), Human-Computer-Interface (HMI))
Grade 11 Sem 2	L1 PDS (1) L1 HIS (2) L1 VOC (3)	L3 SYS (2) L2 NET (3)		L1 CON (2) L3 ADP (3)	**Applied Informatics** Production of Digital Media (PDM), Spreadsheets and Visualizing (SPV), Search, Selection and Organisation of Information (SSO), Communication and Cooperation (COM))
Grade 11 Sem 1		L2 SYS (1)	L1 SSO (3) L2 SPV (2)	L2 ADP (2) L1 DBS (4)	**Practical Informatics**
Grade 10 Sem 2		L1 NET (3)	L1 SPV (3)	L2 ADP (2)	Concepts of Information Processing (CON), Algorithms, Datastructures and Programming (ADP) , Data models and Database Systems (DBS), Intelligent Systems (INS))
Grade 10 Sem 1		L1 SYS (2) L1 OSS (3)	L1 PDM (3) L1 COC (2)	L1 ADP (3)	

All 16 main content areas from the existing competence model in Table 1 are represented. Algorithms, data structures and programming (ADP) can be found in all semesters with 16 out of 71 descriptors, covering a constitutive part of informatics. The topic databases (DBS) with 4 descriptors is provided to be taught only in the first semester of grade 11.

Actually, this proposed curriculum is essentially a rearrangement of the competence model and its content areas and learning objectives into 5 semesters. The last semester in grade 12 is intended to serve for integrating and repeating the subject areas.

The next years will prove if and how this loss of freedom for teachers in planning informatics lessons throughout three years will be commonly accepted.

5   Discussion

Curriculum issues play a very important role in any educational system, in particular with respect to informatics education. In contrast to other traditional disciplines and due to a comparatively new and still dynamic and fuzzy field, the challenges now and ahead are considerable.

> *"Given the importance of informatics as the scientific and engineering basis for the information society, and the ubiquitous political discourse about the importance of innovation, high technology and IT, one might expect that informatics education would by now have found its natural place in the curriculum of industrialized countries, particularly in Europe. Unfortunately, and paradoxically, this is not the case. In fact, informatics education has retreated in most European curricula since pioneering efforts in the 1970 and 1980s".*

This citation from Informatics-Europe [15] can be applied in particular to the Austrian situation. From the perspective of experts, it expresses concerns about the insufficient representation of digital education at all levels of school education except for special areas of vocational education. However, the next years with approved new curricula, accompanied by professional teachers training and appropriate teaching material, will be a challenge.

Seen from a more general and abstract point of view, there is evidence that a certain "vocationalization" of general school curricula not only in the field of informatics takes place [16], a phenomenon which is also addressed in this paper. The shift of from education (in German "Bildung") to an unconditioned and maybe exaggerated competence orientation, to a sort of "utilitarism" and a loss of teaching freedom are increasingly discussed by some teachers and education experts.

Finally, some questions are still up to discussion. Who controls and influences the expert groups who develop models and curricula? Who is in charge for the implementation, and above all, how it is ensured that the enacted models, curricula and educational standards correspond with the teachers' expectations and students' attainments? Obviously, these questions also apply to traditional subjects. With respect to informatics and digital education, we should be, in the first place, so modest to agree at least on a widely accepted balanced curricular coverage of secondary education.

References

1. UNESCO: Training Tools for Curriculum Development. A Resource Pack, http://www.ibe.unesco.org
2. Marsh, C.J., Willis, G.: Curriculum: Alternative Approaches (1999)
3. Taba, H.: Curriculum development: theory and practice. Harcourt, Brace & World, New York (1962)
4. EQF – European Qualification Framework (2008). http://www.accreditedqualifications.org.uk/european-qualifications-framework-eqf.html
5. Brunner, M., Angelo, M.: Competence orientation in vocational schools – the case of industrial information technology in austria. In: Gülbahar, Y., Karataş, E. (eds.) ISSEP 2014. LNCS, vol. 8730, pp. 88–99. Springer, Heidelberg (2014). doi:10.1007/978-3-319-09958-3_9
6. Federal Ministry of Education and Women's Affairs, General Directorate for Vocational Education and Training, Adult Education and School Sports: VET schools and colleges in Austria. Information brochure. https://www.abc.berufsbildendeschulen.at/download/2032/E_Gesamtbroschüre.pdf
7. Micheuz, P.: A competence-oriented approach to basic informatics education in austria. In: Kalaš, I., Mittermeir, R.T. (eds.) ISSEP 2011. LNCS, vol. 7013, pp. 43–55. Springer, Heidelberg (2011). doi:10.1007/978-3-642-24722-4_5
8. Micheuz, P.: Towards a competence model for ICT and Informatics in general education at secondary level. In: Manchester Metropolitan University (ed.) IFIP Working Conference. Addressing Educational Challenges: The Role of ICT. Manchester Metropolitan University, Manchester, pp. 12–21 (2012)
9. DIGIKOMP. http://www.digikomp.at
10. BIFIE. http://www.bifie.at
11. Informatics Curriculum Upper Secondary Level Austria (2003). http://www.bmbwk.gv.at/medienpool/11866/lp_neu_ahs_14.pdf
12. Marzano, R.: What works in schools? What Works in Schools: Translating Research Into Action, Verlag SCD (2003)
13. Micheuz, P., Sabitzer, B.: Selected spotlights on informatics education in Austrian schools. In: Proceedings of the ISSEP 2015 Conference, Ljubljana, pp. 153–164 (2015). https://issep15.fri.uni-lj.si/files/issep2015-proceedings.pdf
14. Bundesministerium für Bildung und Frauen: Die kompetenzorientierte Reifeprüfung Informatik (2013). https://www.bmbf.gv.at/schulen/unterricht/ba/reifepruefung_ahs_lfinf_24984.pdf
15. Informatics-Europe: Informatics education report. http://europe.acm.org/iereport/informatics-education.html

16. Mintz, S., Tirozzi, G., Holsinger, D.B: Secondary Education. In: Encyclopedia of Education (2002). http://www.encyclopedia.com/doc/1G2-3403200550.html

17. Akker, J.: A curriculum perspective on plurilingual education, for the document "Guide for the development and implementation of curricula for plurilingual and intercultural education". Published by the Council of Europe (2010)

18. McCartney, R., Tennenberg, J.: ACM Transactions on Computing Education (TOCE) - Special Issue on Computing Education in (K-12) Schools, **14**(2) (2014)

19. Digicheck – Austrian Questionnaire for Digital Competences (Lower secondary Level). http://digikomp8.digicheck.at

Modelling Competency in the Field of OOP: From Investigating Computer Science Curricula to Developing Test Items

Matthias Kramer[1(✉)], David Tobinski[2], and Torsten Brinda[1]

[1] Computing Education Research Group, University of Duisburg-Essen, Essen, Germany
{matthias.kramer,torsten.brinda}@uni-due.de
[2] Cognitive and Educational Psychology, University of Duisburg-Essen, Essen, Germany
david.tobinski@uni-due.de

Abstract. In this paper, we describe the results of a thorough analysis of 44 K12 computer science curricula and standards documents conducted as part of an ongoing research project aiming at the development of a competency structure model and measurement instruments in the field of object-oriented programming (OOP). The curricula analysis builds upon a first model draft derived theoretically from a literature analysis in prior work. The model draft is 4-dimensional and consists of the four competency dimensions (1) OOP knowledge and skills, (2) Mastering representation, (3) Cognitive processes and (4) Metacognitive processes. We used these dimensions and the belonging sub-dimensions as a coding scheme and coded competency facets concerning OOP contained in the curricula and standards documents using the method of qualitative content analysis according to Mayring. This way, we could firstly successfully prove the curricular validity of our model draft and secondly, after a step of paraphrasing the identified competency facets, use these descriptions to initiate the process of item development to operationalize our competency model draft.

Keywords: Competency modelling · Item development · Competency measurement · Object-oriented programming · K12 education

1 Introduction

One of the current trends in educational research is the defining and measuring of learning outcomes in terms of competencies [1, 2]. Besides various competency modelling approaches in different disciplines in Germany (e.g. [3–5]), on an international level a lot of research has been performed in the context of the Programme for International Student Assessment (PISA) by the Organisation for Economic Co-operation and Development (OECD) which – since the year 2000 – focusses every three years on competencies in the areas of mathematics, science and language. Formerly defined post-hoc (e.g. [6]), the assessed competencies now rely partly on empirically founded competency models [7]. The results of these regular assessments are used to compare the educational levels of different countries or federal states. An expertise which analysed the

© IFIP International Federation for Information Processing 2016
Published by Springer International Publishing AG 2016. All Rights Reserved
T. Brinda et al. (Eds.): SaITE 2016, IFIP AICT 493, pp. 37–46, 2016.
DOI: 10.1007/978-3-319-54687-2_4

"shocking" results (at least from the German perspective) of the first PISA studies under consideration of the different national educational systems came to the key conclusion that those countries performed best which oriented their educational systems at the intended learning outcomes [8] (and not at detailed curricula as before) and recommended (besides other aspects) the development of empirically founded competency models for all educational fields.

Concerning computer science education (CSE), the demand for competency models is still up to date. Although different normative models have been developed as educational standards in the past years (e.g. [9, 10]), empirically founded competency models in the CSE field are still rare (e.g. [4]). So, we have started a project to develop such a competency structure model and appropriate measuring instruments for the field of object-oriented programming (OOP), which is widely included in many K12 computer science curricula worldwide. The long-term goal of this research is to develop instruments to compare the learning outcomes in the CSE field nationally and internationally between different student populations.

2 Background and Related Work

2.1 On the Concept of Competency

In the context of competency modelling and assessment the term competency is often used according to the definition of Weinert. In his expertise for the OECD [11] he defined competencies 2001 as "the cognitive abilities and skills possessed by or able to be learned by individuals that enable them to solve particular problems, as well as the motivational, volitional and social readiness and capacity to use the solutions successfully and responsibly in variable situations". Despite the awareness that metacognitive factors can have major impact on learning results, these aspects of competencies are quite difficult to assess. Hence, Klieme et al. used a more economic definition in a priority programme of the German research foundation on competency modelling by defining competencies as "context-specific, cognitive dispositions of achievement which are functionally related to situations and requirements of certain domains in the sense of specific learning and action fields" [12]. In this context, competency models are used to describe the cognitive dispositions that learning individuals need to solve tasks and problems in a specific content or requirement area. Klieme et al. distinguish between modelling the structure, the level and the development of competencies in corresponding competency models [1]. Schecker and Parchmann [13] distinguish between normative (which describe the behaviour learners should show after a specific period of education, usually found in educational standards) and descriptive competency structure models (which describe the cognitive processes that occur in specific learning situations).

2.2 The COMMOOP Project

Our project COMMOOP aims to develop a normative competency structure model [1, 13] and appropriate measurement instruments for beginners, such as secondary school or undergraduate students, in the field of object-oriented programming (OOP).

We started by reviewing existing literature on competency modelling in other subject areas (such as mathematics, science, humanities, arts, computer science and problem solving) regarding the development methodology as well as the model structures (for a detailed description of this process, see [14]). We identified the areas of knowledge structures, content representation, cognitive processes as well as metacognitive influences as common, recurring structural elements, and verified, expanded and refined these based on an extensive literature analysis on theoretical and empirical studies on teaching and learning as well as on psychological aspects in the field of OOP. As theoretically derived candidates for potential competency dimensions we identified:

1. *OOP knowledge and skills*
    1.1. *Data structure (graph, tree, array)*
    1.2. *Class & object structure (object, attribute, association)*
    1.3. *Algorithmic structure (loops, conditional statement)*
    1.4. *Notional machine (data, working memory, processor, statement, program, automaton)*
2. *Mastering representation (language, syntax, semantics)*
3. *Cognitive process*
    3.1. *Problem solving stage (understanding the problem, determine how to solve the problem, translating the problem into a computer language program, testing and debugging the program)*
    3.2. *Cognitive process type*
        3.2.1. *Interpreting (Remember, Understand, Analyze, Evaluate)*
        3.2.2. *Producing (Apply, Create)*
4. *Metacognitive processes*

The proposed dimensions span a multidimensional competency space. Each competency candidate that is contained therein covers a certain subspace that is limited by fixed values on some dimensions that can be assigned to this competency. For example, the competency candidate *"be able to program arrays in Java"* might cover a subspace that is limited by the following fixed values: 1.1 Array, 2 Java, 3.1 Translating the solution in a computer program and 3.2. Understand and Apply. The remaining dimensions might be covered in total by this competency. It has to be noted that, due to national regulations of Java being one of the predominant languages in schools, our research will first focus on this language.

The theoretically derived model draft was validated based on various competency descriptions in terms of applicability and completeness. For this purpose, we identified competency descriptions related to OOP in 44 computer science curricula and standards from several countries and compared these with our model (see Sect. 3). In 2015, an international working group at the ACM ITiCSE conference analysed 14 case studies on K12 computer science education in 12 different countries, which resulted in 247 extracted competency descriptions. Out of these, 119 were related to programming and could be fully integrated in our model. Finally, the structure model was aligned with the results of a survey among 59 computer science teachers and teacher students on learning difficulties. Their views on which skills and abilities someone needs, to become a competent programmer as well as their point of view on typical problems during that learning process could be also fully integrated in our model.

During this process, we had to adjust our theoretically derived model only in minor subsections (see Sect. 3).

2.3   Learning Metrics, Psychometric Models and Item Development

The discussion around coding to be the new literacy is vivid and the way to a proficiency scale in computer literacy is in its first stages. In PISA the development of scales followed six steps: (1) Identifying possible scales, (2) Assigning items to scales, (3) Skills audit, (4) Analysing field trial data, (5) Defining the dimensions and (6) Revising and refining with main survey data.

In a first step, we identified OOP as an important subscale [14]. Currently we're dealing with the construction of items as well as bringing them on their way to first field trials. For this stage of development, a more functional concept of competency is followed. This perspective is more interested in abilities to cope with challenges in specific situations rather than in the generative and cognitive systems behind [15]. From this background items have a single achievement threshold; the derived information only distinguishes dichotomously between correct and incorrect answers. Thus, the Rasch model can be applied to the raw data, in PISA a generalized form of the Rasch model has been used [16].

The Rasch model is "the only model to date that provides the tools for approximating objective reproducible additive measures in the human sciences." [17, p. 8]. It follows the concept that data conforms a reasonable hierarchy on a single continuum of interest. The most important fact is the measuring of a single variable with a map of persons (ξ_v) and items (σ_i) on the same scale, therefore the relationship between the participant and the item is probabilistic. The resulting model can be regarded as a model of competency levels. While those levels have already been regarded in the step of item construction, they will be precised by the step of skills audit and the analysis of the field trial data. At this stage numerical scores and terms of content, which describe what persons who achieve a specific level know and can do, can be reported. The final assessment of COMMOOP will be a computerized adaptive test (CAT), wherefore the Rasch model is essential [18].

Generative and structure models are more interested in the components behind the specific ability in a concrete item [1]. Modelling latent variables, like working memory or intelligence, comes into the focus, which is mostly driven by cognitivism. These models are rather the result of small experimental designs than of large-scale assessments. Modelling the cognition behind competencies is nowadays a challenge. One of its fruits will be the improvement of intelligent tutorial systems (ITS) and the rise of cognitive tutors. A pioneer of this type of modelling is John R. Anderson and his ACT-R Theory [19, 20]. Anderson and his colleagues have realized different ITS considering the cognitive limitations of the learner, one specific ITS is about learning to code in LISP. At a later stage COMMOOP will regard cognitive models for code trainings. The prior testing will combine the most promising items with different working memory, intelligence and planning scales.

3   Analysis of K12 Computer Science Curricula and Standards

A key step in our model development process (see Sect. 2.2) was a thorough analysis of K12 computer science curricula and educational standards. Altogether, we analysed 44 documents (German and international ones) and extracted competency facet descriptions concerning OOP from them. We performed this step because of two main reasons: first, we wanted to check the applicability of our theoretically derived normative competency model draft by trying to assign the competency facet descriptions to the proposed model categories to check and to ensure "curricular validity". This was an important step also in other competency modelling projects (cf. e.g. [3, 4]). Second, we wanted to prepare the operationalization of our model draft by starting to develop test items suitable to measure the competency facets found in the curricula.

Since we plan to measure OOP competency first in German schools, we included all publically available computer science curricula of Germany's 16 federal states as well as national standards documents of the Board of Federal Ministers of Education and Cultural Affairs and the German Informatics Association in the analysis. If a federal state had different curricula e.g. for lower and upper secondary computer science education, we included both documents in the analysis. To ensure the applicability of our model also in the international context, we also investigated important documents published in English language by other nations, such as the "Computing at school" curriculum (UK), as well as recommendations of international organizations, such as the ACM/IEEE curriculum and the CSTA K12 standards. We included documents from secondary and higher education, because we aim to model and to measure competencies of programming novices regardless of the educational level.

Curricula and standards documents are usually highly structured documents, in which intended learning outcomes are ordered e.g. by age level or by fields of the discipline (such as "algorithms" or "impact on society"). We used scientific definitions of the term "programming" taken from the literature (e.g. [21–23]), extracted possible search terms from them, such as "writing" and "implementing", and searched each of the documents for the sections, in which relevant OOP competency facets were located. Within these sections we performed a qualitative content analysis (QCA) according to Mayring [24] using the tool MAXQDA. We used the dimensions and subdimensions of our theoretically derived normative competency model draft as our category system and coded each OOP competency facet found in the documents with its belonging category. The QCA was performed deductively and inductively (cf. [25]), so the theoretically derived category system was extended inductively whenever a new category candidate was found in the documents.

Since we cannot present the whole coding process and its results in detail here, we give two examples. The text fragment "*By the end of this course, students will [...] use constants and variables, including integers, floating points, strings, and Boolean values, correctly in computer programs*" (taken from the Ontario curriculum for Computer Studies in grades 10 to 12, Canada) was coded with the category *OOP knowledge & skills*, respectively with the subcategory *data structure*. The expected outcome that students should "*know the basics of object-oriented programming, e.g. inheritance, polymorphism and encapsulation*" (taken from the computer science curriculum of Saxony, Germany) was assigned to the subdimension *class and object structure*.

Overall, our model draft proved to be well applicable for the classification of most of the OOP competency facets found in the documents, which contributes to the curricular validity of our approach. Still there are three places, in which we modified it during the coding process: First, we found competency descriptions relating to the ability of being able to evaluate a different solution approach for a problem, so we added a subdimension "*Evaluating different strategies*" in the proposed competency dimension *Problem solving stage*. Second, it became obvious that syntax and semantics are almost inseparable and that third, there was a need to code competency facets relating to "*Documenting and maintenance*" (both: top-level dimension *Mastering representation*) to cover text fragments relating to the use of comments in the code as well as to writing clear and maintainable code. Especially because of the inseparability of syntax and semantics we decided to combine the subcategories belonging to *Mastering representation* in the top-level category and to analyse its inner structure in future work. Table 1 shows the distribution of codings at the end of the coding process.

Table 1. Coding results of the curricula analysis.

Competency dimensions	Subdimension	Number of codings
OOP knowledge & skills	Data structure	104
	Class & object structure	74
	Algorithmic structure	164
	Notional machine	15
Mastering representation	Semantics	36
	Syntax	43
	Programming language	37
	Documenting & maintenance	27
Cognitive processes	Understanding the problem	67
	Determining a plan	103
	Translating the problem solution into a program	116
	Testing and debugging	108
	Evaluating different strategies	11
Metacognitive processes		4

The next important step of the QCA according to Mayring [24] is the paraphrasing and summarizing of specific categories. The aim of this step is to combine similar competency facet formulations in fewer distinct joint formulations. Table 2 shows the result of this process within the dimension "*OOP knowledge and skills*".

It must be noted here that composite competency facet formulations like "*Students are able to assign values to variables of primitive and compound data types as well as more complex data structures*" were coded with more than one category.

Table 2. Categories formed in the subdimensions of the dimension OOP knowledge & skills by paraphrasing and summarizing the competency facet formulations

Subdimensions	Categories	Number of codings
Data structure	Data representation/structure in general	52
	Primitive data types	29
	Composite data types	36
	Dynamic data structures	27
Class & object structure	OO in general	20
	Fundamental OO-concepts (class, object, attributes, methods)	48
	Higher OO-concepts (polymorphism, encapsulation, inheritance)	19
	Using predefined structures	14
Algorithmic structure	Algorithms in general	45
	Fundamental algorithmic structures (sequence, selection, repetition)	91
	Subprograms (methods, procedures, functions)	21
	Recursion	24
	Searching/Sorting	22
	Algorithmic optimization	19
Notional machine		15

It is not surprising, that fundamental algorithmic structures can be found most often in the documents, since neither does every country or state follow an object-oriented paradigm nor, in case they do, is the objects-first approach the most dominant one.

4   Developing Test Items

The next step on the way to an empirically validated competency structure model for OOP (see Sect. 2.2) is the operationalization of the competency facets of our theoretically derived model by describing specific situations that require a certain behaviour that persons show who are competent in this area.

While competency formulations describe a subspace of skills and abilities limited by certain parameters (see Sect. 2.2), the items should only test for a distinct competency dimension in the model to prove that the assumed multidimensionality of the model can be shown empirically. Moreover, the items have to be constructed in a way that solving them correctly will indicate the underlying competency. Hence, many test items of varying difficulty are required. Furthermore, it is necessary to take into account the probands' previous knowledge to ensure the validity of the results. In Germany, students at the end of grade 12 should have the necessary competencies when they have gone through upper secondary computer science education or when they completed an "Introduction to OOP" course at university level.

As a result of the curricula analysis we have collected numerous formulations describing OOP competency facets and abstracted those in the paraphrasing step (see Sect. 3). These descriptions are now used to construct test items, respectively to gain access to programming competencies and hence to validate the assumed theoretical competency structure on an empirical level. In the following, we give two examples of test items to be used at the end of an introduction to OOP. Item 1 is a considerably easy item addressing the understanding of classes as templates, objects as instances, attributes as characteristics and methods as modifiers of attribute values:

Item 1: *You are given the following source code:*

```
class House{
  Triangle roof;
  Square apartment;
  public House(){
    roof = new Triangle();
    apartment = new Square();
    roof.setLength(12);
  }
  public void adjust(){
    apartment.setLength() = roof.getLength();
  }
}
```
Mark all appearing class identifiers in red.

Item 1 can also be extended by various other tasks, such as *"If objects are created, please write down the respective line number"* or *"Please write down all the attributes and methods a House-object can access"*.

Item 2: *You are given the following source code:*

```
public class A {                      public class Z{
  void doThis(){                        public static void main
    System.out.println("A");            (String[] args){
  }                                       A[] z = new A[7];
}                                         z[0] = new A();
                                          z[1] = new B();
public class B extends A {                z[2] = new C();
  void doThis(){                          z[3] = new B();
    System.out.println("B");              z[4] = new A();
  }                                       z[5] = new C();
}                                         for(A e : z){
                                            e.doThis();
public class C extends B {                }
                                        }
}                                     }
```
Predict the output, which is generated by the main method of class Z.

To raise complexity, it is reasonable to choose more advanced concepts, to differ in the respective task, to use more abstraction, etc. Item 2 is a more complex task addressing the understanding of inheritance, polymorphism and encapsulation. The correct solution of item 2 can indicate a correct understanding of inheritance along with a corresponding concept for polymorphism. As well as item 1 item 2 can be varied, e.g. by adding one *doThis* method in class C and asking to predict the correct output, by writing a new subclass *D*, using *super* to refer to attributes and methods in super classes and so on.

The items will finally be evaluated by means of Item Response Theory. Hartig and Frey [26] already showed that for a multidimensional competency modelling this is a valid approach.

5   Summary and Outlook

In this paper, we gave an overview of the current state of our project COMMOOP, in which we aim to develop an empirically founded competency structure model for the field of object-oriented programming. We focussed on a curricula analysis, which we conducted to identify competency descriptions concerning OOP. We used these descriptions in a first step to check the applicability of our theoretically derived competency model draft for the classification of these descriptions. Second, we used the competency descriptions assigned to the subdimension "OOP knowledge and skills" to start the operationalization of our model by developing first test items to measure the proposed competencies. The process of item development is continuing under consideration of aspects, such as item difficulty and variety, suitability for adaptive testing and test length restrictions. Several iterations of pretests with the items will be conducted next on the way to develop a test instrument to validate the proposed competency structure.

References

1. Klieme, E., Hartig, J., Rauch, D.: The concept of competence in educational contexts. In: Hartig, J., Klieme, E., Leutner, D. (eds.) Assessment of Competencies in Educational Contexts. Hogrefe & Huber Publishers, Toronto (2008)
2. Hartig, J., Klieme, E., Leutner, D. (eds.): Assessment of Competencies in Educational Contexts. Hogrefe & Huber Publishers, Toronto (2008)
3. Jordan, A.-K., Knigge, J.: The development of competency models: an IRT-based approach to competency assessment in general music education. In: Brophy, T.S. (ed.) The Practice of Assessment in Music Education: Frameworks, Models and Designs, pp. 67–86. GIA Publications, Chicago (2010)
4. Linck, B., Ohrndorf, L., Schubert, S., Stechert, P., Magenheim, J., Nelles, W., Neugebauer, J., Schaper, N.: Competence model for informatics modelling and system comprehension. In: Proceedings of the Global Engineering Education Conference 2013, pp. 85–93. IEEE (2013)
5. Schecker, H., Parchmann, I.: Modellierung naturwissenschaftlicher Kompetenz. Zeitschrift für Didaktik der Naturwissenschaften **12**, 45–66 (2006)
6. Neumann, K., Kauertz, A., Lau, A., Notarp, H., Fischer, H.E.: Die Modellierung physikalischer Kompetenz und ihrer Entwicklung. Zeitschrift für Didaktik der Naturwissenschaften. **13**, 101–121 (2007)
7. Neumann, K., Fischer, H.E., Kauertz, A.: From PISA to educational standards: the impact of large-scale assessments on science education in Germany. Int. J. Sci. Math. Educ. **8**(3), 545–563 (2010)

8. Klieme, E., Avenarius, H., Blum, W., Döbrich, P., Gruber, H., Prenzel, M., Reiss, K., Riquarts, K., Rost, J., Vollmer, H.J.: The Development of National Educational Standards. An expertise. Federal Ministry of Education and Research, Berlin (2003)
9. Brinda, T., Puhlmann, H., Schulte, C.: Bridging ICT and CS: educational standards for computer science in lower secondary education. ACM SIGCSE Bull. **41**(3), 288–292 (2009)
10. Seehorn, D., Carey, S., Fuschetto, B., Lee, I., Moix, D., O'Grady-Cunniff, D., Boucher Owens, B., Stephenson, C., Verno, A.: CSTA K-12 Computer Science Standards: Revised 2011. ACM Technical report, New York (2011)
11. Weinert, F.E.: Concept of competence: A conceptual clarification. In: Rychen, D.S., Salganik, L. (eds.) Defining and Selecting Key Competencies. Hogrefe & Huber, Seattle (2001)
12. Klieme, E., Maag-Merki, K., Hartig, J.: Kompetenzbegriff und Bedeutung von Kompetenzen im Bildungswesen. In: Hartig, J., Klieme, E. (eds.) Möglichkeiten und Voraussetzungen technologiebasierter Kompetenzdiagnostik, Bonn (2007)
13. Schecker, H., Parchmann, I.: Modellierung naturwissenschaftlicher Kompetenz. Zeitschrift für Didaktik der Naturwissenschaften **12**, 45–66 (2006)
14. Kramer, M., Hubwieser, P., Brinda, T.: A competency structure model of object-oriented programming. In: Proceedings of the Fourth International Conference on Learning and Teaching in Computing and Engineering (LaTiCE), pp. 1–8. IEEE (2016). (in press)
15. McClelland, D.C.: Testing for competence rather than for intelligence. Am. Psychol. **28**, 1–14 (1973)
16. OECD: PISA 2012 Technical report, PISA. OECD, Paris (2014)
17. Bond, T., Fox, C.: Applying the Rasch Model. Lawrence Erlbaum Ass., London (2001)
18. Frey, A., Kroehne, U., Seitz, N.-N., Born, S.: Multidimensional adaptive measurement of competences. In: Leutner, D., Fleischer, J., Grünkorn, J., Klieme, E. (eds.) Competence Assessment in Education: Research, Models and Instruments. Springer, Heidelberg (in press)
19. Anderson, J.R., Bothell, D., Byrne, M.D., Douglass, S., Lebiere, C., Qin, Y.: An integrated theory of the mind. Psychol. Rev. **111**(4), 1036–1060 (2004)
20. Anderson, J.R., Corbett, A.T., Koedinger, K., Pelletier, R.: Cognitive tutors: lessons learned. J. Learn. Sci. **4**, 167–207 (1995)
21. Blackwell, A.F.: What is programming? In: Kuljis, J., Baldwin, L., Scobl, R. (eds). Proceedings of the 14th PPIG, pp. 204–218 (2002). http://www.ppig.org
22. Böszörményi, L., Weich, C.: What is programming? In: Böszörményi, L., Weich, C. (eds.) Programming in Modula-3. Springer, Heidelberg (1996)
23. Williamson, I., Dale, R.: What is programming? In: Williamson, I., Dale, R. (eds.) Understanding Microprocessors with the Science of Cambridge Mk14. Macmillan Education UK, pp. 13–17 (1980)
24. Mayring, P.: Qualitative content analysis–research instrument or mode of interpretation. Role Res. Qual. Psychol. **2**, 139–148 (2002)
25. Bortz, J., Döring, N.: Forschungsmethoden und Evaluation für Human- und Sozialwissenschaftler. Springer, Heidelberg (2006)
26. Hartig, J., Frey, A.: Sind Modelle der Item-Response-Theorie (IRT) das "Mittel der Wahl" für die Modellierung von Kompetenzen? Zeitschrift für Erziehungswissenschaft, 16 (Sonderheft 18-2013), pp. 47–51 (2013)

Introducing Collaborative Practices
to Undergraduate Studies

Jaana Holvikivi[1]($\boxtimes$), Minna Lakkala[2], and Hanni Muukkonen[2]

[1] Helsinki Metropolia University of Applied Sciences, Helsinki, Finland
jaana.holvikivi@metropolia.fi
[2] University of Helsinki, Helsinki, Finland
{minna.lakkala,hanni.muukkonen}@helsinki.fi

Abstract. The changes in software industry and software development methods call for appropriate teaching methods in academia. In addition to theoretical knowledge and coding practice, familiarity with common practices in the industry is expected from the graduates. Teamwork, collaboration and communication skills are essential demands for software engineers. These skills take years to develop, and therefore, this study presents how collaborative practices were introduced right in the beginning of information technology studies. The results of project based courses were encouraging in terms of student achievements and course completion rates. Additionally, feedback from students through an extensive survey was largely positive.

Keywords: ICT education · Collaborative practices · Professional competences · Project-based learning

1 Introduction

Software industry and software development practices have undergone tremendous changes in the last decades. These changes have not entered software engineering education in academia with the same force. Much of higher education still depends on very traditional teaching practices and conventional curricula. Several attempts to bring real-life engineering practices into education have been made, most notably the CDIO initiative by a number of technical universities worldwide [1] and the Aalborg Project Based Learning model [2]. Even though the theoretical backgrounds of these efforts differ, the practical implementation usually follows similar patterns on applying a project development cycle to course work, and concentrating on a problem and its solution instead of listed curriculum items (contents, skills, competences).

The Helsinki Metropolia University of Applied Sciences has a long history of undertaking curriculum changes to address a severe problem of low retention in information technology and engineering studies [3]. As long as the university funding from the government depended largely on the number of students, the motivation for implementing changes was low but when the funding scheme was changed to be based on study completions and graduations, the dilemma had to be addressed seriously three

T. Brinda et al. (Eds.): SaITE 2016, IFIP AICT 493, pp. 47–55, 2016.
DOI: 10.1007/978-3-319-54687-2_5

years ago [4]. Therefore, the university appointed a team of teachers in various disciplines to explore educational innovations in other European universities. The Aalborg model as an overall solution was chosen as the starting point for curriculum reform, which was implemented for the 2014-15 study year. The general guideline for the whole university encompassed larger study modules (5-15 ECTS credits), flexible curriculum choices as well as problem and project based learning methods.

Currently, the education at the university aims at developing the knowledge, skills, ethics, communication, and emotional component of the professional expertise to meet the need for highly integrated competence in the present day working environments. Dialogue with companies has revealed that education has failed to fully respond to the new requirements in the software industry. Demands from companies increasingly stress abilities for collaboration, efficient teamwork and professional communication. Therefore, project-based methods were included into most modules in the new curriculum. Additionally, the concepts of progressive inquiry [5] and problem-based learning were applied in course design. Moreover, participatory on-line learning environments were used to support the learner's development of understanding through collaborative construction of a shared product [6].

In information technology education, the first study year was divided into four 15 ECTS modules. Each module had a theme that introduced different major options of the studies: networks, programming and web-development, electronic devices and object-oriented programming. The project work in each module was supported by a varying amount of basic and theoretical studies such as mathematics.

The aim was to change studies in a way that makes entering the information technology profession a natural and exciting process regardless of the student background. In this paper, we discuss the results of applying working life practices immediately in the beginning of the studies.

2   Educational Practices at Metropolia

The studies in IT were previously loosely structured. In the old curriculum, students had 8 small courses in the fall semester that were partially studied in a large group (50 or 90 students). The incoming groups started with short courses in mathematics, physics, and the basics of information technology or media technology. Most courses were from 3 to 5 ECTS credits, and they consisted of lectures to a large audience and laboratory practice for groups of 24 students. If students failed courses, they could retake them during the following academic years. Unfortunately, this freedom and independence did not result in good retention, on the contrary: nearly 40% of students interrupted their studies already after the first year and only 40–49% graduated in 5 years (see Table 1). Interrupting studies is quite common in Finland where higher education is free. However, the high dropout rate became costly for the university, causing losses of income from the government when the funding depended on ECTS credits and graduates.

Table 1. Retention rates at Metropolia in all engineering degree programs.

Year	2009	2010	2011	2012	2013
Retention	42%	40%	43%	45%	49%

In the reform 2014, the curriculum was swapped around to include team projects and product development already in the beginning, whereas mathematics and physics were taught all along the studies. This was very different from the previous curriculum where first year was devoted mainly to basic scientific studies, languages, and other rudimentary skills. The drop-out after first year before the reform was regularly around 40%, as many students could not cope with the amount of physics and electronics that was required, and they lost interest in the profession.

The majority of students in the undergraduate programmes discussed here come directly from high school or after their military service year. In August each year, about 210 Finnish students, and 50 international students who study in English begin their studies. The majority of students, around 85%, are male. Currently, about a half of the students in the international group come from Vietnam, and 20% from Nepal. Others come from various countries, especially form Eastern Europe. Their former high school studies have followed a very traditional mode of teaching, including lectures, home work and examinations [7].

Opposed to the previous organization of studies, the new curriculum was based on large 8 week modules that take full time. Each class of 25 to 30 students had one fixed classroom where they had all lessons except certain laboratory sessions that needed special equipment. The classrooms were furnished with small tables that could easily be rearranged. There were also movable white boards and connections for laptop chargers [8, 9].

3   Research Methods

The Metropolia University of Applied Sciences conducted this educational reform in a very short time and with a loose outline. Therefore, the implementations of the new curriculum were quite diverse in different departments. The follow-up of results requires collection of a big amount of data and various evaluation methods. Some of the data are presented in this study.

The outcomes of the studies were measured by several means. Most obvious measurement was the study completion rate. The statistics were gathered in four successive years, of which two represented the previous curriculum and two the new curriculum. Student and teacher views on learning of collaborative knowledge work practices were collected using a validated questionnaire.

The Collaborative Knowledge Work Practices Questionnaire (CKP) is designed for investigating students' self-reported evaluation of collaborative working practices and competence development in courses [10]. In particular, aspects of collaboration and the use of digital technology are targeted as central components in modern knowledge work. These include learning to collaborate on shared objects (e.g., reports, products, designs), iterative development through feedback, integrating individual and collaborative working, understanding various disciplines and practices, interdisciplinary collaboration and communication, and learning to exploit technology. The questionnaire is based on the theoretical framework of the trialogical approach on learning that emphasises collaborative knowledge creation [11].

The questionnaire was available online and had 27 statements on Likert scale plus three open questions. The 5-point statements were of the type: "During the course/study unit I have learned … e.g. – to develop products collaboratively by using technology." The answer choices were: "Not at all (1); Just a little; Somewhat; Quite a lot; Very much (5)".

The questionnaire was answered by students and teachers in 13 modules of the new curriculum, including 24 teachers and 198 students who started the study in the year 2014/15. Students' and teachers' scores on the seven scales of the CKP questionnaire were compared statistically (t-test). The teachers answered the same questionnaire items with the instruction "In my opinion, students learned during the course … e.g., to define sub-goals for the collaborative work".

Moreover, qualitative methods were included in the evaluation of the results, such as the analysis of open-ended questionnaire responses, student work results, and teacher and student interviews that help in explaining statistical results. The readiness for teamwork and other basic abilities were mainly evaluated based on classroom performance.

4   Results

4.1   Retention Rates

The initial passing rate of the 15 ECTS modules of the new curriculum was 85–100%. More importantly, the retention after first year was equally high, practically all students continuing their studies in the second year [12].

The ECTS credit accumulation was investigated by examining students who stayed on track with their studies, completing the expected 30 credits in the two study periods of the first semester (Tables 2 and 3). As can be seen from the figures, the amount of students with at least 30 ECTS increased from 48% in 2013 to over 80% in the years 2014 and 2015 in the Finnish groups. The positive effect of the new curriculum model was even stronger in the international groups, where earlier completion rates were between 17% and 31% (Table 3).

Table 2. Course completions of Finnish study groups in IT (one campus)

	2012 n = 143	2013 n = 149	2014 n = 106	2015 n = 107
1–14 ECTS credits	14%	11%	0%	2%
15–29 ECTS credits	26%	41%	14%	9%
30->	59%	48%	86%	89%

Table 3. Course completions of international study groups in IT

	2012 n = 74	2013 n = 76	2014 n = 45	2015 n = 48
1–14 ECTS credits	23%	14%	0%	2%
15–29 ECTS credits	46%	68%	20%	8%
30->	31%	17%	80%	90%

Equally, other degree programmes in engineering reveal a similar pattern. The Electrical Engineering and Automation Technology results after the first semester show that the new curriculum significantly improved results, and more than 93% of the students in these degree programmes passed all the courses in time compared to the relatively low values of 70% in 2013 and 50% in 2012 [4].

In addition to a good passing rate, course grades were also exceptionally high, especially in the international groups where the average grade was 4.0 (of 5), Table 4.

Table 4. Grade averages in international study groups in IT 2014–15

Course	N	Average grade
Networks A	27	4.3
Networks B	24	4.5
Games A	27	3.5
Orientation A	22	3.9
Orientation B	26	3.8

A comparison between international and Finnish students reveals that the international students were more ambitious and targeted at good grades, which they also achieved. The grade average in the Finnish groups in the spring term 2015 was 3.4 (of max. 5).

4.2 Questionnaire Answers

Student and teacher opinions on the learning in the new modules were collected using the same questionnaire after each module. The responses of students and teachers from 13 modules were compared on each of the seven scales of the CKP questionnaire (Fig. 1). There were no statistical differences between the scale scores. Students and teachers gave the highest scores to learning about collaborating on shared objects (e.g., plans, designs, reports), integrating efforts in collaborative working, development through feedback, persistent efforts, and exploiting technology. Lower scores were given to understanding about various disciplines and practices as well as learning about interdisciplinary collaboration and communication.

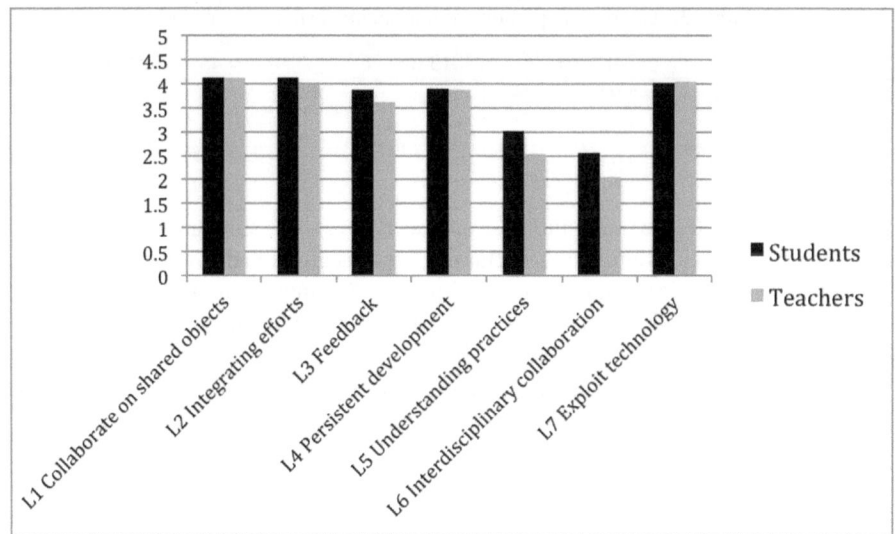

Fig. 1. Students' and teachers mean responses on the scales of the Collaborative Knowledge Practices Questionnaire. (Not at all = 1, Very much = 5).

The questionnaire contained also three open-ended questions. According to a thematic analysis, in the open-ended questionnaire responses the students addressed the following aspects as positive or impressive in the courses (233 mentions in general):

- *Working methods (90)*: Practical tasks (24), Group work (30), Learning community and atmosphere (17), Working methods in general (11), Project work (4), Freedom of choice (4);
- *Teaching and guidance (52)*: Good teachers and teaching (36), Teachers' positive attitude (7), Guidance and feedback from teachers (9);
- *Content (31)*: Interesting and useful content (31);
- *Outcomes (28)*: Learnt new things (21), High-quality products (7);
- *Organization (28)*: Good entity (15), Appropriate phase of work (7), Good integration of subjects (6);
- *Facilities (4)*: Good study premises and equipment (4).

The negative aspects were partially the same, or sometimes the other side of the coin (180 mentions in general):

- *Organization (70)*: Tight timetable and heavy workload (24), Uneven workload (13), Confusing and incomplete arrangements (12), Poor integration of subjects (12), Poor communication practices (9);
- *Working methods (60)*: Problems in group work (18), Too little teaching of theory (13), Challenging working methods (10), Restless classroom (5), Too much group work (7), Too much teaching of theory (4), Compulsory attendance (3);
- *Content (42)*: Difficult content (29), Not interesting or useful content (13);

- *Teaching and guidance (27)*: Poor teachers and teaching (13), Too little guidance and feedback (6), Unclear goals and evaluation criteria (8);
- *Facilities (8)*: Poor study premises and equipment (8).

As was noted before the arrangements of the modules were varied, therefore some aspects such as amount of theory or guidance could be very different between modules.

4.3   Adoption of Teamwork

According to student interviews in the classroom, none of the international students had previous experience in teamwork or team projects. However, the transition to university studies seemed to make the students open to a new way of learning, and all approached the teamwork mode positively. As contrasted to students who had previous university studies particularly in Finland, they adapted quickly to self-directed project work. Only students who had started university studies elsewhere and transferred to our university, found the new mode difficult. Many of them had problems in adapting to regular attendance and shared responsibility of teamwork. Interestingly, even one year of previous studies had fixed their study habits.

Teamwork and project work were more challenging to assess fairly than individual deliverables. Teams of six or seven students were problematic in this respect but unfortunately the lack of equipment forced to do some projects in such large teams. Most projects were executed in teams of four. Instructors tried to avoid unfair situations by choosing half of the deliverables as individual assignments (such as mathematics, programming exams and student home pages). Moreover, the continuous presence of teachers in the classroom gave them an understanding of each student's skills. At the end of some projects, students were requested to indicate how much each team member contributed to the project. In most cases, students gave a fair assessment of each other and even downplayed their own part.

As teamwork is not completely new in the curriculum, the results can also be compared with earlier experience. Numerous reports show that project work has always had several benefits such as better course completion and student satisfaction [13, 14]. On the other hand, it had no discernible overall impact on retention and graduation when it was only a small part of the curriculum.

The orientating courses of the first year enabled students to acquire basic knowledge of the study environment together. The collaborative practices developed during the first courses could later be observed when the students proceeded with their studies. How well the teamwork and collaboration skills persisted during the second academic year, was monitored and the results varied depending on the arrangements in the subsequent modules. When courses were built on collaboration the effect was positive, but when they followed traditional learning patterns, the students also reverted to those.

5   Discussion and Conclusion

The new study modules were by no means similar to each other. Much of the realization depended on the teacher team, some of whom preferred to divide the module into smaller parts among each other. All modules except one had a larger project, though. From the students' point of view, having a permanent home class was a significant difference to earlier years. Arguably, belonging to a group could have been a decisive factor in student retention. Despite the fact that the students were split to new groups according to the major subject selection the second year, where only part of the former classmates followed, they already had a network of study mates.

As the curriculum contents also changed in the reform, the results can be challenged in claiming that the students passed because of low requirements. However, the teachers involved would not agree, as actually the workload and requirements were set high. On the other hand, the number of individual deliverables within courses was certainly lower than before, which made the management of studies easier than before. Peer pressure within teams presumably added to the amount of work that was actually done because individuals were denied the privilege of procrastination. In particular students who had weaker self-regulation skills benefitted from a well-organized study mode. They had no choices to make in the first year, and the schedule for a week was always nearly similar.

According to the survey results, the teachers' and students' responses to the scales evaluating students' learning of knowledge work competences during the study modules were aligned. The average scores were quite high except the two scales that measured understanding practices and knowledge of various disciplines and interdisciplinary collaboration, which were not emphasized in the first-year studies. Open-ended responses revealed that students valued especially the working methods as well as teaching and guidance. They found disturbing particularly the organization of working, which might reflect the novelty of the implementation of teaching in larger modules together with a team of teachers. Also, various working methods were mentioned by students as unsatisfactory, including challenges in group work. However, it is encouraging that there were, in all, clearly more mentions about positive than negative aspects of the study experiences.

The main aims of the reform such as improved retention rate and high rate of completed study modules were achieved in an impressive manner. Despite the great variation of methods in course organization and teaching, the collaborative mode of learning and teaching seemed to contribute to a successful beginning of studies, and in particular to student enthusiasm and goals. Additionally, there were some indications that students adopted collaborative working practices that are expected by the software industry. Further research could address teachers' team teaching and the variation of course designs, their execution and related learning outcomes. Further, how students continue in their study programs is of interest to see; whether the reorganization of the first year of studies has continuous effects in terms of retention, or the completion of study credits. Further research could document the development of collaboration skills and other working life competences and aim to follow the students through their future transition to industry.

Acknowledgments. The study was partially supported by the Lifelong Learning Programme of the European Union under Grant KA3MP-2013-4764/001-001 (Promoting Knowledge Work Practices in Education; the KNORK project; http://knork.info).

References

1. Crawley, E.F., Malmqvist, J., Östlund, S., Brodeur, D.R.: Rethinking Engineering Education: The CDIO Approach. Springer, New York (2007)
2. Dalsgaard, F., Du, X., Kolmos, A.: Innovative application of a new PBL model to interdisciplinary and intercultural projects. Int. J. Electr. Eng. Educ. **47**, 174–188 (2010)
3. Schrey-Niemenmaa, K., Karhu, M., Ristola, A., Sirkjärvi, J.: The metropolia adaptation of CDIO in all 20 of its engineering study programmes. In: Proceedings of the 6th International CDIO Conference, École Polytechnique, Montréal, 15–18 June 2010
4. Valmu, H., Vartia, R., Kupila, E., Heikkinen, T.: Significantly improved student progression results by means of course integration and collaborative pedagogy in the degree programmes of electronics, electrical engineering and automation technology of the Helsinki Metropolia UAS. In: Proceedings of 19th International Conference on Engineering Education, ICEE 2015, pp. 32–40 (2015)
5. Muukkonen, H., Lakkala, M.: Exploring metaskills of knowledge-creating inquiry in higher education. Int. J. Comput.-Support. Collaborative Learn. **4**(2), 187–211 (2009)
6. Paavola, S., Hakkarainen, K.: Trialogical approach for knowledge creation. In: Tan, S.C., So, H.J., Yeo, J. (eds.) Knowledge Creation in Education, pp. 53–73. Springer, Singapore (2012)
7. Holvikivi, J.: From theory to practice: adapting the engineering approach. In: Proceedings of International Conference on Engineering Education, Turku (2012)
8. Hjort, P., Holvikivi, J., Vesikivi, P., Lukkarinen, S.: Student collaboration and independence from day one in higher education. In: Proceedings of the 43rd Annual SEFI Conference, Orléans, France (2015)
9. Lukkarinen, S., Holvikivi, J., Hjort, P., Mäkelä, M., Lakkala, M.: Creation of a collaborative study community in engineering studies. In: Proceedings of 19th International Conference on Engineering Education, ICEE 2015, Zagreb, Croatia, pp. 597–603 (2015)
10. Muukkonen, H., Lakkala, M., Toom, A., Ilomäki, L.: Assessment of competencies in knowledge work and object-bound collaboration during higher education courses. In: Kyndt, E., Donche, V., Trigwell, K., Lindblom-Ylänne, S. (eds.) Higher Education Transitions: Theory and Research. EARLI. New Perspectives on Learning and Instruction (2016)
11. Paavola, S., Lakkala, M., Muukkonen, H., Kosonen, K., Karlgren, K.: Trialogical learning: The roles and uses of design principles in a project on trialogical learning. Res. Learn. Technol. **19**(3), 233–246 (2011)
12. Vesikivi, P., Hjort, P., Lakkala, M., Holvikivi, J., Lukkarinen, S.: Adoption of a new project-based learning (PBL) curriculum in information technology. In: Proceedings of the 43rd Annual SEFI Conference, Orléans, France (2015)
13. Markkanen, H., Holi, M., Benmergui, L., Bauters, M., Richter, C.: The knowledge practices environment: a virtual environment for collaborative knowledge creation and work around shared artefacts. In: EdMedia: World Conference on Educational Media and Technology, Vienna, Austria (2008)
14. Muukkonen, H., Kosonen, K., Marttiin, P., Vesikivi, P., Kaistinen, J., Nyman, G.: Pedagogical design for knowledge creating inquiry in customer projects. Knowl. Manage. E-Learn. **5**(3), 278 (2013)

Teacher Education - Key Stakeholder Practices

Introducing Blended Learning MOOC – A Study of One bMOOC in Norwegian Teacher Education

Inger Langseth[1] and Halvdan Haugsbakken[2(✉)]

[1] Department of Teacher Education, Norwegian University of Science and Technology, Trondheim, Norway
Inger.Langseth@ntnu.no
[2] Department of Sociology and Political Science, Norwegian University of Science and Technology, Trondheim, Norway
Halvdan.Haugsbakken@ntnu.no

Abstract. Although MOOCs have been around for a decade, the use of MOOCs in teacher training is a new development. In 2015, a Norwegian teacher education received internal funding to develop a MOOC intended for blended learning, which we call bMOOC. The bMOOC consisted of four different modules, and the course content was created internally by highly competent teacher trainers. One goal with the bMOOC was to familiarize teacher students and teacher educators with the concept of blended learning. Another goal was to support students' academic writing processes across courses and possibly take some of the workload connected to instruction and feedback off the teacher trainers. The article analyzes the outcome of the implementation of the bMOOC, which shows low user adoption rate and low course completion. The study questions whether teacher educators see the pedagogical value in MOOCs and whether teacher students have enough digital competence to make use of online learning objects in formal learning.

Keywords: Teacher education · Blended learning · MOOC · Digital competence

1 Introduction

Our study discusses the introduction of a blended learning MOOC in teacher education, with an emphasis on the relationship between digital learning and teacher education. Although there is broad agreement that developing teacher students' digital competence is important, digital pedagogical innovation occurs primarily in the practice field and rarely in teacher education [1]. Moreover, when teacher students and teacher educators are offered the possibility to use new digital learning objects (DLO), both groups tend to prefer more traditional practices, thereby missing out on the benefits of developing their digital competences. If this is the case, institutional practices in teacher education contribute to a status quo and the reproduction of the technology-practice gap in education, something that the field has been criticized for [2]. One possible consequence of this contradiction is that teacher education will lag further behind schools in the use of

© IFIP International Federation for Information Processing 2016
Published by Springer International Publishing AG 2016. All Rights Reserved
T. Brinda et al. (Eds.): SaITE 2016, IFIP AICT 493, pp. 59–71, 2016.
DOI: 10.1007/978-3-319-54687-2_6

digital technology for teaching and learning and make goals set in national educational policies difficult to reach. Another peculiarity is that while teacher educators succeed in developing teachers' competencies in schools [3, 4], they seem to struggle when developing digital competencies internally, among their own staff.

To illustrate some of the complexity of the challenges above, this paper analyzes the introduction and experiences of a blended learning MOOC (bMOOC) containing several learning objects in four modules. The bMOOC was implemented as an integrated course across subjects in Norwegian teacher education in the fall 2015. Our research question is: What happens when a bMOOC is introduced in teacher education?

To show our argument, we will first define the paper's conceptual framework, by focusing on recent and relevant MOOC research. We will frame what we mean by the bMOOC concept. Second, we will describe our methodological approach, where we outline the research strategies we used to analyze the data we collected in our study. Third, we will present our research findings. Finally, we will draw some conclusions.

2   A Need to Address Blended Learning in MOOCs

To frame what we mean with the bMOOC concept in teacher education, we will contextualize the concept in recent developments in the MOOC literature.

In terms of educational philosophies, the interest in MOOCs has developed across two trajectories over the last decade. On the one hand, from 2009, one saw the rise of cMOOCs. The cMOOC is characterized by the introduction of Connectivism and the work of Canadian scholars [5]. Later, the cMOOC was described as connectivist, due to its "loose" design, meaning that there is no standard technology platform, no formal course content and no formal assessment [6]. Learning is interest-driven with an emphasis on social learning and based on networking and discussions among participants on social media. On the other hand, from 2012, a new scholarship, the xMOOC, emerged [5]. Here, the educational philosophy differs, in the sense that learning focuses on transferring pre-defined information from expert to novice. In this sense, xMOOCs are more "behavioristic", involving instruction by means of video lectures, automated feedback and assessment (by peers) [6]. They are intended for global and scalable courses and offer a certificate upon completion. They also offer the possibility of big data analysis. The xMOOC is a development fronted by American elite universities and commercial actors.

There is a vast emerging body of research literature on MOOCs. In brief, the research literature investigates the outcomes of MOOCs that are offered to off-campus students, and develops around particular research streams. Looking at relevant research streams, studies that examine *the social background of participants*, report the reoccurring finding that students are males who have completed higher education and have an average age around 30 [7]. Furthermore, user demographics show that MOOC courses are U.S. and Europe based and few studies in English show MOOC experiences from African and Asian countries [8, 9]. MOOC research papers also examine *learner perspectives*, focusing on what it means to teach for large online audiences and why MOOCs have low completion and high dropout rates. In some studies, scholars break down course populations and analyze different types of user commitment [10]. For example, Milligan et al. [11] classified three different types of participant groups – passive participants, lurkers, and active participants, a categorization indicating levels of student engagement. Many studies report that the dropout rate is at 94% on average [12, 13], but researchers identify the various reasons why students drop out and suggest strategies to make MOOC courses more sustainable [14]. Researchers attempt to establish the *learning outcomes* of a MOOC, something that has proven difficult to determine. Particular studies compared MOOC courses in mathematics with a similar on-campus course at an American university and found no significant difference [15]. Other studies show that the MOOC idea of being "large" is itself a challenge for learning. Large classes can lead to information-overload and loss of overview [16, 17], something which is also proven in studies on discussion forums [18]. Here, studies recommend some type of online intervention, for example in the form of a moderator that can guide students [19]. Recent studies have explored the idea of *gamification* [20], which is a method to award students with badges as motivation to complete courses. Here, studies claim that gamification can increase user enrolment and increase user engagement [21, 22].

MOOC is clearly a flexible concept that is under development. According to Bates [6], there seems to be three distinct patterns within the development of MOOC courses: (1) the transfer of best practices from credit-based online courses, like the use of moderated discussion groups, (2) the opening up of regular campus classes to non-registered students and (3) the use of blended learning. Our study elaborates on blended learning and the bMOOC concept in teacher education.

The bMOOC is based on a social and connectivist approach to learning [23], where online and campus-based teaching and learning merge to improve educational outcomes. We suggest a definition of six concepts in order to describe how technology integrates with teaching and learning in bMOOCs in the following educational philosophy:

(1) Digital competence building: When online MOOC content is blended with on-campus courses, pedagogical uses of new technologies are modeled, scaffolded and explored. It is of vital importance that teacher students develop their digital competence in formal educational contexts in their pre-service training in order to be able to contribute to the digital competency development in schools when they graduate. Digital literacy is one of several concepts that try to capture what a pedagogical use of technology involves:

The awareness, attitude and ability of individuals to appropriately use digital tools and facilities to identify, access, manage, integrate, evaluate, analyse and synthesise digital resources, construct new knowledge, create media expressions, and communicate with others, in the context of specific life situations, in order to enable constructive social action; and to reflect upon this process [24].

(2) Joint knowledge-construction: bMOOCs facilitate new ways of collaborative teaching and learning in formal education. Teacher educators can co-construct MOOC modules in subject areas that are taught across courses, something which facilitates both content validity and quality and collaborative learning and competence building among novices and experts in an area of study. Examples are MOOC

modules in academic writing and scientific methods. Likewise, teacher students get constant access to pre-selected information in multiple modalities (text, video, visuals etc.), and they can share ideas and get timely feedback from a larger group of students and educators in the discussion forums.

(3) Time saving design: The bMOOC design is time saving, in the sense that teacher educators can spend less time on content development and more time interacting with students, either online or in class, which according to Bates [6] is important if students are to develop deep understanding, transformative learning, evidence-based critical thinking and high level decision making.

(4) Transparency: The design is transparent, in the sense that bMOOC content - information, questions, feedback and user statistics and research data - is shared. The data informs teacher educators about troublesome knowledge, participation rates etc. in the learning processes and makes it possible to modify courses based on research and learning analytics.

(5) 21st Century skills: bMOOCs encompass social elements like collaboration, cooperation, sharing, curating and social media use, which are powerful skills in the 21st Century.

(6) Scalable and social: The bMOOC has its strength in the social fabric that potentially exists in and between the two learning spaces. It is possible to offer high quality information to scalable groups of students in the MOOC and provide scaffolding and feedback to individuals and smaller groups of students in the courses on campus, thus combining best practices from both MOOC technology and campus-based pedagogy.

The bMOOC concept has implications for how new educational practices are implemented in teacher education. The commonly used strategies, where stakeholders are informed by e-mail, in meetings or in a research and development project design, may not serve the purpose. For example, the reflection-on-action approach is typically based on previous experience in a learning context upon which participants are invited to reflect, thereby thinking in new ways, seeing things from other angles and using general theories to see possibilities for change and improvement in their teaching [25]. In new digital surroundings, participants may well be void of previous experiences with new digital teaching and learning to reflect upon. Moreover, due to the speed of the technological development, it is only partially possible to conduct theory informed teaching and learning in new digital contexts. Research says much about what has promoted formal learning, less about what promotes learning in today's and tomorrow's technology informed educational cultures [26]. Consequently, participants in their first bMOOC are exposed to some level of risk taking, and lack of confidence in their own digital competences and resistance to change might impede the learning process.

There is a need for a different approach to research-based education in digital contexts. One possible approach is to base development on reflection-in-action [25], where participants reflect while spending time to learn to master the new technologies and to move out of their own comfort zone and engage in "risk taking" activities that involve collaboration and sharing in one simultaneous action. This implies that reflection takes place in a situation where "all the events, together, are experienced at once, at the same time" [25]. Reflection is then demanded by digital conditions and stimulated by native curiosity in an ongoing process, also described in Schön's concept of reflection-in-action as spontaneous, common, real thinking that may make sense to the practitioner. In connectivist terms, learning then happens when patterns gradually emerge from chaos while engaging in a network of nodes [27].

3   Methods

Our data analysis is based on a mixed research approach. We used quantitative and qualitative methods. Our data is triangulated to check for reliabilities and valid measurements. This research strategy has consisted of comparing our research findings from our quantitative data analysis with research results from our qualitative data analysis.

Our quantitative research strategy consisted in collecting and analyzing course data from an LMS, which made up the technological platform of the bMOOC. After course completion, we reviewed registered course data on user participation to exclude invalid data. A total of 326 users or cases were registered at the start of the course, but 46 users were excluded from our data analysis, reducing our final data sample to 280, divided into 256 teacher students and 24 teacher trainers. From there, we derived an overview on descriptive statistics on user participation among teacher student and teacher trainers.

Our qualitative research approach consisted of collecting and analyzing data on user participation in the LMS and qualitative interviews with teacher students and teacher educators. The interviewees were randomly selected among volunteers present at one lecture and in one meeting. In total, twelve interviews were completed, six individual interviews with teacher students and six individual interviews with teacher educators. We used a semi-structured interview guide, where we asked a number of simple, short questions; how they learned about the MOOC, whether they accessed the MOOC, how they used the learning objects, and their thoughts on module contents. The interviews lasted from 15 to 30 min. The interviews were recorded on a digital audio recorder. Our data was collected from October to December 2015.

After completing the interviews, they were transcribed and translated into English. We used a constant comparative method [28] and open coding strategy to analyze the data from the interviews. We looked for patterns in our interview data. After coding our data material in several rounds, we arrived at some categories. We grouped the teacher students' and teacher educators' answers into larger categories in an interrelated method, where two researchers worked together. We used direct quotations to give our informants a voice.

The study is based on informed consent. The teacher education and the informants involved in the study have been made anonymous [29].

4   Data Analysis – Presentation of Research Findings

We have divided our data analysis into three sections. The first part describes the background and the context for the bMOOC and its overall course content. The second part presents research findings from our quantitative data analysis. The analysis focuses on course data and provides simple descriptive statistics on a number of defined variables, which are meant to highlight online activity or traffic in the bMOOC. The third part focuses on the study's qualitative data. Here, we provide an analysis of user experiences, where we analyze teacher students' and teacher trainers' use and evaluation of the bMOOC, including user experiences of one separate module on academic writing.

4.1   The Background for Initiating the bMOOC

The teacher education, which has about 450 teacher students and 70 teacher educators, is located in an urban area and is part of a Norwegian university. During the spring of 2015, the teacher education received internal funding to develop a blended learning MOOC, where the goal was to improve teaching and learning in higher education. There were several reasons for initiating the blended learning MOOC project. In order to improve the quality of the foundation courses on campus, one aim was to familiarize teacher students and teacher educators with the concept of blended learning. Another aim was to support students' academic writing processes across courses and possibly take some of the workload connected to instruction and feedback off the teacher trainers. The bMOOC was inspired by a "flipped classroom" model and involved the use of multimodal learning objects, student-based activities, sharing, cooperation and collaboration in the learning processes. The bMOOC intended to develop a community of digitally competent teacher educators and teacher students, who in the long term could contribute to changing existing teaching and learning processes in schools in the Norwegian K-12 system.

Looking at the design and the content in the bMOOC, it was intended as an online resource across subjects that teacher students and teacher educators could use throughout the semester, and additionally as a supplement to teacher students' individual competence development. Each of the four modules in the bMOOC intended to scaffold teacher students' key competences in their future professional career as teachers. The bMOOC modules were: how to master the art of academic writing, how to develop a personal learning network (PLN), how to master digital note taking and collaborative writing and the use of digital blackboards. Each module was estimated to 1–3 h' work online. For example, the academic writing module discussed the pitfalls of academic writing. It consisted of texts, videos, discussions and an evaluation of the module. In addition, there were "reflection tags" indicating where teacher trainers could make use of the course on campus (blending). The module was divided in three sections: (1) an introduction to academic writing, intended to be read once (2) a presentation of the academic text structure, which was intended to be used in the writing process and (3) help when students experience a writer's block, which was specially intended for students who struggle with academic writing. The amount of time each student teacher or teacher trainer would spend in the bMOOC depended on previous experience with digital tools and academic writing. Taking the bMOOC was estimated to about 5 h.

4.2   Quantitative Data Analysis of the bMOOC

We stress that our quantitative data analysis is not complete, only preliminary. In general, the analysis suggests that the bMOOC's online activity shares several traits seen in Social Network Sites (SNS) or online communities. For example, it is not uncommon that online communities experience a rapid adoption rate among users, but later have challenges to become sustainable and create active online engagement. This often results in an equal drop-down rate as online communities lose popularity. In our study, we find little data suggesting that teacher students and teacher educators initiate online contact with peers and engage in an online discussion in the bMOOC modules, something that one could expect in our case. There appears to be a small core group of users who have completed the four modules in the bMOOC. In our data set, the bMOOC has a high online activity in September, but this declines as the course progresses.

A pattern emerges when we look at distinct variables, like the teacher student's total time spent online in the bMOOC, as shown in the LMS analytics. When breaking down the mentioned variable on a more detailed level, interesting research findings emerge. We have for example divided the teacher students' online activity into four time subcategories or values. This division shows that 27% of the teacher students spent between 0–5 min, 41% used between 5–60 min, 22% spent between one to five hours, and 10% spent five hours or more. Largely, female teacher students have recorded most online activity. This means that the most expected characteristic user pattern consists of login on and engagement with the course material for an hour or two, before dropping out never to return. The data also demonstrates a "thinning" of number of teacher students, when an increase in recorded online time is considered. Only 22 teacher students have logged more than five hours of online activity.

Analyzing our course data on the teacher educators' use and online engagement, we see a similar user pattern. The teacher educators' total time spent on the bMOOC is somewhat similar to that of the teacher students. Of the 24 teacher trainers, 12.5% spent between 0–5 min, 37.5% used about 5–60 min, 37.5% recorded 1–5 h, and 10% spent five hours or more on the bMOOC. Our data suggests that the teacher educators exhibit the same user behavior as those they intend to educate; many teacher educators seem to register and take a look at the bMOOC but never return to work with the online material.

Our initial observations are confirmed in other variables in our data set. Another way to conceptualize online activity is to look at the variable page views. Page views is a variable indicating how many times a web page in the bMOOC has been loaded. Descriptive statistics from the LMS analytics used to organize the bMOOC show that there were 4314 page views in September, 2239 in October, 641 in November, and 91 in December. Here, we can also observe a progressive decline in online activity, where the peak starts in September and follows a steady drop, as the bMOOC progresses.

4.3 Qualitative Data Analysis of the bMOOC

The qualitative data also confirms user experiences and online patterns established in our preliminary quantitative data analysis. Our qualitative data is only preliminary.

In our interviews, we explored the teacher students' user experiences. One surprising research finding was the teacher students' view on the value of online learning and the bMOOC. Some teacher students stated that online learning and the use of digital resources bring little benefit, and that they prefer other approaches to learning. This suggests a contradictory view on technology in education. On the one hand, teacher students are brought up in a digital world, but on the other hand, they approach and frame digital learning from a textbook perspective. Our data suggests that the teacher students are inexperienced with online learning and the demanding work it involves.

Data collected from the LMS confirms the above pattern. The course data shows that the teacher students did not actively participate in the academic writing module in the bMOOC. Course data from the module establishes that there are few online discussion entries, comments and replies.

The teacher students' low and passive online participation is utterly elaborated on in the evaluation of the academic writing module. Five of the seven teacher students who evaluated the module were women. Five of them reported that they took the whole module, while one took about half and one took selected elements. The respondents said that the module was useful to them, referring to different elements in the module. They were most positive about the middle section made for the more hands-on writing process, but all the three sections were considered relevant to them. They report that they to some extent understood more about the writing process after taking the bMOOC. The data shows that there was no collaboration in the discussion forums, even though they reported that they were willing to collaborate online with other participants.

In the online evaluation, student teachers reported that they had not been properly informed about the bMOOC. In the interviews, the teacher educators reported that only a few students were present when the bMOOC was introduced. Moreover, the presentation was optional. Six of the seven teacher students reported that their teacher educator had briefly informed them about the academic writing module, meaning that they never used the bMOOC actively in the course.

In the interviews, the teacher students reported that working in the bMOOC was too time-consuming. Consequently, the online material in the bMOOC was considered of little relevance to their exams in academic writing and learning. They preferred other approaches, like traditional feedback from the tutor and peer assessment on campus. This female teacher student favored writing an academic text on paper by herself, completing it the "old fashion way, in order to save time and get on with other things":

> I opened the MOOC and no, can't be bothered. It will take less time to just write the text yourself. Surely, a good thing, but it takes more time than you will get back from doing it, and you must read it, that is time better spent on writing the academic text itself or doing other things.

The interviews show that the teacher students had varying approaches and prior experiences with academic writing. In the module evaluation, two of seven teacher students reported that they had only been taught to write in secondary school, whereas five had been instructed in academic writing in higher education in previous courses. This finding is elaborated on in the interviews, where teacher students commented upon the relevance of a bMOOC in formal learning in academic writing.

We asked the teacher students to explain how they learned to write academic texts. They suggested different methodological approaches involving help from peers and tutors on campus, but very few saw the value of online collaborative learning:

> We get feedback on the first draft. Some teacher trainers have given very concrete feedback that helps. Students can also give peer reviews. That is not in all subjects, but in many. I think it helps, I get new perspectives and new ways of forming sentences. It is also scary. If it is good, I am afraid that the other students will steal my idea, if I think it is a bad text, it is a bit awkward.

The teacher educators' user experiences are different from those they are set to train as future teachers. The teacher educators saw and emphasized the potentially positive educational benefits with MOOCs, but this is contradicted in practice. A theme running through our interviews was the lack of information about the bMOOC itself. Six teacher educators explained that they had to a variable extent received information about the bMOOC and how to sign up for it. For example, they had challenges in remembering where to find URL links, which would enable them to login in to the bMOOC.

The teacher educators have a dual relationship with the bMOOC concept. On the one hand, they acknowledge the importance of the digital learning environment. On the other hand, they prefer the social and relational aspect on campus. This applies especially to feedback on teacher students' academic text production. For example:

> I think the f-2-f-relation we have with our students is important. I think direct contact with me is more important, and therefore we used the MOOC on 2nd year students. I believe these online resources can make our work on feedback easier. We have high scores on student evaluations, and that is because we spend a lot of time on relations.

The teacher educators underlined that the bMOOC could have a positive impact on the amount of time they spend giving feedback to the teacher students. Here, they saw the MOOC as a positive contribution to students' writing process and a valuable resource in their work:

> I use a lot, lot of time to give feedback on students' academic texts. It takes time to give many students feedback with notes: You need more references, you need to include theory before the end, you need to structure your text etc. My God, I spend a lot of time giving feedback. I spent two hours on one text today. Later in the studies, it is easier. I spend some 1–2 h per text. Students have asked for help online. I see that we need to give more information about academic writing.

Finally, the teacher trainers emphasized that the success and impact of a bMOOC, depends upon certain organizational factors. Like any new practice introduced into an education system, the bMOOC must have legitimacy and support from the teaching institution. For example, when a bMOOC is implemented, it needs the support from the top-management. Suitable routines to inform all stakeholders must be established, so that potential users are aware of the existence of the bMOOC. In other words, the teacher trainers emphasized the need for better management strategies in the implementation of the bMOOC.

5   Discussion and Conclusion

Initially, we asked what happens when a bMOOC is introduced in teacher education. Our study tries to answer the research question by raising some questions that we wish to discuss, and that we believe might contribute to the research on MOOCs in teaching and learning. First, our research confirms previous research findings on social media and MOOCs. On the one hand, several studies have pointed out that many MOOCs have a low completion rate, with an estimated dropout rate of 94% [16, 17]. Therefore, our data analysis appears only to confirm previous studies. On the other hand, there is a tendency in educational research on social media, for example, to question whether today's adolescents are truly "digital natives" [30]. Some scholars have hinted that this is an ascribed myth that needs to be challenged. Various scholars point out both in studies [31, 32] and research reviews [33–35] that students in higher education might have a digital upbringing, but they seldom live up to expected standards defined in formal, digital learning. Rather, adolescents appear to be passive consumers of digital content and frame the educational online world from a textbook oriented approach. We see evidence of this in our analysis. The majority of teacher students and teacher trainers are inexperienced with formally structured online learning and seem to perceive the bMOOC as only vaguely beneficial to education and learning.

Second, as an extension of the above, we believe that our study brings interesting nuances as to how teacher students reflect upon how to develop their academic competences. Two features related to "reflection-on-action" [25] emerge in our study: that of time and effort. In a situation where teacher students have limited experiences with formal learning in digital surroundings, their reflection on how to improve their academic writing seems to exclude MOOCs. They also report that the time and effort they choose to spend on their academic papers is in line with the results they assume that they will obtain. Consequently, they conclude that there is no need to look deeper into yet another learning object in the bMOOC. Theoretically speaking, they experience a balance in the situation where they carry out the assignment [25]. From this follows that (1) extending teacher students campus based artefacts to also include online MOOCs seems to be too much of an effort. Our study shows that they enter the MOOC, spend a limited amount of time and leave, never to come back. (2) Behind our findings related to the low adoption rate of the bMOOC, we also find that teacher students' reflection on their own competence development seems to a large extent to be related to personal goals to reduce study hours. (3) Our study also reveals that when confronted with an academic writing assignment, teacher students prefer the" trial and error" strategy to theory informed and research based strategies in the bMOOC. At the same time, teacher educators report that teacher students to a variable extent make use of feedback from educators in their writing processes on campus. These findings suggest a gap between student teachers' perceived and actual competence in academic writing and a lack of strategies to close it. Contrary to this trend, we find another pattern. (4) Among the few teacher students who have made use of the bMOOC, they report to a large extent that they find academic writing hard work, and that the bMOOC is worth the effort when completing the academic writing assignment. Our findings suggest that these students have made their reflection-on-action based on previous experiences with online learning and a realistic assessment of their own academic writing skills. Summing up, when deciding what actions to take, teacher students seem to consider whether the bMOOC is worth the time and effort based on previous experiences with online learning and perceived level of confidence in their own academic writing. In previous studies, Dysthe [36], for example, found that Norwegian students had a form of "resistance" towards obligatory activities that were not graded, and that students invested the least possible effort to pass requirements set by their teachers. Our study extends Dysthe's findings to digital surroundings and graded assignments. In the interviews, the teacher educators state that students' competence in academic writing needs to be developed and that they spend a lot of time giving basic feedback on features that, we argue, could have been learned in the bMOOC.

Third, this pattern of beliefs and behavior reproduces the theory-practice gap that we initially described, and the pattern is strengthened when the implementation strategy in the institution is not adequate. We suggest that introducing MOOCs in formal education needs to be more organized and emphasized through active participation in "reflection-in-action" [25]. In order for teacher students to reflect upon the value of online learning, like in the bMOOC, they must be introduced to it on campus, by teacher educators who make advantage of the benefits of social networking and multimedia learning objects. This presupposes that teacher educators are familiar with the MOOC concept. If this is not the case, like our research findings suggest, the possibility of extending the students' learning context to involve online learning and collaboration can be lost. The question that needs to be asked is how to implement digital competence in teacher education. We suggest that the more traditional approach that involves reflection-on-action is not adequate, since it is based on a limited set of digital knowledge and skills. Reflection will then not lead to creativity and invention, which is necessary for change. We suggest that new technologies be introduced in a blended learning approach, where teacher educators jointly are allocated time to develop their digital competence. Two of the participants in our study, who had previously participated in a bMOOC, reported on results that affected their teaching, learning and assessment strategies on campus.

Fourth, as with any research, our study has limitations that have to be acknowledged at this point. This case study contains data that is to a limited extent generalizable to other educational contexts. Other studies can attain other research results. We believe however that our research findings might contribute to a better understanding of the challenges connected to implementing blended learning in educational cultures. Another limitation is that this study is only preliminary. In addition, we did not conduct any research in the classrooms or campus lectures.

The goal of this paper has been to introduce the bMOOC concept into current research on MOOCs and push the field in a new direction. Our study suggests that teacher education has work to do to enhance future teacher students and teacher teachers' digital competences. If the technology-practice gap is not addressed, we are afraid that we can see a widening of this gap in our K-12 education system.

References

1. Haugsbakken, H.: Using Social Media The Inside Out; A Aualitative Study of Four Different Local Models for Organizing Social Media in Organizations. NTNU, Trondheim (2016)
2. Irgens, E.J.: Rom for arbeid: lederen som konstruktør av den gode skole. In: Andreassen, R.A., Irgens, E.J., Skaalvik, E.M. (eds.) Kompetent Skoleledelse, pp. 125–145. Tapir, Trondheim (2010)
3. Postholm, M.B.: Teachers developing practice: reflection as key activity. Teach. Teach. Educ. Int. J. Res. Stud. **24**(7), 1717–1728 (2008)
4. Riksaasen, R., Langseth, I.: Endringer av Praksis i Klasserommet. En Artikkelsamling om Utviklingsarbeid, Aamarbeid, Erfaringer og Forskning. Akademika Forlag, Trondheim (2014)
5. Ebben, M., Murphy, J.S.: Unpacking MOOC scholarly discourse: a review of nascent MOOC scholarship. Learn. Media Technol. **39**(3), 328–345 (2014)

6. Bates, T.: Teaching in a aigital age. University of British Columbia (2016)
7. Ho, A.D., Chuang, I., Reich, J., Coleman, C.A., Whitehill, J., Northcutt, C.G., Williams, J.J., Hansen, J.D., Lopez, G., Petersen, R.: HarvardX and MITx: the first year of open online courses. In: HarvardX and MITx Working Paper, No. 1 (2014)
8. de Waard, I., Abajian, S., Gallagher, M.S., Hogue, R., Keskin, N., Koutropoulos, A., Osvaldo, R.C.: Using mLearning and MOOCs to understand chaos, emergence, and complexity in education. Int. Rev. Res. Open Distance Learn. Spec. Issue-Connectivism: Des. Delivery Soc. Networked Learn. **12**(7), 94–115 (2011)
9. Kop, R.: The challenges to connectivist learning on open online networks: learning experiences during a massive open online course. Int. Rev. Res. Open Distance Learn. Spec. Issue-Connectivism: Des. Delivery Soc. Networked Learn. **12**(3), 59–74 (2011)
10. Anderson, A., Huttenlocher, D., Kleinberg, J., Leskovec, J.: Engaging with Massive Online Courses. In: WWW 2014 - Proceedings of the 23rd International Conference on World Wide Web, Seoul, Korea. ACM, New York (2014)
11. Milligan, C., Littlejohn, A., Margaryan, A.: Patterns of engagement in connectivist MOOCs. Merlot J. Online Learn. Teach. **9**(2), 216–227 (2013)
12. Koutropoulos, A., Gallagher, M.S., Abajian, S.C., de Waard, I., Hogue, R.J., Keskin, N. O., Rodriguez, C.O.: Emotive vocabulary in MOOCs: context & participant retention. Eur. J. Open Distance E-Learning 1, (2012)
13. Jordan, K.: Initial trends in enrolment and completion of massive open online courses. Int. Rev. Res. Open Distance Learn. **15**(1), 133–160 (2014)
14. Gomez-Zermeno, M.G., Aleman De La Garza, L.: Research analysis on mooc course dropout and retention rates. Turkish Online J. Distance Educ. **17**(2), 3–14 (2016)
15. Colvin, K., Champaign, J., Liu, A., Zhou, Q., Fredericks, C., Pritchard, D.E.: Learning an introductory physics MOOC: all cohorts learn equally. Int. Rev. Res. Open Distrib. Learn. **15**(4) (2014)
16. Liyanagunawardena, T.R., Adams, A.A., Williams, S.A.: MOOCs: a systematic study of the published literature 2008–2012. Int. Rev. Res. Open Distance Learn. **14**(3), 202–227 (2013)
17. Knox, J.: Digital culture clash: 'Massive' education in the e-learning and digital cultures. Distance Educ. **35**(2), 164–177 (2014)
18. Firmin, R., Schiorring, E., Whitmer, J., Willett, T., Collins, E.D., Sujitparapitaya, S.: Case study: using MOOCs for conventional college coursework. Distance Educ. **35**(2), 178–201 (2014)
19. Dillenbourg, P.: MOOCs: Two years later. In: Research Workshop (Keynote no Printed Record Available), EDEN, Oxford (2014)
20. Crisp, G.T.: Assessment in next generation learning spaces. In: International Perspectives on Higher Education Research, pp. 85–100 (2014)
21. Vaibhav, A., Gupta, P.: Gamification of MOOCs for increasing user engagement. In: Proceedings of the 2014 IEEE International Conference on MOOCs, Innovation and Technology in Education, Thapar University, Patiala, Punjab, India. IEEE MITE (2014)
22. Chang, J.W., Wei, H.Y.: Exploring engaging gamification mechanics in massive online open courses. Educ. Technol. Soc. **19**(2), 177–203 (2016)
23. Siemens, G.: Connectivism: a learning theory for the digital age. Int. J. Instr. Technol. Distance Learn. **2**(1), 3–10 (2005)
24. Martin, A.: Digital Literacy Needed in an "e-permeated" World-Progress Report of DigEulit Project (2006). http://www.idunn.no/ts/dk/2006/02/
25. Clarà, M.: What is reflection? Looking for clarity in an ambiguous notion. J. Teac. Educ. **66**(3), 261–271 (2015)

26. Biesta, G.: Reclaiming a language for education in an age for learning. Nord. Pedagogikk **24**, 70–82 (2004)
27. Siemens, G.: Knowing Knowledge: The leadership Perspective Key Note 12. November, Skolelederkonferansen, Lillestrøm, Norway (2010)
28. Strauss, A., Corbin, J.: Basics of Qualitative Research: Techniques and Procedures for Developing Grounded Theory. Sage Publications, Inc., Thousand Oaks (1998)
29. NESH. Forskningsetiske Retningslinjer for Samfunnsvitenskap, Jus og Humaniora [Research Ethical Guidelines for Social Science, Law and the Humanities] (2006). http://www.etikkom.no/no/Vart-arbeid/Hvem-er-vi/Komitefor-samfunnsvitenskap-og-humaniora/
30. Prensky, M.: Digital natives, digital immigrants. On the Horizon **9**(5), 1–6 (2001)
31. Junco, R.: The relationship between frequency of facebook use, participation in facebook activities, and student engagement. Comput. Educ. **58**(1), 162–171 (2012)
32. Selwyn, N.: Faceworking: exploring students' education-related use of facebook. Learn. Media Technol. **34**(2), 157–174 (2009)
33. Aydin, S.: A review of research on facebook as an educational environment. Educ. Technol. Res. Dev. **60**(6), 1093–1106 (2012)
34. Hew, K.F.: Students' and teachers' use of facebook. Comput. Hum. Behav. **27**(2), 662–676 (2011)
35. Manca, S., Ranieri, M.: Is it a tool suitable for learning? A critical review of the literature on facebook as a technology-enhanced learning environment. J. Comput. Assist. Learn. **29**(6), 487–504 (2013)
36. Dysthe, O.: Pedagogiske endringer etter kvalitetsreforma og konsekvensar for læring. Utfordringar og Strategiar Videre. Uniped **30**(3), 29–44 (2007)

cMOOC: How to Assist Teachers in Integrating Motivational Aspects in Pedagogical Scenarios?

Aïcha Bakki[1,2(✉)], Lahcen Oubahssi[1], Chihab Cherkaoui[2], and Sébastien George[1]

[1] LIUM, UBL, University of Maine, Le Mans, France
{aicha.bakki,lahcen.oubahssi,sebastien.george}@univ-lemans.fr
[2] IRF-SIC Laboratory, FSA, Ibn Zohr University, Agadir, Morocco
c.cherkaoui@uiz.ac.ma

Abstract. From the very beginning of MOOCs, education stakeholders and researchers in the field of technology enhanced learning (TEL) considered closely the issues related to dropout of learners in these environments. In a detailed analysis of this question, several authors pointed out that this dropout is due to a lack of learners' motivation, a lack of learners' engagement, the isolation, etc. These dropout rates can also be associated with inadequate tools, models and mechanisms allowing personalization and/or adaptation of learning activities. According to these studies, a highly promising solution consists in looking to achieve the supporting of learners' motivation and engagement via adaptation of pedagogical scenarios. This paper goes in this direction by examining and trying to analyze the literature around the dropout issue in MOOCs. It mainly focuses on finding some possible solutions to adapt teaching scenarios and therefore motivate learners. More precisely, these solutions are essentially based on the connectivist approach, by taking into account four dimensions of educational activities, that is: aggregation, remixing, repurposing and feed forward.

Keywords: cMOOC · MOOC · Educational scenario building · Connectivism

1 Introduction

The MOOC (Massive Open Online Courses) movement seems to promise a reinvention of online education to reverse the production and dissemination of knowledge [1].

The model of MOOCs constitutes a significant educational innovation, related in particular to massiveness, openness, peer assessment, etc. Massiveness generates serious questions about how to manage large heterogeneous groups. The heterogeneity, in this context, refers to the diversity of those who enroll, an opening to all, without any distinction of: prerequisites, diplomas, language, etc. This suggests, in a certain way, a true "democratization" of access to online resources. In addition, the certification creates new business models [2]. Finally, if a consensus on the benefits of this educational model seems to be established, it generates new questions. The problematization of these issues create revisited fields, with specific constraints associated to MOOCs, such as: peer assessment, educational scenario building of MOOCs, nature and profiles of learners, motivation and dropout, etc.

© IFIP International Federation for Information Processing 2016
Published by Springer International Publishing AG 2016. All Rights Reserved
T. Brinda et al. (Eds.): SaITE 2016, IFIP AICT 493, pp. 72–81, 2016.
DOI: 10.1007/978-3-319-54687-2_7

The goal of our work is to conceive and develop various tools which consider complementary and plural aspects of online learning, through individual and/or adaptive, collaborative, fun and massive dimensions. Therefore, the perspective of this work is to refine our approach in order to provide models, tools and techniques to assist teachers (pedagogical teams) to improve pedagogical scenarios in MOOCs taking into account further motivation and adaptation issues.

The main purpose of this paper is not to examine the contribution of MOOCs in achieving the guidelines traced at the beginning, but to propose solutions to the new issues raised, especially dropout rates. Indeed, most authors point out a success rate that does not exceed 10% [3]. We note, however, that dropout in MOOCs differs from classroom-based courses or event-online diploma courses. The research community have explained this difference by the relative isolation of the learner in MOOC environments, the goals of the course or even the qualification of the course (certificate or diploma), etc.

We present in Sects. 2 and 3 a literature review as follow: an instance of the main fundamentals of MOOCs and educational scenario building concepts in these environments, then we discuss the issues related to dropout. We will analyze synthetically the various causes, issues raised and proposed solutions. In Sect. 4, we present as a discussion our problematic and positioning related to mentioned work and research.

2 Research Context

2.1 MOOC: Massive Open Online Course

MOOC is an acronym that can be approached in two different ways. First, regardless of the underlying ideology, MOOCs are essentially a platform [4]. In other words, MOOCs represent a technical support on which courses are hosted. On the other hand, MOOCs designate the courses themselves. The MOOC acronym comprises four terms that represent a divergence in the research community. They assign different meanings to each word, related to learning and/or online education. Anderson [5] gives a short description according to the features of each word. He defines Massive, not only by the large number of participants, but also by the capacity of the MOOC to scale. Scalability refers here to the capacity of the course to expand to large numbers, without causing disruption to any of the components or activities of the educational experience. For Open, he postulates that most MOOCs are open in the sense of allowing participation anywhere, to anyone and are open free for participation. However, MOOCs may or may not be open in the sense of allowing access to course content or in allowing and encouraging open communication of ideas and ideals.

Moreover, the origins of MOOCs have used acronyms distinguishing a typology of these courses: cMOOCs [6] and xMOOCs [7]. Each of these types of MOOC have their own technological and pedagogical characteristics. As illustrated in Fig. 1, xMOOC is most of the time comprising traditional approaches of teaching and learning, it places the teacher as the main leader in the pedagogical scenario process, whereas the cMOOC is more collaborative. It integrates the learner in a dynamic multi-actors' process of instructional scenario building. According to this, we believe that the cMOOC offers a search field better adapted to our vision and approach. That consists in providing to the

teacher (in this case even learners who can be potential "teachers") resources and services to innovate their pedagogical scenarios to motivated learners.

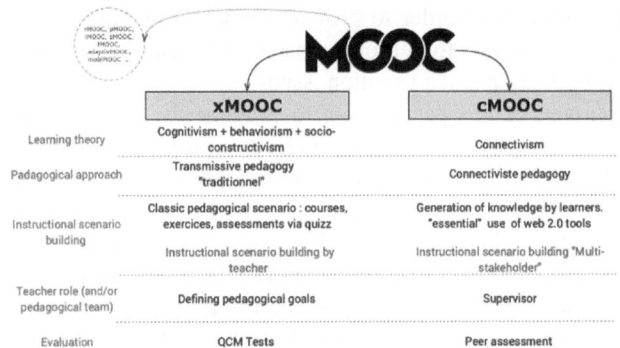

Fig. 1. xMOOC vs. cMOOC

2.2 MOOC: Educational Scenario Building

Educational scenario building is a process of modeling the learning situation. It "is
primarily a content design work, resource organization, planning of the activity and
mediation to induce and support learning and orchestration" [8]. A scenario implies
notions of role, resources, activities and orchestration. It aims to organize and structure
the learner's activity, to define the role of each actor and the relationship with the used
tools and resources.

To define globally a pedagogical scenario, we transcribe below Pernin and Lejeune's
definition: "The learning scenario represents the description, performed *a priori* or *a
posteriori*, in conducting a learning situation or learning unit for the appropriation of a
specific set of knowledge, it has to specify the roles, activities and the knowledge of
handling resources, tools, and services related to activities' implementation" [9].

Overall, in the MOOCs, educational scenario building requests innovative and
appropriate approaches of teaching and learning to meet the needs of this new concept.
It should consider two aspects: massiveness and openness.

Specifically in cMOOCs, connectivism aims to promote learning through collaboration, production, sharing and creating connections between peers; in almost total
openness. In this environment, learners have freedom of choice of learning objectives,
from which connections emerge between individuals sharing the same learning objectives. Starting from this point, the connected communities are formed by creating a
wealth of resources; personalized courses (paths) are emerging. These paths result from
the contributions of each participant and from networks that are formed throughout the
course. Such courses are based on four principles: *aggregation* of information and
resources, a *reflection* on those resources that could be linked to new knowledge, redi-
recting resources by *creating* new ones, and finally *sharing* new resources produced.

Openness of cMOOCs suggests that a pedagogical scenario is not needed and would
even go against the underlying principles. Contrary to this assumption, we believe that

designing the course connectivists implements educational scenario building practices. Indeed, despite this opening, it seems necessary to establish conditions that are conducive to the emergence of connectivist activities.

The success of a connectivist course suggests promoting and supporting learner autonomy to gain control of their learning and thus promote the creation and emergence of new resources. Autonomy cannot be taken for granted, "It presupposes abilities that all people are not equally capable or willing to mobilize" [10]. Learners must create and produce new resources and knowledge; we believe that they must be guided and oriented during this process to develop and promote their autonomy. In this line, De Figueiredo [11] postulates that:

> The dependence of the students from "canned" knowledge and their lack of autonomy, proactivity and initiative has reached unbelievable levels It is vital and urgent to break the vicious circle of dependence and lack of autonomy (...) The use of the technologies has contributed significantly to help manage autonomy. The need to instrument autonomy is also beginning to be understood (...) Once some degree of autonomy is gained, more systematic delegation of assessment can be started, then needs to be instrumented the locus of control may then be gradually transferred to the student to let them participate to the actual development of the course.

As part of connectivism implementation Armatas et al. [12] stipulate that "learning activities are structured to assist students to become independent and autonomous learners while at the same time providing students with opportunities to develop a range of technical and professional skills". From all these points, the need for educational scenario building in these open environments which depends on the learners' production is justified.

The problematization of these findings leads to these questions about the conception process, deployment and adaptation of cMOOCs:

- Which solutions can be provided to teachers to take into account the massiveness of cMOOCs, connectivism principles, the plurality of profiles, the emergence of the educational scenario and finally, the uniqueness of each (course) path?
- Which tools do we have to provide to teachers to conceive a pedagogical cMOOC-oriented scenario?
- Which tools or dispositives may allow learners to have a control on their learning and also to visualize the scenario and to adapt it according to their needs?
- How can we design an educational scenario building support which takes account of the dynamics, flexibility and opening of cMOOCs while maintaining the learners' autonomy?

3   Dropout Issue in MOOCs: State of the Art

Characterizing precisely the dropout issue is not that easy. One of the possible ways that we propose to approach it, follows this plan: possible causes of dropout, different research about the learners' profiles in this environments and proposed solutions to dropout.

Many researchers examined the dropout issue in MOOCs. Clow [13] explains the dropout rate by the demotivation of learners. The view of Cisel [14] covers the initial motivation of the participant. Indeed, he says that the interaction of the participant with the MOOC differs according to his/her post-registration intent and objective. This was supported by Anderson [5], who emphasized that several participants "enroll" just to satisfy their curiosity without any intention to complete the course. Other research is in place around the engagement of learners in a MOOC; we cite in particular the work of Kizilcec et al. [15]. The authors carried out an empirical study about lack of engagement of learners and its causes in MOOCs; but also the lack of interaction between participants using the MOOC. In the same sense, the fact that the participants are isolated is considered by many authors as one of the main reasons behind the weak participants' engagement.

3.1   Research/Studies on Learners' Profiles

To examine the issues of dropout in MOOCs, we examined work related to learner profiles in MOOCs. We note the work of Kizilcec et al. [15] and Hill [16] who proposed classifications of learners that interact with the platform. For illustration, we summarize here the work of Hill [16]. In this work a classification of participants in a MOOC according to their degree of involvement in five categories was proposed:

No-Shows – These students appear to be the largest group of those registering for a Coursera-style MOOC, where people register but never login to the course while it is active.

Observers – These students login and may read content or browse discussions, but do not take any form of assessment beyond pop-up quizzes embedded in videos.

Drop-Ins – These are students who perform some activity (watch videos, browse or participate in discussion forum) for a selected topic within the course, but do not attempt to complete the entire course. Some of these students use MOOCs informally to find content that helps them meet course goals elsewhere.

Passive Participants – These are students who view a course as content to consume. They may watch videos, take quizzes, read discuss forums, but generally do not engage with the assignments.

Active Participants – These students fully intend to participate in the MOOC and take part in discussion forums, the majority of assignments and all quizzes and assessments.

In a more recent work, Ferguson et al. [17] describe different "clusters" of learners from an empirical study of learners' engagement in different types of MOOCs. The authors define 7 clusters of learners: *Samplers, Strong Starters, Returners, Midway Dropouts, Nearly there, Late completers* and *Keen Completers*. These clusters are different according to types of MOOCs. This study shows also that "engagement patterns are related to pedagogy and course duration" [17].

In our view, these classifications are important for several reasons. The first one is to understand the types of MOOC learners and evaluate their engagement. The second is to research methods and practices that can be applied in order to sustain learners' motivation and engagement, and consequently reduce dropout rate. The third reason is to identify specific needs of learners to adapt the content and learning modalities. These are the solutions discussed below.

3.2 Some Possible Solutions Against Dropout

Based on a literature review, we can distinguish four different approaches to minimize the dropout rate:

Pedagogical Strategies Approach. This approach is represented by a number of theoretical strategies validated by empirical studies. Among the pedagogical strategies discussed in the literature, we highlight the work of Williams [18], of adding motivational messages to students when solving mathematics problems on the platform [19]. An example of a message in an activity is: "Remember, the more you practice, the smarter you become". According to this author, this has led to impressive results that were validated in practice. A second strategy is to encourage participants to answer questions and generate explanations before, during and after the activities [18]. Another method is support learners to manage their time on MOOC platforms [2]. This strategy argues that non-experience in e-learning and bad time management involve dropout.

Personalization and/or Adaptivity Approach. Several research studies focus on the importance of personalization to avoid dropout. In this context, we can mention the PERSUA2MOOC project [20]. This project provides a system for personalization of learning outcomes in MOOCs. PERSUA2MOOC is a project that aims to "adapt" the learning activities considering the individualities and teachers' educational activities. Another interesting work related to personalization is proposed by Williams et al. [21]. The authors propose a platform-independent framework "MOOClet" that allows supporting randomized experimentation and adaptive personalization of content in MOOC platforms. Other works, such as Gutiérrez-Rojas et al. [22], present a scheduling algorithm to suggest dynamically the optimum time for learners to learn, considering their profiles, preferences and priorities. This algorithm is implemented by an adaptive scheduler named MyLearningMentor, which provides a sequence of scheduled tasks. Other studies use the model of Felder and Silverman [23] to identify learning styles to provide an adaptive navigation strategy. Another solution is proposed by Cherkaoui et al. [24] with a model of adaptation in Online Learning Environments including MOOC platforms; the aim of this work is to propose an architecture of adaptation model taking into account several dimensions: individual dimension, the massive dimension, the social dimension and the fun dimension.

Gamification Approach. Integrating games into the learning process is a solution to capture a larger audience, to motivate and maintain learners' motivation and engagement during the learning activity. Indeed, the coupling of learning, virtual reality and video games allows us to consider the integration of serious games in the online learning process, mentioned in research work [25, 26].

Technological Approach. Finally, we note that in addition to video, MOOCs also follow technological ascent, implementing other web2.0 tools, namely, social networks, wikis, forums, etc.

In our view, identifying these works is important for several reasons: (1) compile and analyze the state-of-the-art in MOOC research that has been conducted on dropout issue in MOOCs; (2) identify the methods and practices that are applied in order to reduce dropout rate; (3) conduct research on how to reduce dropout in MOOC environments by investigating new models; and (4) examine the context within which further work can take place by identifying opportunities that lie ahead in this research area and make a significant contribution to future research.

Although many research works have addressed the need to reduce dropout rates in MOOC environments, there is not yet any tangible research that focuses on educational scenario building via a teacher-centered process in particular, by introducing and implementing motivational aspects and practices into pedagogical scenarios.

4   Our Work: Positioning and Methodology

The emergence of cMOOCs is constrained by creating favorable conditions and environments for teachers to design their courses and for learners to increase their autonomy.

Our hypothesis lies in the proposal of an adequate process of educational scenario building that is suitable with connectivist aspects. From this point of view, the proposal for cMOOC course authoring tools seems to us a solution to encourage teachers to move towards this model, which to date does not have as much success as the xMOOC.

Our work stems from a need to improve cMOOC environments by supporting the implementation of situations and educational activities based on a connectivist approach through a structured and dynamic pedagogical scenario. We aim to provide conceptual and technical tools for teachers to design pedagogical scenarios, and for teachers and students to adapt their scenarios. This is what we describe in the rest of this chapter.

To meet the requirements above, we propose a cMOOC-oriented cycle (Fig. 2) that will consider on the one hand the pedagogical scenario building and its implementation. In our context, this process will rebuild the interdisciplinary connections by introducing concrete contexts of application based on the main activities of connectivism (formalization and deployment phases), and, on the other hand, the dynamic adaptation to learners' progression through tools that allow drawing up a progressive, emergent course scenario and knowledge consolidation (adaptation process phase).

1. **Formalization**: The aim of this phase is to provide teachers with tools and/or models to assist them in the design of formalized cMOOC-oriented scenarios. Our first contribution, arising from these needs, lies in proposing a meta-model of a connectivist pedagogical scenario taking into account the massiveness aspect of cMOOC environments. Our model will be built in several layers. The first level of abstraction is represented by the four activities of connectivism cited previously (aggregation, remixing, repurposing and feed forwarding). Technically, in this phase, we aim to develop a cMOOC-oriented scenario editor in a common language that can be used

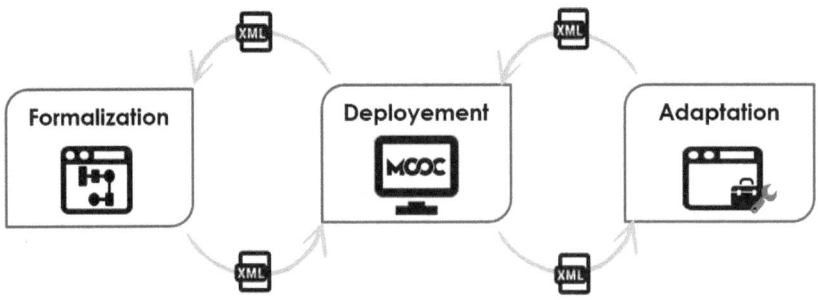

Fig. 2. cMOOC-oriented cycle

by different actors involved in the implementation process of learning systems to meet the starting educational intentions all over the design process.

2. **Deployment**: The aim of this phase is to operationalize pedagogical scenarios in a cMOOC platform. Our contribution lies in the proposal for an operationalization process allowing teachers to create deployable learning scenarios. This phase is to provide a solution (or set of solutions) that allows deployment of pedagogical scenarios generated during the "formalization" phase on a MOOC platform. We will offer elements and services that allow the dynamic implementation of built scenarios: any change on the workflow will be included on the platform and *vice versa*.

3. **Adaptation**: This phase is designed to permit compliance with one of the connectivism aspects through our proposal: the learner is an actor of his learning, he is not anymore a consumer of resources but a creator. The learner is dynamically involved in the instructional scenario building process. As mentioned above, the educational scenario building process, in connectivist environments, is immersing throughout the learning session. Thus, our objective is to bring solutions to the emergence of needs (motivational, functional, etc.) throughout the learning process. Our contribution is to offer an adaptation model, that takes into account:

   - The plurality of profiles, the uniqueness and respect of their personal learning objectives.
   - A real-time adaptation solution.
   - The possibility of the integration of motivational aspects.

5 Conclusion

This paper first presented the two axes related to our work, namely: cMOOCs and educational scenario building in those environments. The synthesis of the literature highlights our views on the approach of dropout along three dimensions: possible causes of dropout, research related to the types of participants and solutions to minimize the dropout rate. The literature review demonstrates that all cited points are complementary and also highlights the importance of motivation as a solution to reduce dropout rate. Analysis of various works highlights several tracks. The objective of our work is to propose an approach, models, methods and techniques to users of MOOCs, to take into account motivation concepts in the design, adaptation and/or personalization of their pedagogical scenarios taking into account specification of cMOOC environments.

References

1. Glance, D.G., Forsey, M., Riley, M.: The pedagogical foundations of massive open online courses. First Monday **18**(5) (2013)
2. Nawrot, I., Doucet, A.: Building engagement for MOOC students, introducing support for time management on online learning platforms. In: International World Wide Web Conference Committee (IW3C2) (2014)
3. Liyanagunawardena, T.R., Adams, A.A., Williams, S.A.: MOOCs: a systematic study of the published literature 2008–2012. Int. Rev. Res. Open Distance Learn. **14**(3), 202–227 (2013). 16
4. Schroeder, R., Levin, C.: eduMOOC: open online learning without limits. In: Annual Conference on Distance Teaching & Learning (2012)
5. Anderson, T.: Promise and/or Peril: MOOCs and Open and Distance Education. Commonwealth of Learning (2013)
6. Downes, S.: Places to go: connectivism & connective knowledge. Innovate J. Online Educ. **5**(1) (2008)
7. Hollands, F.M., Tirthali, D.: MOOCs: expectations and reality. Center for Benefit-Cost Studies of Education, Teachers College, Columbia University, New York, NY. p. 34 (2014)
8. Henri, F., Compte, C., Charlier, B.: La scénarisation pédagogique dans tous ses débats. PROFETIC. Revue internationale des technologies en pédagogie universitaire **4**(2), 14–24 (2007)
9. Pernin, J.P.: LOM, SCORM et IMS-Learning Design: ressources, activités et scénarios. In: actes du colloque «L'indexation des ressources pédagogiques numériques», Lyon, vol. 16 (2004)
10. Linard, M.: Autoformation, éthique et technologies: enjeux et paradoxes de l'autonomie. Autoformation et enseignement supérieur, pp. 241–263 (2003)
11. De Figueiredo, A.D.: Onlife learning and the role of the stakeholdere. In: IFIP TP3 Conference (2016)
12. Armatas, C., Spratt, C., Vincent, A.: Putting connectivist principles into practice: a case study of an online tertiary course. Am. J. Distance Educ. **28**(2), 81–91 (2014)
13. Clow, D.: MOOCs and the funnel of participation. In: Proceedings of the Third International Conference on Learning Analytics and Knowledge, pp. 185–189. ACM (2013)
14. Cisel, M.: MOOC: Ce que les taux d'abandon signifient. Blog de Matthieu Cisel (2013)
15. Kizilcec, R.F., Piech, C., Schneider, E.: Deconstructing disengagement: analyzing learner subpopulations in massive open online courses. In: Proceedings of the Third International Conference on Learning Analytics and Knowledge, pp. 170–179. ACM (2013)
16. Hill, P.: Some validation of MOOC student patterns graphic (2013). http://mfeldstein.com/validation-mooc-student-patterns-graphic
17. Ferguson, R., Clow, D., Beale, R., Cooper, A.J., Morris, N., Bayne, S., Woodgate, A.: Moving through MOOCS: pedagogy, learning design and patterns of engagement. In: Conole, G., Klobučar, T., Rensing, C., Konert, J., Lavoué, É. (eds.) EC-TEL 2015. LNCS, vol. 9307, pp. 70–84. Springer, Heidelberg (2015). doi:10.1007/978-3-319-24258-3_6
18. Williams, J.J.: Applying cognitive science to online learning. In: NIPS Data-Driven Education Workshop (2013)
19. Khan Academy. http://www.KhanAcademy.org

20. Clerc, F.: Mise en Place de la Personnalisation Dans le Cadre des MOOCs. Mémoire de master, Université Claude Bernard Lyon 1 - LIRIS (2014)
21. Williams, J.J., Kim, J., Maldonado, S., Heffernan, N., Li, N., Whitehill, J., Chu, L., Pechenizkiy, M.: The MOOClet Framework: Improving Online Education through Experimentation and Personalization of Modules (2014)
22. Gutiérrez-Rojas, I., Alario-Hoyos, C., Pérez-Sanagustín, M., Eony, D., Delgado-Kloos, C.: Scaffolding self-learning in MOOCs. In: Proceedings of the Second MOOC European Stakeholders Summit, EMOOCs, pp. 43–49 (2014)
23. Fasihuddin, H.A., Skinner, G.D., Athauda, R.I.: Boosting the opportunities of open learning (MOOCs) through learning theories. GSTF J. Comput. (JoC) 3(13), 1–6 (2013)
24. Cherkaoui, C., Qazdar, A., Battou, A., Mezouary, A., Bakki, A., Er-Raha, B., Mamass, D.: A model of adaptation in online learning environments (LMSs and MOOCs). In: Tenth International Conference on Intelligent Systems (2015)
25. Romero, M., Usart, M.: Serious games integration in an entrepreneurship massive online open course (MOOC). In: Ma, M., Oliveira, M.F., Petersen, S., Hauge, J.B. (eds.) SGDA 2013. LNCS, vol. 8101, pp. 212–225. Springer, Heidelberg (2013). doi:10.1007/978-3-642-40790-1_21
26. Freire, M., del Blanco, A., Fernández-Manjón, B.: Serious games as edX MOOC activities. In: Global Engineering Education Conference (EDUCON), pp. 867–871. IEEE (2014)

Using Images as a Stimulus to Explore the Identity of Student Teachers in Computing

Eleanor Overland[✉]

Faculty of Education, Manchester Metropolitan University, Manchester, UK
e.overland@mmu.ac.uk

Abstract. The computing curriculum in English secondary education is now officially in its second year of implementation. A new, specialist group of student teachers are being trained to be able to deliver the new, rigorous computing curriculum. In this emerging curriculum area, it is essential teachers explore their own identity, beliefs and values in order to deliver effectively and ensure enjoyment for both themselves and the pupils they teach. In this study, the student teachers engage with images and place them in a hierarchy to stimulate honest discussion and exploration of computing teacher identity. Whilst the student teachers resonate with approaches in the classroom, such as group work, engagement with the computing curriculum topics themselves are limited and show an area which may require more attention and challenge in the computing teacher training programme.

Keywords: Computing education · ICT education · Student teachers · Identity

1 Introduction

The National Curriculum in England has undergone a significant shift; from September 2014 ICT education was withdrawn and replaced with computing [1]. As a result, Initial Teacher Education (ITE) courses have been updated to reflect the requirement for new, specialist teachers to enter the profession. Secondary trainee teachers in England now follow courses in 'Computing' or 'Computing with [Information and Communication Technologies] ICT'. The courses attract a range of graduate applicants, some direct from computing-related degree courses and others from industry and computer-related employment. For some applicants their computing subject knowledge is broad and in sufficient depth to teach to the highest levels, others may have more specialist backgrounds and so need to follow a computing subject knowledge enhancement course prior to teacher training. The opportunity to teach the 'new' subject attracted 878 students in England between 2013 and 2015 [2]. The availability of bursaries to support career change and the availability of subject knowledge enhancement courses has brought in a wide range of students, differing in age, background and expectations. Added to the eclectic mix of students are a range of school-based mentors, many of whom are not computing specialists themselves but may have been teaching an ICT-based curriculum for considerable time. Those that are computing specialists may have found themselves

T. Brinda et al. (Eds.): SaITE 2016, IFIP AICT 493, pp. 82–91, 2016.
DOI: 10.1007/978-3-319-54687-2_8

teaching mathematics or more science-based subjects so the opportunity to engage with their specialism is also a new experience. Although a rapidly developing area, finding trainee teachers an experienced school-based mentor who is a computing specialist is a challenge.

The context of change and curriculum reform adds an additional layer of complexity for trainee computing teachers. Developing an identity as a teacher, whilst a changeable and evolving process, is crucial as part of any ITE where students are given the opportunity to explore their values and beliefs, how they are learning and the context in which they will work; a process of becoming [3]. The computing trainees may well receive mixed messages from mentors, university tutors, the media and pupils themselves. All those involved in the curriculum change will also be identifying their own role and position within it so therefore, whilst thinking primarily of their own position, the trainees are also subject to mixed rhetoric from those around them. Exploring identity within this context is therefore more crucial yet more challenging than for many other subject areas at this time.

2   Exploring Identity

2.1   The Importance of Identity Construction

Studies have found supporting teachers in the exploration of their identity has allowed teachers to 'grow in service to students', develop better teaching, renew practice and ultimately enjoy the role [4, 5]. Leuhmann prioritised 'recognition work' with student science teachers in order to provide opportunities for the student teachers to explore their identity through personal reflection and exploratory processes such as keeping journals and engaging in discussion. The methods of exploring teacher identity vary in nature but are similar in aim, in order to identify external influences (including prior experience and own education), professional factors, personal factors and uncovering a set of values, beliefs and goals held by the teacher [6].

Ni and Guzdial [6] carried out a study exclusively with teachers of computer science in the United States of America (USA). They found varied identities, with particular differences in motivation and confidence with the subject of computer science. Respondents in the survey very much attached themselves to labels such as programming, computer science and the complexities of the subject. With the current government rhetoric in England there is a danger of current student teachers in computing finding themselves attached to the lexicon rather than the underlying values and priorities they have as computing teachers. There is a drive for computing to portray itself as having far more academic rigour and challenge than its predecessor, ICT, and current student teachers are very much part of this emerging landscape [7].

Assessment practices are also developing. The national qualifications in England taken by school pupils at age 16 years now require 80% of assessment to be completed through written examinations. This results in very little of the two-year course being practical requiring 'project based' computing solutions. For student teachers this may be at odds with their own experience in industry before training to be teachers or in their own personal experience of being engaged in the 'maker movement' or 'hackerthon' type events. In these, constructivism is very much favoured with participants 'playing' and exploring to discover new learning [8].

Support during the teacher training course and in negotiating a path through the range of conflicting influences, terminology and rhetoric is provided by school-based mentors. School-based mentors help shape the teacher the student becomes through the communication of classroom practice-based values that the student may then receive or reject. At the same time, the students will need to feel valued by their mentors in order to feel self-worth in their development as teachers [9]. Where the student teachers may have greater subject knowledge than their mentors this may add complexity to how mentors support the development of student teacher identity. Subject knowledge may become less of a priority for the students or could even lead to them devaluing the beliefs and advice of the mentors and so seek values from alternative sources.

2.2   Image as a Provocation

In an attempt to break away from the lexicon of the emerging computing curriculum, a visual approach to exploring identity is being taken. The theoretical frameworks for this study are varied yet interwoven. The study draws on identity theory and on semiology; how is identity portrayed or interpreted? The study also 'borrows' from art theorists. This section outlines the frameworks that are drawn upon in this study but also explores the overlaps within the fields.

Foucault considers a painting of a pipe, which features a blackboard stating 'this is not a pipe' within the image, depicting yet another pipe. The reading of this image by Foucault outlines a number of ambiguities [10]. The discussion extends for some time and raises a number of questions about the painting. What is clearly illustrated is the non-relation, or the very complex relation between the painting and its title. The intention of the artist, Magritte, is to challenge the viewer of the image and focus their attention on the very act of naming. The tension between the naming of the painting and the objects portrayed, resemblance and affirmation, is where the viewers (or 'reader' of the image) are forced to think, to devise meaning and consider their own view. Without the text, the painting would be accepted by most as a representation of a pipe.

The tension that can be created through visual representation and opposing text can also be initiated through contradictory images. In an attempt to move away from lexicon, the same tensions can be developed and so similar commitment from the 'reader' is required. Two images are presented, using the anchorage 'pupils at work'; firstly an image of children sitting in rows, working on paper without evident speech or movement; secondly, a small group of children clearly talking and focussed on a central resource. A choice needs to be made, which one is most representative of 'pupils at work'. For this to happen, as a reader of the images, you would need to draw on your own experiences, your understanding of 'work' and which image most resonates. The comparative process aids the reader, not only to view the image, but consider their own position and so new understanding of it.

There is a concern that this process of comparing and selecting images is simplistic and limited in scope. The images may be isotopic in nature so the comparison becomes superficial, a tangle of words and images with little contradiction to sustain a purposeful discourse [11, 12]. However, within this process of comparing images, the multiplicity of layers and 'readings' on an image adds further value and legitimacy to the method. Even the most naive of images (produced without intention or message, if this is indeed possible) will convey characteristics of a message; even if not substantial these will be relational in some way to the 'reader' [12]. Without applying their own experience and prior understanding to the reading, signs would not be understood and the image would be unintelligible to the reader. Each reading of an image is therefore individual, based on experience and understanding, so in exploring one's own readings of signs, a consideration of one's own experience, beliefs and identity will be required.

3   Methodology

The study involved 40 trainee computing teachers from two different cohorts between September 2014 and December 2015. The students worked in pairs to discuss, respond and reflect on the process.

Participants were given 18 images and requested to select only 9 to feature in their completed diagram. This first part of the process required the trainee teachers to act as 'readers' of the images. They discussed what each of the images meant to them and agreed half of the images to be discarded. They were instructed to keep the 9 that most resonated with them as teachers of computing. By working in pairs, the students were required to articulate their view of each image and come to a consensus as to which images are given priority.

The images selected for the process were varied in nature and included a selection of photographs from classroom situations, topics delivered within ICT or computing classrooms, and pupil work. Each image was numbered for purposes of analysis but these were allocated randomly. The students were given the images as a shuffled pile of cards. The students were given no further information on what the images depicted, although they were much larger than the examples presented below. Students were asked to annotate, wherever appropriate, to provide an insight into their reading or positioning of the image. A copy of all images is available online [13].

Depicting pupil activity within learning settings (Fig. 1):

- **Image 4** is a view of a typical examination setting. All English national computing qualifications will require 80% assessment through a written examination.
- **Image 9** is a pupil connecting a MakeyMakey with Scratch running on screen.

Depicting pupil work in computing or ICT lessons:

- **Image 2** shows a hand-drawn flow chart.
- **Image 6** shows a pupil working on a tablet, here using the Beebot application.

Depicting classroom display or on-screen presentation of pupil work from computing and ICT lessons:

- **Image 3** shows two pieces of hardware along with moveable printed labels.
- **Image 10** is a hand-drawn poster depicting 'Internet Safety Girl'.

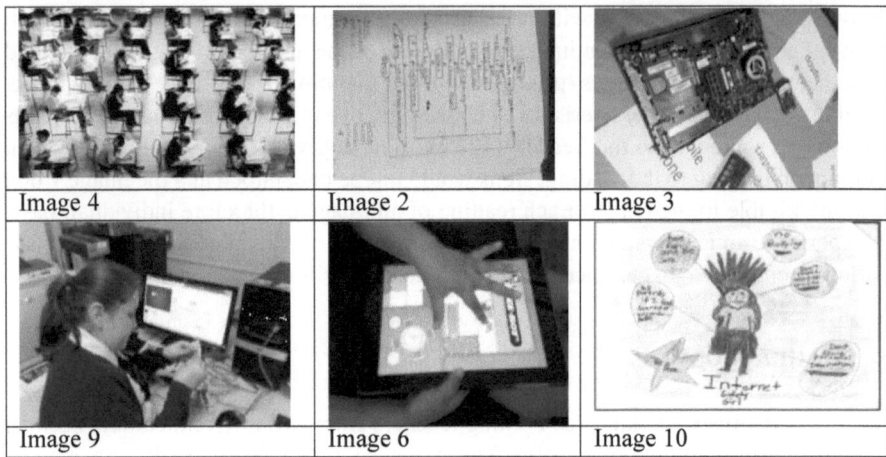

Fig. 1. Examples of images from the study

Following the discussion and selection of an agreed 9 images, the students were given a 'Diamond 9' shape as shown in Fig. 2.

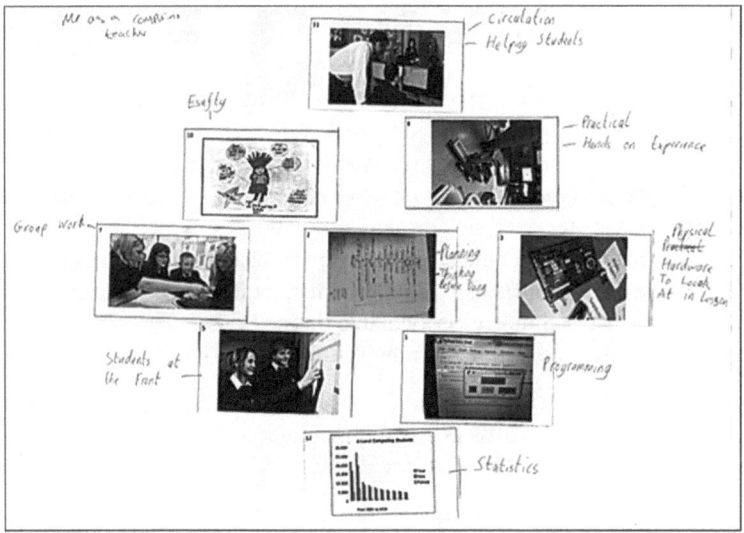

Fig. 2. An example of a completed diamond 9

They were requested to place their images within the hierarchical structure, the most important being at the top of the diamond and the least at the base. This time, rather than just being 'readers' of images, the students were required to draw on their beliefs, values and classroom practice to prioritise images. This process has been used successfully to develop discussion and identify tacit thoughts of abstract concepts, particularly with school age children [14, 15].

4 Results and Findings

Approaches to analysis of the data are three-fold. The first two make use of a basic statistical analysis to identify patterns and trends in the selection and placement of the data. The first looks at the overall usage of each image using a weighted score dependent on the position anywhere within the Diamond (Fig. 3).

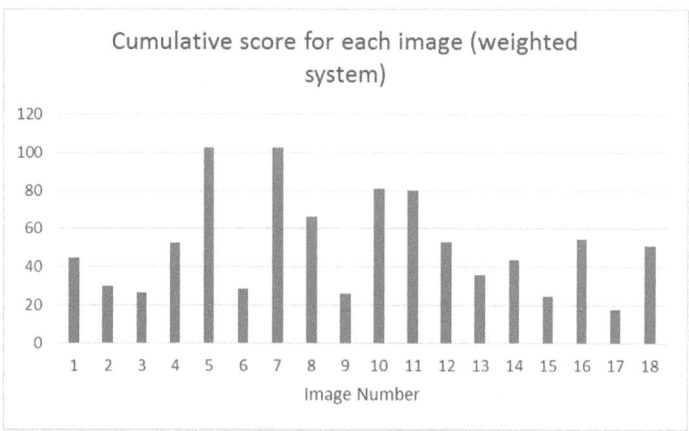

Fig. 3. Summary data showing weighted scores for each image based on overall use within the diamond 9

The second simply identifies the images most commonly used in the top 3 rows of the diamond formation (Fig. 4). Thirdly the Diamond 9 responses are compared to consider the annotation added by the participants.

Images 5 and 7 are most prevalent in their use within the diamonds. One depicts pupils clearly conversing and working together around a laptop. It is labelled throughout the responses with appropriate 'buzz words' (for example, Fig. 5). These are terms that currently feature prominently across much teacher training and development across all curriculum areas. These descriptors include 'peer learning', 'group work', 'interactive learning', 'learning by doing', 'active learning' and 'experimental learning'. Also featuring highly are practical work, pupil-led learning and teacher support.

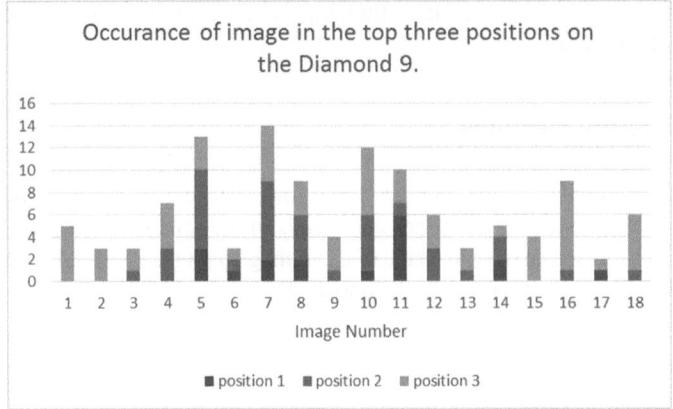

Fig. 4. Summary data showing frequency of images used in the top three positions within the diamond 9

Fig. 5. Annotated image 7 labelled as group work, peer teaching and active learning

Image 10 also featured strongly throughout many of the diamonds. Interestingly, it is one of the few images that does not depict a computer or some aspect of specific computing subject knowledge. The image portrays a hand-drawn 'super hero girl' who knows how to stay safe online. The annotations (Fig. 6) mainly feature an 'e-safety' label, never alluding to a reading of the image other than the safety message.

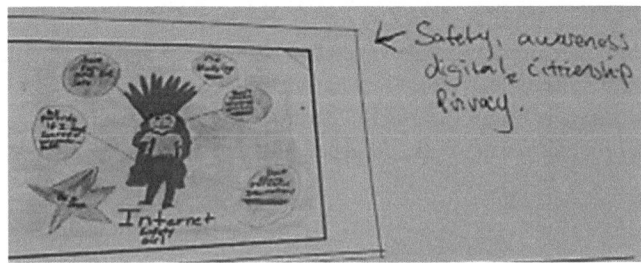

Fig. 6. Annotated internet safety girl

The trainees are reading this image as the pupil illustrator intended and have held fast to the message. They have identified safeguarding as being one of their top-most priorities as a teacher, the need to protect and even nurture the pupils in their use of the internet. This notion of the caring nature of the role resonates strongly with some of the findings Walkerdine identified from her own exploration of teacher identity [16].

Interestingly, code, assessment and curriculum seldom featured or were placed in low positions on the Diamond. Where they were included the annotation was very basic, often including straightforward terms such as 'programming' and 'coding'. Very few of the wider terms and content featured in the National Curriculum Computing document were included in any of the annotation and images that may have suggested these were placed very low in the hierarchy or not featured. These omissions are the terms most associated with current 'measures' of the English computing education through Ofsted and government-led computing curriculum rhetoric. What was clearly apparent, however, was the rejection of 'ICT' both as a curriculum subject and in the wider context. Only one image displayed use of a mobile device and there is a clear dislike for traditional ICT-type tasks such as the annotated database shown in Fig. 7.

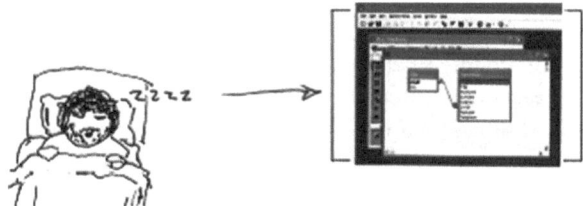

Fig. 7. Database structure with student annotation

The student teachers were also asked to note any omissions they felt they were unable to represent from the images with which they were provided. Not all felt the need to take this opportunity; however, some were listed: cross curricular, inclusion, marking, differentiation, behaviour, class discussions and the internet. It is interesting how this list features some of the more challenging aspects of teaching and yet none of the images have been annotated in a way to suggest they have been 'read' as a negative feature of teaching as a profession. This is due to the nature of the study with student teachers being asked to prioritise and look at importance. This suggests the process may lend itself to being used in different ways, for example, specifically addressing curriculum design or teacher challenges.

One of the most revealing aspects of this research process was the participant response. The trainee teachers fully engaged with the process and were fascinated by the outcome, both their own and those of others. Following the task they requested to look at each other's work and discussed and justified their own decision making process. It also allowed university-based teacher educators to have a greater understanding of the student teacher identity and support areas they felt may be worth further discussion and exploration.

By only recording the final annotated diamonds for this study, much rich data was lost. Recording the discussions the trainees were having during the process would have provided additional insight into the process and the actual awakening of teacher identity occurring within the group. With the second cohort the student teachers were asked to volunteer to record their discussions. Only one pair did and after a short while asked if they could stop the recording. They felt their discussions were less honest and free flowing as they were conscious that university staff may listen to what they said. It may be more appropriate for student teachers to develop their own personal reflections following the discussion to contribute towards the understanding of the process. Also revisiting this activity at a later date would add another insight into identity development amongst the student teachers. What is most important is that student teachers have the opportunity to construct and re-construct their identity as part of their teacher training programme [17].

5   Conclusion

A main finding from the Diamond 9s is the lack of priority given to subject specific topics or classroom activity. Student teachers are clearly more engaged in the 'how' of their teaching rather than the 'what'. Maybe this is where student teachers feel they have the most freedom and ability to develop their own practice, whereas the computing curriculum is a given. Conflicts between personal identity and the mandated curriculum can really hamper teacher development, a sense of achievement and so job satisfaction [18]. In the new field of computing education in English high schools, it is important any conflicts are explored, particularly to ensure the growing number of specialist teachers are able to contribute their ideas and beliefs to the development of the curriculum and to ensure retention of this new group of teachers. It is essential time is given to this within computing teacher training programmes and student teachers are able to explore where they may have ownership and influence in curriculum development in schools.

What is clear is the images have been a valuable stimulus for discussion. A move to images has ensured the student teachers have been able to have jargon-free, open discussions and really explore the aspects of teaching they most resonate with rather than paying lip service to computing curriculum rhetoric or the assessed requirements of the course. In this study the images have been collected and issued to the students. Expanding the process to encourage student teachers to take their own images, through a photo journal, may encourage them to 'look' at their teaching practice from a different perspective. This way the process would develop to be more personally reflective and explore identity over a period of time.

The process embraced within this paper, whilst at an early stage of development, is already appreciated by student teachers and student teacher educators. The process of engaging with the images has allowed a space for discussion and exploration which may otherwise be missed. It is important, particularly in the developing area of training computing teachers, that identity continues to be explored.

References

1. Department for Education (DFE,b): National Curriculum from September (2013, 2014). https://www.gov.uk/government/collections/national-curriculum. Accessed 14 Mar 2014
2. Department for Education (DFE,a): Initial teacher training: trainee number census – (2014, 2015). https://www.gov.uk/government/statistics/initial-teacher-training-trainee-number-census-2014-to-2015. Accessed 23 Feb 2016
3. Britzman, D.: Practice Makes Practice: A Critical Study of Learning to Teach. State University of New York Press, New York (2003)
4. Luehamnn, A.L.: Identity development as a lens to science teacher preparation. Sci. Educ. **91**(5), 822–839 (2007). Wiley InterScience, University of Rochester
5. Livsey, R.C., Palmer, P.J.: The Courage to Teach: A Guide to Reflection and Renewal. Jossey-Bass, California (1999)
6. Ni, L., Guzdial, M.: Who am I? Understanding high school computer science teachers' professional identity. In: SIGCSE 2012, Raleigh, NC, 29 February–3 March 2012
7. Royal Society: Shut Down or Restart? The way forward for computing in UK Schools. The Royal Society, London (2012)
8. Martinez, S.L., Stager, G.S.: Invent to Learn: Making, Tinkering and Engineering in the Classroom. Constructing Modern Knowledge Press, Torrance (2013)
9. White, B.E., Lemieux, A.: Reflecting selves: Pre-service teacher identity development explored through material culture. Learn. Landscapes **9**(1), 267–283 (2015)
10. Foucault, M.: This is Not a Pipe. University of California Press, Berkeley (1983)
11. Manghani, S., Simons, J., Piper, A.: Images: A Reader. Sage Publications, London (2006)
12. Barthes, R.: Image Music Text. Fontana Press, London (1977)
13. Online copy of all images used within the study. https://drive.google.com/drive/folders/0B0iqB-MoHnQ_MENQMkZyazNJWUk
14. Clark, J.: Using diamond ranking as visual cues to engage young people in the research process. Qual. Res. J. **12**(2), 222–237 (2012)
15. O'Kane, C.: The development of participatory techniques: facilitating children's views about decisions which affect them. In: Christensen, P., James, A. (eds.) Research With Children: Perspectives and Practices, Falmer Press, London (2000)
16. Walkerdine, V.: Schoolgirl Fictions. Verso, London (1990)
17. Trent, J.: Teacher education as identity construction: insights from action research. J. Educ. Teach. **36**(2), 153–168 (2010)
18. Connelly, F.M., Clandinin, D.J.: Shaping a Professional Identity: Stories of Educational Practice. Teachers College Press, New York (1999)

Developments in Educational Management

Datafication in Education: A Multi-Level Challenge for IT in Educational Management

Andreas Breiter[✉]

Institute for Information Management, University of Bremen, Bremen, Germany
abreiter@uni-bremen.de

Abstract. While data-driven decision-making has become a new paradigm for school development and accountability, research on the underlying ICT infrastructures and the ICT management processes have been less prominent. With the trend of datafication, educational management gains new options but also requires adequate controlling mechanisms to take care of the data and to account for privacy and security. The information management cycle can be used to define all relevant aspects of the management process. This is adopted to the specific situation of educational institutions and furthermore extended to account for the different levels of educational governance. This leads to a new concept of educational technology governance as a necessary frame for supporting datafication processes.

Keywords: Educational governance · ICT management · Datafication · Information technology governance

1 Datafication: A Societal Trend

In the past decade, an increasing trend to measure social life in numbers can be observed as part of the so-called 'audit society' [1]. With this turn, almost all aspects of social life have become measured and quantified. Originating from the business sector, large-scale data have attracted the attention of many education scientists as a basis for decision-making aiming at education improvement. Decision support systems in the field of education have started to emerge in which student data are used in a feedback loop to improve student performance. Datafication raises expectations concerning increasing transparency for the public, accountability and civic participation but also associated fears with respect to surveillance and privacy [2]. This is also addressed in recent critical studies on 'big data' [3–6].

Educational decision-making processes are increasingly linked to the collection, processing and visualization of data [7–9]. These data practices relate to schools' performances and student achievements, which are compared on a national and international scale. They affect salaries of teachers and school managers, which are adjusted according to test scores as well as decision-making of parents for school choice or control of teachers. The general idea is twofold: data can be used for school improvement [8–10], but also for accountability [11–14]. This is part of a larger output-orientation of

T. Brinda et al. (Eds.): SaITE 2016, IFIP AICT 493, pp. 95–103, 2016.
DOI: 10.1007/978-3-319-54687-2_9

education measured by standardized achievement tests (high stakes), which started in the U.S., Australia and the UK and has a growing importance all over the world [15]. This output-orientation goes hand in hand with increased control (governance) of school systems [11], also based on neo-liberal reforms for 'new public management' [16]. Selwyn [17] points out that data are being generated and processed in increased volume, velocity and variety, resulting in what is known as large-scale data or big data. This trend has increasingly led to discussions on data mining and analytics in business, science and government. Williamson [18] speaks of 'governing software' and the 'emergence of "digital governance" in public education' (p.83). He argues that educational decision-making is increasingly being delegated to database-driven analytics software and states that 'software has now become a significant social actor that can govern and shape people's lives' [18].

Within the educational context, more data and more heterogeneous data are being generated—deliberately—for monitoring, surveillance or evaluation purposes but also—automatically—through routine operations of digital devices and systems [17]. They range from computer-based tests to learning analytics on large-scale data in complex information systems. They allow the 'recording, storage, manipulation and distribution of data in *digital* form' [17, emphasis in original]. Digital data are distinct from pre-digital forms as they may be exhaustive in scope, highly detailed and can be combined in a flexible manner. Datafication has to be understood in different dimensions. As more and more media are based on computer devices and software, we generate 'digital traces' [19] by using them. This can be aggregated and processed automatically. A rather new trend is learning analytics and educational data mining. While some embrace the new opportunities for improving teaching and learning [20–22], others refer to the challenges of an education system which is defined algorithmically [23–25].

2   Datafication and Educational Governance

Eynon [26] points out that the use of big data observed in the educational sector is not a new phenomenon, as it has been widely applied in the commercial sectors, where data sets are combined to understand markets, as well as in the field of natural sciences. In the business sector, customer satisfaction is usually utilized to measure how well a company performs. The more satisfied the customers are with the service provided by a company, the more profits are likely to be gained. Likewise, in the education sector, students' performance is usually used to measure the quality of education, i.e., the better the students perform, the better the quality of education is usually perceived to be. Education itself brings profit to a country from the perspective of improvement of human capital. In this context, educational government bodies can be seen as the main organizations that provide services to society in the form of education. Especially in education, the governance structure of the education system has a strong explanatory power to understand changes from the classroom level (micro) to the organizational level (meso) to the policy level (macro). ICT has to be embedded in each of these levels and has its impact across the levels. We follow the framework model of educational governance [27, 28] and contextualize it to the role of ICT in schooling [29]. The three-tier model of educational technology governance allows a broader view on the intertwined processes on the macro, meso and micro level.

On the macro level, in most countries, public pressure on changing education policy enforced by international non-governmental organizations (like OECD or IEA) can been observed since the publication of PISA results in the 1990s. Martens et al. [15] explained different reactions of nation states to these pressures – from adoption of achievement tests in the national education policy, to ignoring it. They even identified a convergence of educational systems to follow the logic of the test systems [30].

Other studies in education policy highlight numbers and evidence-based policy as the mode of educational governance in Australia [31]. They point out that from a socio-logical point of view, it is necessary to be aware of the social construction behind the numbers, which come to constitute education policy, as an understanding of the socially constructed nature of data leads to the identification of its weaknesses and strategies to improve. On the meso level of the district (or region), comprehensive information systems have been built in order to cope with increasing data [32–34]. This level is rather under-researched as intermediaries are less in focus but also the differences of educa-tional governance across countries are particularly strong. Depending on the level of autonomy of the schools, the centralization or decentralization of the national school system as well as the size of the school system to be attractive for commercial software companies varies. Hence, the micro level of the school according to data practices and school information systems has been studied extensively. This ranges from technology adoption of school information systems [35, 36] by administrators and teachers to different uses of information systems for performance feedback [37–39] to learning analytics [20, 25]. In this paper, we argue that all information systems and the underlying infrastructures need to be managed, i.e. planned, organized and controlled.

3   Educational Technology Governance for a Datafied Education System

3.1   Educational Information Management

Data are a carrier of information that can be turned into knowledge when they are inter-preted in a particular context by humans. This knowledge may lead to action by indi-viduals or organizations when it is perceived as referring to a certain context [10]. Data, information and knowledge can be seen as a continuum where information management is rooted in an efficient and reliable infrastructure for data processing [40]. In the enter-prise world, the purpose is to make an enterprise as intelligent as possible by valuing its knowledge assets for success. Choo [40] defines an intelligent organization as one, which is able to learn from its internal and external environments, by detecting and correcting errors between outcome and expectation. Internal environment in this context refers to any available data or information that originates from within the organization. Applying this to the educational sector, student performance can be improved by learning from data or information that resides in the information system the educational institution operates.

While in general information systems can be understood as technologies and associated people and processes, Visscher [41] defines an information system in the context of education as any computer or set of computers with data bases that enable users to record, process, retrieve and distribute data. Breiter et al. [42] make a clear distinction of the following types of school information systems: (1) Assessment information system, (2) Learning management system, (3) Administrative school information system, and (4) Electronic school directory. An assessment information system is aimed at presenting the evaluation results of students and schools. Drawing on self-evaluation tests, classroom-based assessments or standardized tests, this information system is accessed by students, teachers, parents, and decision-makers. Learning management systems are about teaching and learning and are addressed at teachers and students, such as e-learning or learning platforms. Administrative school information systems are used for administrative or management purposes of school staff. Electronic school directories cover school master data, such as school profiles or addresses, which are usually made available to the public.

Information systems are means to the end for better decision-making, based on an ICT infrastructure (networks, databases etc.) which itself needs to be managed (Fig. 1). Anagnostopoulos et al. [12] define the underlying information infrastructure as an assemblage of people, technology and policy. This infrastructure is described as being similar to the physical infrastructure of cities or states, which includes canals, traffic and street intersections. For an efficient transportation across countries or regions, this infrastructure needs people to design, build and maintain it continuously, including its rules, norms, and underlying assumptions about its use. The term infrastructure itself is defined as something big, layered, and complex, where adjustment involves aspects dependent on the context applied [43, 44]. Information infrastructures can be regarded as institutions or formative contexts on the basis that they 'constitute the background condition for action, enforcing constraints, giving direction and meaning, and setting the range of opportunities for undertaking action' [45]. The implication is that as they are 'infused with value', they become more taken for granted and less expendable. When it comes to decision support systems in the education area, Anagnostopoulos et al. [12] define the underlying information infrastructure as an assemblage of people, technology and policy, using the famous term of Latour [46]. This infrastructure is described as being similar to the physical infrastructure of cities or states, which includes canals, traffic and street intersections. For an efficient transportation across countries or regions, this infrastructure needs people to design, build and maintain it continuously, including its rules, norms, and underlying assumptions about its use. The information infrastructure itself is pointed out to have economic, social, political and cultural impacts. It is more than just technology, as it is (re)shaped through the interaction of individual, social, political and technological forces.

As in business, we can find additional cross-sectional educational management processes on the leadership level such as strategic development, human resources and staff development, organizational issues and controlling. On the top level, the availability of data to make informed decisions as well as the demand for this data has to be managed. Further research suggests that this is not a static concept but has to be regarded as an ongoing process across the levels. As we know from generic

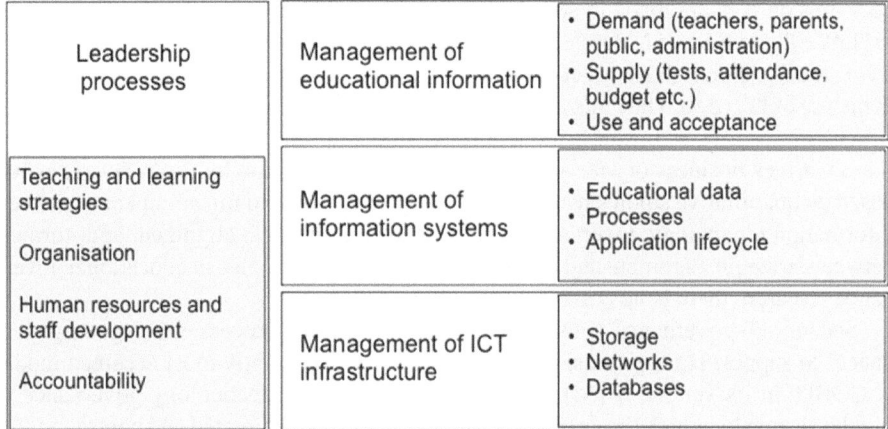

Leadership processes	Management of educational information	• Demand (teachers, parents, public, administration) • Supply (tests, attendance, budget etc.) • Use and acceptance
Teaching and learning strategies Organisation	Management of information systems	• Educational data • Processes • Application lifecycle
Human resources and staff development Accountability	Management of ICT infrastructure	• Storage • Networks • Databases

Fig. 1. Information management in education (adaptation from [49])

technology acceptance models [47, 48], as well as from research on school information systems [41], perceived usefulness and ease of use are predictors for integrating technology in everyday activities.

According to Choo [40], the information management cycle consists of a continuous loop with six distinct steps. It starts with (1) the identification of information needs, which basically consists of answering the questions of what kind of data are needed for which purposes. This is then followed by (2) information acquisition (data collection), (3) information organization and storage (data storage), (4) development of information products and services and (5) data distribution, which is executed by data organizers with the help of ICTs, and then (6) information use.

From an educational management perspective, input data in this system are not limited to student achievement data only, but the system can also be fed with other kinds of related data. Student achievement assessments have been widely accepted as the standard to evaluate student performance for class, school or international levels of comparison. Additionally, budget data, process data, students' e-portfolios or computer-generated data like logfiles [24] or from learning analytics [20, 25] can be added to build a heterogeneous data set with different formats, time span, from structured to non-structured and in different aggregation levels. These are typically all characteristics of "big data" [50].

3.2 Educational Technology Governance

The process character of the management cycle and the relevance of data for decision making on the different levels of educational governance illustrates the necessity for an overall plan and control mechanism. As this is already in place following the Deming-cycle of plan, do, check and act (PDCA) in IT Governance, the next step is to account for the special aspects of IT in educational management. Usually, the term information technology governance is used in two different directions: First, as a description of how decisions on ICT are made in complex organizations in order to align IT and business [51]. Weill and Ross [52] define information technology governance as follows: 'Specifying the decision rights and accountability framework to encourage desirable behavior in the use of IT' (p.8). They make a distinction between different forms of organizational structures: from IT or business monopoly in which one defines the action of the other (i.e. IT drives business or vice versa) to duopolies and to anarchy. Empirical research based on quantitative studies research shows a positive and significant linkage between information technology governance mechanisms and strategic alignment and, further, between strategic alignment and organizational performance [53]. In educational governance research, there is no correspondent research, yet.

Second, IT governance is used as a definition of meta-processes for 'good governance' to support strategic business development. The currently most accepted model is COBIT in its version 5 [54]. In COBIT 5, information technology governance is '… the system by which the current and future use of ICT is directed and controlled' (p. 3). The standard identifies three core elements: (1) Evaluate: checking for current and future use of IT; (2) Direct: defining directives to prepare and implement strategies, plans and guidelines to secure IT business alignment; (3) Monitor: controlling the implementation and the capabilities. COBIT encompasses altogether 37 sub-processes, which are defined with activities, metrics and input-output relations. Furthermore, a maturity level can be assigned to each process in order to monitor quality for continuous improvement.

Transferred to educational technologies, this would mean to implement governance processes on both the strategic and the operational level, focusing on teaching and learning as well as on educational management.

4   Conclusions

As we have highlighted, the rise of data for decision-making on all levels of educational governance has not only implications for preventing unintended consequences but also for processes of ICT management. The information management cycle needs to be reflected on all three levels of educational governance. It is part of educational policy making, requiring adequate data provision, which allow national and international comparisons. This demand is built into information systems, which are based on ICT infrastructures (e.g. national indicators, ranking systems, databases by state and non-governmental organizations, state-wide information systems). On the meso level of the school district, district-wide information systems are in place, serving for the needs of administrators and policy makers. On the micro level of the school, building management needs data, implemented in school information systems and based on ICT infrastructure. Additionally, there are cross-sectional processes on each level and, as a distinct characteristic of the school system, also across levels. Not only the data provision is bottom-up from the school to the policy level (e.g. as reports and achievement test results) but also from school to district and from district to school, and vice versa. Furthermore, specific requirements to process sensible educational data such as grades, performance levels or attendance need to be embedded into an overall policy of privacy and security.

As we concluded, the strategic processes need to be implemented, managed and monitored. In order to cope with the challenge of datafication on a large scale, strategic processes of governance for educational technologies are necessary. This is relevant for both the administrative data practices and teaching and learning. Education systems and policy makers could save time and energy by adopting existing models from business. This would lead education and educational technology to the next level of professional management.

References

1. Power, M.: The Audit Society: Rituals of Verification. Oxford University Press, Oxford (1999)
2. Hope, A.: Governmentality and the "selling" of school surveillance devices. Sociol. Rev. **63**(4), 840–857 (2015)
3. Kitchin, R.: The Data Revolution: Big Data, Open Data, Data Infrastructures and Their Consequences. SAGE, Thousand Oaks (2014)
4. Borgman, C.L.: Big data, little data, no data: Scholarship in the networked world. The MIT Press, Cambridge (2015)
5. Gitelman, L. (ed.): "Raw Data" is an Oxymoron. The MIT Press, Cambridge (2013)
6. Boyd, D., Crawford, K.: Critical questions for big data. Inf. Commun. Soc. **15**, 662–679 (2012)
7. Piety, P.J.: Assessing the Educational Data Movement. Teachers College Press, New York (2013)
8. Mandinach, E.B., Honey, M.: Data-Driven School Improvement: Linking Data and Learning. Teacher College, Columbia University, New York (2008)
9. Schildkamp, K., Lai, M.K., Earl, L.: Data-based Decision Making in Education: Challenges and Opportunities. Springer, Dordrecht (2013)
10. Breiter, A., Light, D.: Data for school improvement: Factors for designing effective information systems to support decision-making in schools. J. Educ. Technol. Soc. **9**, 206–217 (2006)
11. Behn, R.D.: Rethinking accountability in education: How should who hold whom accountable for what? Int. Public Manag. J. **6**, 43–73 (2003)
12. Anagnostopoulos, D., Rutledge, S.A., Jacobsen, R.: The Infrastructure of Accountability: Data Use and the Transformation of American Education. Harvard Education Press, Cambridge (2013)
13. Sellar, S.: Data infrastructure: a review of expanding accountability systems and large-scale assessments in education. Discourse Stud. Cult. Polit. Educ. **36**, 765–777 (2014)
14. Wong, K.K.: Politics and governance: evolving systems of school accountability. Educ. Policy. **27**, 410–421 (2013)
15. Martens, K., Nagel, A.-K., Windzio, M., Weymann, A.: Transformation of Education Policy. Palgrave, Basingstoke (2010)
16. Pollitt, C., Bouckaert, G.: Public Management Reform: A Comparative Analysis. Oxford University Press, Oxford (2000)
17. Selwyn, N.: Data entry: towards the critical study of digital data and education. Learn. Media Technol. **40**, 64–82 (2015)
18. Williamson, B.: Governing software: Networks, databases and algorithmic power in the digital governance of public education. Learn. Media Technol. **40**, 83–105 (2015)

19. Karanasios, S., Thakker, D., Lau, L., Allen, D., Dimitrova, V., Norman, A.: Making sense of digital traces: An activity theory driven ontological approach. J. Am. Soc. Inf. Sci. Technol. **64**, 2452–2467 (2013)
20. Berland, M., Baker, R., Blikstein, P.: Educational data mining and learning analytics: applications to constructionist research. Technol. Knowl. Learn. **19**, 205–220 (2014)
21. Papamitsiou, Z., Economides, A.A.: Learning analytics and educational data mining in practice: A systematic literature review of empirical evidence. Educ. Technol. Soc. **17**, 49–64 (2014)
22. Greller, W., Drachsler, H.: Translating learning into numbers: A generic framework for learning analytics. Educ. Technol. Soc. **15**, 42–57 (2012)
23. Reimann, P., Markauskaite, L., Bannert, M.: e-Research and learning theory: What do sequence and process mining methods contribute? Br. J. Educ. Technol. **45**, 528–540 (2014)
24. Schulz, A.H., Breiter, A.: Monitoring user patterns in school information systems using logfile analysis. In: Passey, D., Breiter, A., Visscher, A.J. (eds.) Next Generation of IT in Educational Management. IFIP Advances in Information and Communication Technology (IFIPAICT), pp. 94–103. Springer, Berlin (2013)
25. Ferguson, R.: Learning analytics: drivers, developments and challenges. Int. J. Technol. Enhanc. Learn. **4**, 304–317 (2012)
26. Eynon, R.: The rise of big data: What does it mean for education, technology, and media research? Learn. Media Technol. **38**, 237–240 (2013)
27. Sergiovanni, T.J., Burlingame, M., Coombs, F.S., Thurston, P.: Educational Governance and Administration. Prentice-Hall, Englewood Cliffs (1987)
28. Altrichter, H.: Theory and evidence on governance: conceptual and empirical strategies of research on governance in education. Eur. Educ. Res. J. **9**, 147–158 (2010)
29. Kozma, R.B.: Comparative analyses of policies for ICT in education. In: Voogt, J., Knezek, G. (eds.) International Handbook of Information Technology in Primary and Secondary Education, pp. 1083–1096. Springer, Berlin (2008)
30. Bieber, T., Martens, K., Niemann, D., Teltemann, J.: Towards a global model in education? Interdisciplinary perspectives on international student assessments and their impact on policies and institutions. In: Hamilton, M., Maddox, B., and Addey, C. (eds.) Literacy as Numbers. Researching the Politics and Practices of International Literacy Assessment Regimes. pp. 165–186. Cambridge University Press, Cambridge (2015)
31. Lingard, B., Creagh, S., Vass, G.: Education policy as numbers: Data categories and two Australian cases of misrecognition. J. Educ. Policy **27**, 315–333 (2012)
32. Wayman, J.C., Jimerson, J.B., Cho, V.: Organizational considerations in establishing the data-informed district. Sch. Eff. Sch. Improv. **23**, 159–178 (2012)
33. Cho, V., Wayman, J.C.: Districts' efforts for data use and computer data systems: the role of sensemaking in system use and implementation. Teach. Coll. Rec. **116**(2), 1–45 (2014)
34. Coburn, C.E., Talbert, J.E.: Conceptions of evidence-based practice in school districts: Mapping the terrain. Am. J. Educ. **112**, 469–495 (2006)
35. Passey, D., Breiter, A., Visscher, A.J. (eds.): Next Generation of IT in Educational Management. Springer, Berlin (2013)
36. Tatnall, A., Kereteletswe, O.C., Visscher, A. (eds.): Information Technology and Managing Quality Education. Springer, Berlin (2011)
37. Breiter, A., Stauke, E.: Assessment information systems for decision support in schools. In: Tatnall, A., Okamoto, T., Visscher, A.J. (eds.) Knowledge Management for Educational Innovation, pp. 9–18. Springer, Berlin (2007)
38. Verhaeghe, G., Vanhoof, J., Valcke, M., Van Petegem, P.: Using school performance feedback: perceptions of primary school principals. Sch. Eff. Sch. Improv. **21**, 167–188 (2010)

39. Visscher, A.J., Coe, R.: School Improvement Through Performance Feedback. Swets & Zeitlinger, Lisse (2002)
40. Choo, C.W.: Information Management for an Intelligent Organization: The Art of Environmental Scanning, 3rd edn. Information Today, Medford (2002)
41. Visscher, A.J.: Information technology in educational management as an emerging discipline. Int. J. Educ. Res. **25**, 291–296 (1996)
42. Breiter, A., Stauke, E., Büsching, N., Lange, A.: Educational Management Information Systems - Case Studies from 8 Countries. Shaker, Aachen (2006)
43. Star, S.L.: The ethnography of infrastructure. Am. Behav. Sci. **43**, 377–391 (1999)
44. Star, S.L., Ruhleder, K.: Steps toward an ecology of infrastructure: design and access for large information spaces. Inf. Syst. Res. **7**, 111–134 (1996)
45. Ciborra, C.U., Hanseth, O.: From tool to gestell. Inf. Technol. People. **11**, 305–327 (1998)
46. Latour, B.: Reassembling the social: an introduction to actor-network-theory. Oxford University Press, Oxford (2007)
47. Davis, F.D.: Perceived usefulness, perceived ease of use, and user acceptance of information technology. MIS Q. **13**, 319–340 (1989)
48. Venkatesh, V., Morris, M., Davis, G.B.: User acceptance of information technology: Toward a unified view. MIS Q. **27**, 425–478 (2003)
49. Krcmar, H.: Information Management. Springer, Berlin (2004)
50. Mayer-Schonberger, V., Cukier, K.: Big Data: A Revolution that will Change How We Live, Work and Think. John Murray, London (2013)
51. Wulf, V., Stiemerling, O., Pfeifer, A.: Tailoring groupware for different scopes of validity. Behav. Inf. Technol. **18**, 199–212 (1999)
52. Weill, P., Ross, J.W.: IT Governance How Top Performers Manage IT Decision Rights for Superior Results. Harvard Business School Press, Boston (2004)
53. Wu, S.P.-J., Straub, D.W., Liang, T.-P.: How information technology governance mechanisms and strategic alignment influence organizational performance: insights from a matched survey of business and IT managers. MIS Q. **39**, 497–518 (2015)
54. ISACA: COBIT 5 - A Business Framework for the Governance and Management of Enterprise IT. Information Systems Audit and Control Association (2012)

IT in Educational Management: Can it Support Solution of e-Cheating Problem?

R. Robert Gajewski[(⊠)]

Warsaw University of Technology, Warsaw, Poland
rg@il.pw.edu.pl

Abstract. The paper tries to answer the question – can IT tools help to solve e-cheating problem during the course of information technologies and computer sciences. The scale of e-cheating leads to the situation that dishonest students have better grades than honest ones. None of the simple solutions known from the literature helped to solve that problem, so IT tools were used. The first part of the paper gives a critical review of the literature of the subject. In the second one comparative analysis of results of the two surveys is performed. The first one was based on a survey conducted in United States, the second in Australia. This analysis shows that there are very big cultural differences in students' attitude to cheating in different countries. The third part presents two software solutions of e-cheating problem investigated during research – monitoring software and safe exam browser. Final remarks are accompanied by raising an open question – will these IT solutions be valuable in the coming decade?

Keywords: Cheating · Plagiarism · Collusion · E-learning

1 Introduction and Literature Review

Cheating is perhaps as old as education. Mavis [1] wrote about college cheating as a function of subject and situational variables in 1962 and Haines [2] about college cheating as an effect of immaturity, lack of commitment, and a neutralizing attitude in 1986 and also ten years later [3]. But nowadays due to the information and communication technology it is much easier to cheat so it starts to be a crucial problem. There were tens of papers written on this subject. The review can be found in [4]. The answer to the important philosophical question why cheating is so wrong can be found in [5]. According to Bouville cheating can be frustrating for the instructors because it can be interpreted as the direct affront. Instructors can also feel betrayed. But the most important reason is the fact that cheating can influence grades which are an information how good a student is. So finally good and fair students can have worse grades than cheaters.

It is very important to distinguish between different forms of cheating. Johnston in [6] precisely defined plagiarism and collusion as forms of cheating and illustrated this in a very intuitive way (see Fig. 1). Plagiarism is "the submission of material (written, visual or oral) originally produced by another person or persons without due acknowledgement so that the work could be assumed to be the student's own". On the other hand, "collusion is the term used to describe any form of joint effort intended to

T. Brinda et al. (Eds.): SaITE 2016, IFIP AICT 493, pp. 104–113, 2016.
DOI: 10.1007/978-3-319-54687-2_10

deceive an assessor as to who was actually responsible for producing the material submitted for assessment." One should also distinguish unintended plagiarism and improper collaboration which can be treated as elements of poor academic practice.

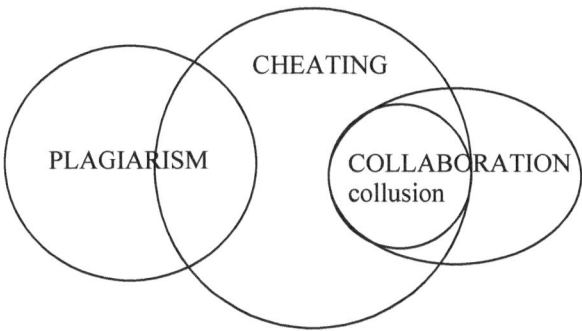

Fig. 1. Plagiarism and collusion as forms of cheating – adapted from Johnston [6].

According to Barret and Cox [7] the line between collusion and collaboration is hazy but at least students are learning something by cheating. A similar problem was investigated by Sutherland [8]. She wrote about crossing the line and raised the fundamental question – collusion or collaboration in the university group work? Dabrovska [9] expanded Johnston's classification of cheating giving various examples of dishonest behavior but the problem of avoiding plagiarism and collusion remained open. Fraser in [10, 11] presented the problem of collaboration, collusion and plagiarism in a computer science coursework. Mahmood in [12] investigated students' understanding of plagiarism and collusion and gave some recommendations for academics. There are also books written about these problems. Carroll [13] wrote a handbook for deterring plagiarism in higher education, while Culvin [14] wrote a book on plagiarism, prevention, deterrence and detection.

There are only a few papers devoted to technical issues. Ajanovski [15] prepared best a practice document on access control and monitoring for campus computer labs. Keresztury [16] warned instructors, that in the electronic teaching era there are many new cheating methods. Khan in [17] wrote in his paper about new e-cheating technologies. Leister in [18] presented how to prevent unwanted communication in ICT-based examinations by using free software. Omer in [19] described network services application to controlling and developing computer laboratories. Uhrakova in [20] investigated the attitude of students towards electronic and non-electronic cheating. Kumar in [21] examined security issues in the learning management system Moodle. Faucher in [22] presented innovative teaching techniques and the detection and prevention of them. Harper in [23, 24] described the problem of high tech cheating in nurse education. None of the solutions from these papers can be directly used during tests in a computer laboratory.

During the last decade different forms of e-cheating were getting more and more popular during the classes in information technologies and computer sciences described in details in [25, 26]. This resulted in a ridiculous situation when cheating students in many cases had better grades than honest students. Simple pedagogical hints given by

McDowell and Brown [27] like: "use strict controls", "make the rules clear and have known penalties", "design assessment instruments that make cheating difficult" and "develop climate that will reduce the likelihood of cheating" did not help to decrease cheating during the last years. So, the main motivation to start this research was a strong will to change this unmoral situation.

2   Two Surveys and Their Results

In order to learn what is the attitude towards cheating among Polish students two surveys were conducted. In order to learn what are the cultural differences between different countries the first survey was based on the survey from Gettysburg in USA and the second was based on the survey conducted in Monash University in Australia. Similar comparative analysis on students' perception and attitudes towards academic dishonesty between the students in China and United States was done by Zou and Lan in [28].

2.1   Comparison of Results with Gettysburg Survey

This survey was conducted during the first week of classes in October 2015. The total number of responses was 203. The number of students registered for the subject was 221. The total number of the questions in this survey was 24. Answers on 18 of them are presented in two tables. Table 1 summarises results for questions about practice of cheating while Table 2 about acceptance of cheating. All results are in percent. Results for Gettysburg are calculated as an average from the years 2008–2014.

Table 1 shows that answers to all questions differ significantly, especially for the last question "did you ever cheat during high school".

Table 1. Comparison of results of surveys – practice of cheating.

Question	Gettysburg			2015 Poland		
	Never	Once	More than once	Never	Once	More than once
Did you ever witness cheating in your high school?	13	10	77	8	5	87
Have you ever reported another student you suspected of cheating?	79	18	3	94	3	3
Have you ever interrupted a student who was cheating?	50	24	26	72	10	18
Did you ever cheat during high school?	60	21	19	30	17	58

Table 2. Comparison of results of surveys – acceptance of cheating.

Question	Gettysburg			2015 Poland		
	Very dishonest	Dishonest, but I do it anyway	Not dishonest	Very dishonest	Dishonest, but I do it anyway	Not dishonest
Forging a teacher's signature?	95	4	1	94	3	3
Forging an administrator's signature	98	1	0	97	1	2
Cheating on a homework assignment	61	34	5	29	56	15
Cheating on a test	95	5	0	39	53	8
Cheating on a midterm or final examination	99	1	0	78	16	6
Fabricating lab data	80	16	4	76	12	12
Completely faking a lab experiment	96	3	1	58	37	5
Plagiarizing a paper or written assignment	99	1	0	58	37	5
Working with another student when instructed to work alone	57	33	9	25	45	30
Signing in for another student who missed class	83	13	4	73	18	9
Lying to protect another student	70	24	6	40	33	27
Lying to get an extension on an assignment	83	16	1	54	33	13
Lying about why you turned in an assignment late	78	20	2	49	35	16
Lying about why you were absent	75	21	4	43	35	21

In Table 2 only answers to the two first questions about acceptance of forging signatures are nearly the same. For the rest of the questions there are big differences. For example, cheating during a test is treated as very dishonest by 95% of students in Gettysburg and only 39% of students in Poland. On the other hand, when results "very dishonest" and "dishonest but I do it anyway" are summed up the difference is not so big: 100% vs 92%. These results show that although the perception of cheating as unmoral is very similar in both countries the actual level of cheating in Poland is much higher than in Gettysburg, so some additional treatment should be undertaken. It seems also that this treatment should be focused on reducing the opportunity to cheat rather than on pedagogical issues.

2.2   Comparison of Results with Monash University Survey

This test was conducted during the last week of classes in January 2016. Total number of responses was 179. Number of students attending classes at the end of semester was 201.

Table 3. Comparison of results of surveys.

Scenario	Acceptability			Practice		
	Australia		Poland	Australia		Poland
	2000 mean	2010 mean	2015 mean	2000%	2010%	2015%
Showing assignment work to a lecturer for guidance	2.07	2.21	1.68	37	42	67
Posting to an Internet newsgroup for assistance	2.07	2.28	1.77	27	34	68
Two students collaborating on an assignment meant to be completed individually	2.54	3.20	2.65	44	36	54
Resubmitting an assignment from a previous subject in a new subject	2.82	2.99	2.49	27	17	41
Submitting a friend's assignment from a past running of the subject	2.86	3.46	3.03	34	20	32
Copying the majority of an assignment from a friend's assignment, but doing a fair bit of work yourself	2.98	3.37	2.98	31	21	39
Not informing the tutor that an assignment has been given too high a mark	3.08	3.29	2.82	17	16	39
Being given the answer to a tutorial exercise worth 5% by a class mate if the computer you used has problems	3.76	4.29	3.03	7	3	9
Copying material for an essay from a text book	3.81	4.19	3.71	22	10	34
Copying material for an essay from the Internet	3.85	4.28	4.29	23	10	33
Obtaining a medical certificate from a doctor to get an extension when you are not sick	3.94	4.02	3.35	12	3	9
Swapping assignments with a friend, so that each does one assignment, instead of doing both	3.96	4.45	3.37	9	3	37
Copying another student's assignment from their computer without their knowledge and submitting	4.18	4.62	3.94	7	3	7
Copying all of an assignment given to you by a friend	4.30	4.62	3.92	10	3	10

(*continued*)

Table 3. (*continued*)

Scenario	Acceptability			Practice		
	Australia		Poland	Australia		Poland
	2000 mean	2010 mean	2015 mean	2000%	2010%	2015%
Hiring a person to write your assignment for you	4.51	4.62	3.97	3	1	6
Using a hidden sheet of paper with important facts during an exam	4.59	4.64	4.32	4	2	53
Hiring someone to sit an exam for you	4.65	4.69	4.32	3	0	5
Taking a student's assignment from a lecturer's pigeonhole and copying it	4.72	4.72	4.29	4	2	3

Questionnaire of this survey is fully based on the questionnaire used in 2000 during the survey conducted in Australia at Monash University and at Swanbourne University which results were published in [29]. The same survey was conducted ten years later and results were compared in [30]. The most important part of both surveys consists of 18 scenarios. For each of them answers are given using a Likert scale [31] with the answers ranging from 1 – acceptable to 5 – not acceptable.

Comparison of results of all surveys is in Table 3. In columns 2000 and 2010 are results from Australia and in column 2015 results from Poland. For acceptability mean value of the answers to the question "how acceptable is this scenario" is calculated and for practice percent of students who answered yes to the question "have you ever done this".

What can be easily learned from Table 3 is that in Australia a positive change has occurred among students over the decade with regard to cheating awareness, acceptability and practice. Results of a survey conducted in Poland are much worse than Australia from the year 2000. Especially big differences are in the case of the three following scenarios:

- Copying material from the book or from the Internet,
- Swapping assignments with another person,
- Using a hidden sheet of paper with important facts during an exam. (In the case of questionnaires concerning computer lab tests "a hidden sheet of paper" means using all types of unauthorized materials e.g. files.)

The first problem can be generally solved by means of plagiarism checkers on the university level. The second one should be mainly solved by instructor manually. The third one which can be generally called as using unauthorized materials during exams can be solved by means of specialized IT tools which will be described below. For the last-mentioned scenario – using unauthorized materials – worth mentioning is the relatively small difference in mean values of acceptability (4.59, 4.64 and 4.32) and very big difference in practice (4%, 2% and 53%).

3 Technical Issues

Comparison of results of the two surveys shows that cheating is a serious and important problem in Poland. Moreover, all instructors who have classes in a computer lab and in a typical class know differences in cheating possibilities. It is much easier to cheat in the computer lab when it is not equipped with specialized software. So, in order to prevent cheating two IT solutions were used. The problem of plagiarism in BSc and MSc thesis is solved on the university level while problems of individual instructors should be solved by themselves. But the solution of plagiarism problem is doubtful. There are many sites which offer automatic rewording.

3.1 Save Exam Browser

In order of prevent cheating during multiple choice tests on MOODLE Safe Exam Browser (SEB) platform was used. SEB is the result of a project lead by the Swiss National Research and Education Network and supported by funds from the ETH Board. According to the information from sebexambrowser.org portal "SEB runs on a local computer and it is connected via the internet to a learning management system (LMS). SEB consists of a kiosk application and a browser part, which are running on an examination computer. The kiosk application locks down the examination computer, the browser part communicates via the internet (or a LAN) with the quiz module of a LMS running on a server." This idea is illustrated by Fig. 2. The kiosk application locks down the computer and starts the SEB browser. The SEB browser connects with the URL of the LMS quiz page. The user interface of the LMS is reduced to navigation necessary for the test. Usage of SEB prevents using Google search engine or PDF files during test exams.

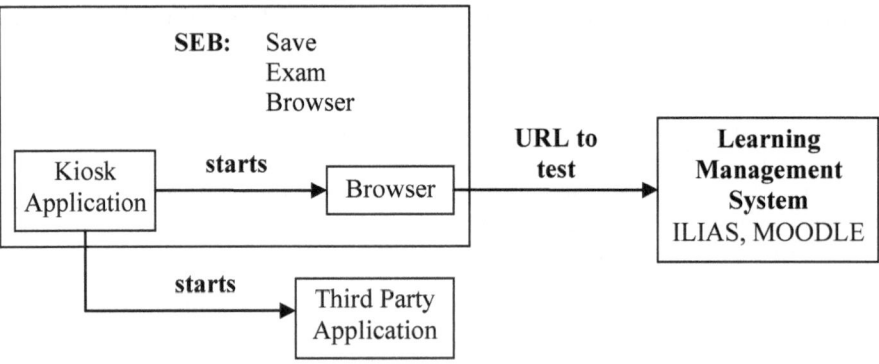

Fig. 2. Schematic illustration of an online exam with SEB and a LMS. Source: based on picture from safeexambrowser.org

3.2   Lan School Manager Lite

In order to prevent cheating during practical tests LanSchool, classroom and desktop movement software was used. Its lite, free of charge version can monitor up to 3000 students by real time computer thumbnail monitoring. Such thumbnails can be arranged and saved to represent the classroom layout. LanSchool Lite enables also to view the students' active application and last visited website as well as a full screen view of the student's monitor. There are much more capabilities in the full version of this software. Screen Feed option allows to monitor details of students' screens from a distance. Other features like Internet History or Keystroke Monitoring create a safe environment for all students. This software reduced nearly to zero cheating in a form of collusion or using unauthorised materials during practical tests – the only authorised materials were help files.

4   Final Remarks and Open Questions

Results of both surveys show that cheating especially in electronic form (e-cheating) is an important issue in higher education. A full solution to this problem can be obtained only by means of cooperation of all stakeholders of education market – university and faculty authorities, instructors and... students. Cases when students force instructors and authorities to act actively against cheating are more and more often. But on the other hand, none of the technical solutions will work forever so continuous research in this field is necessary.

Two suggested and discussed IT solutions decreased radically levels of cheating. Although the difficulty level of tests was not changed (namely questions and practical problems were in fact the same) in this year nearly 20% of students had to retake a lecture test, while one year ago only 2% of students had to do this. Similar results were obtained for practical tests. In this case retakes did not help too much due to the fact that it is easier to memorize answers on the questions rather than understand how a spreadsheet or computer algebra system works and solve a unique computing problem. So, the final conclusion is: IT can support the solution of e–cheating problem.

Acknowledgments.   The author would like to thank all Students who participated in surveys and filled two long questionnaires. Research was conducted within a frame of grant No. 504/01921/1088/40.

References

1. Mavis, E., Feldman, S.E.: College cheating as a function of subject and situational variables. J. Educ. Psychol. **55**, 212–218 (1964)
2. Haines, V.J., Diekhoff, G.M., LaBeff, E.E., Clark, R.E.: College cheating: immaturity, lack of commitment, and the neutralizing attitude. Res. High. Educ. **25**, 342–354 (1986)
3. Diekhoff, G.M., LaBeff, E.E., Clark, R.E., Williams, L.E., Francis, B., Haines, V.J.: College cheating: ten years later. Res. High. Educ. **37**, 487–502 (1996)

4. Ercegovac, Z., Richardson, J.V.: Academic dishonesty, plagiarism included, in the digital age: a literature review. Coll. Res. Libr. **65**, 301–318 (2004)
5. Bouville, M.: Why is cheating wrong? Stud. Philos. Educ. **29**, 67–76 (2009)
6. Johnston, W.: The concet of plagiarism. Learn. Teach. Action. **2**, 1–9 (2003)
7. Barrett, R., Cox, A.L.: At least they're learning something: the hazy line between collaboration and collusion. Assess. Eval. High. Educ. **30**, 107–122 (2005)
8. Carroll, J.: A Handbook for Deterring Plagiarism in Higher Education. OCSLD, Oxford (2013)
9. Dobrovska, D.: Avoiding plagiarism and collusion. In: Proceedings of the International Conference on Engineering Education - ICEE 2007. Coimbra, Portugal (2007)
10. Fraser, R.: Collaboration, Collusion and Plagiarism in Computer Science. University of Waterlo, Waterloo (2013)
11. Fraser, R.: Collaboration, collusion and plagiarism in computer science coursework. Inform. Educ. **13**, 179–195 (2014)
12. Mahmood, Z.: Students' understanding of plagiarism and collusion and recommendations for academics. WSESAS Trans. Inf. Sci. Appl. **6**, 1349–1358 (2009)
13. Sutherland-Smith, W.: Crossing the line: collusion or collaboration in university group work? Aust. Univ. Rev. **55**, 51–58 (2013)
14. Culvin, F., Lancaster, T.: Plagiarism, Prevention, Deterrence and Detection. The Higher Education Academy (2001)
15. Ajanovski, V.: Access Control and Monitoring for Campus Computer Labs: Best Practice Document. Faculty of Computer Science and Engineering, Skopje (2015)
16. Keresztury, B., Cser, L.: New cheating methods in the electronic teaching era. Procedia - Soc. Behav. Sci. **93**, 1516–1520 (2013)
17. Khan, Z.R., Balasubramanian, S.: Students go click, flick and cheat: E-cheating, technologies and more. J. Acad. Bus. Ethics. 6 (2012)
18. Leister, W., Fretland, T., Solheim, I.: Preventing unwanted communication in ICT-based exams by using free software. In: Proceedings of Norwegian Symposium on Information Technology and Organisations 2009, pp. 27–38. Curran Associates, Inc, Trondheim, Norway (2009)
19. Omer, M.K.A.: Network services application to controlling and develop institute computer LABs. Int. J. Innov. Technol. Explor. Eng. IJITEE. **5**, 29–33 (2015)
20. Uhrakova, E., Podaril, M.: The attitude of students towards electronic and non-electronic cheating. In: The Future of Education Conference Proceedings 2011. Simonelli Editore (2011)
21. Kumar, S., Dutta, K.: Investigation on security in LMS moodle. Int. J. Inf. Technol. Knowl. Manag. **4**, 233–238 (2011)
22. Faucher, D., Caves, S.: Academic dishonesty: Innovative cheating techniques and the detection and prevention of them. Teach. Learn. Nurs. **4**, 37–41 (2009)
23. Harper, M.G.: High tech cheating. Nurse Educ. Today **26**, 672–679 (2006)
24. Harper, M.G.: High tech cheating. Nurse Educ. Pract. **6**, 364–371 (2006)
25. Gajewski, R., Wlasak, L., Jaczewski, M.: IS (ICT) and CS in civil engineering curricula: case study. In: Proceedings of the 2013 Federated Conference on Computer Science and Information Systems, pp. 717–720. IEEE, Krakow (2013)
26. Gajewski, R.R., Jaczewski, M.: Flipped computer science classes. In: Federated Conference on Computer Science and Information System, pp. 795–802. Warsaw (2014)
27. McDowell, L., Brown, S.: Assessing students: cheating and plagiarism. The Higher Education Academy (2001)

28. Zhou, H., Lan, S.S.: A comparative analysis on Students' perceptions and attitudes towards academic dishonesty between students in China and in The United States. In: Proceedings of the Spring 2007 American Society for Engineering Education Illinois-Indiana Section Conference (2007)
29. Sheard, J., Dick, M., Markham, S., Macdonald, I., Walsh, M.: Cheating and plagiarism: perceptions and practices of first year IT students. ACM SIGCSE Bull. **34**, 183–187 (2002)
30. Sheard, J., Dick, M.: Computing student practices of cheating and plagiarism: a decade of change. In: The 16th Annual SIGCSE Conference on Innovation and Technology in Computer Science Education, ITiCSE 2011, Darmstadt, Germany, June 27–29, 2011, pp. 233–237 (2011)
31. Likert, R.: A technique for the measurement of attitudes. Arch. Psychol. **22**, 1–55 (1932)

Business Process Management (BPM) and e-Government: An Experience at University of Las Palmas de Gran Canaria (ULPGC)

Pablo Hernández-Bolaños(✉) and Jorge Rodríguez-Díaz(✉)

University of Las Palmas de Gran Canaria, Las Palmas, Spain
phernandez@dede.ulpgc.es, jorge.rodriguez@ulpgc.es

Abstract. The development of business process management (BPM) is a key factor to launch e-Government in a public organization. This development requires first identifying the components that make up the business process management and, second, implementing them. It is just this implementation which has been presented as one of the most complex milestones in the development of BPM. In this paper the authors show how to implement the components of BPM successfully based on construction that deploys an organizational initiative that addresses directly a problem expressing the organization and indirectly the implementation of BPM. This methodology is justified by a case study carried out in the ULPGC.

Keywords: e-Government · Business Process Management (BPM) · Success critical factors

1 Introduction: Need for BMP to Implement the ULPGC e-Government Project

The University of Las Palmas de Gran Canaria (ULPGC) promoted in 2010 the e-Government project, whose purpose was the implementation and promotion of e-Government within this public organization.

The different actions carried out within this project represent a significant evidence of the deployment of e-Government in the ULPGC, as this university has an electronic office system for the identification and authentication of both, citizens and administrative bodies, in the exercise of its powers [1], electronic register, electronic notifications, ability to recognize the validity of an electronic document, electronic management of procedures, availability of electronic information for citizens about the status of procedures and possibility of cooperation between administrations for the promotion of e-Government [2]. All this provides evidence that the ULPGC is capable of supporting an electronic service delivery.

However, the objective of this work has not been directly the implementation of e-Government, but the implementation of the Business Process Management (BPM) as an essential element to promote e-Government in public organizations [3, 4]. This article

T. Brinda et al. (Eds.): SaITE 2016, IFIP AICT 493, pp. 114–123, 2016.
DOI: 10.1007/978-3-319-54687-2_11

highlights a methodology to implement the BMP in these organizations consisting of starting an initiative to solve a concrete organizational problem of the institution itself, while the BPM components are developed. This paper also describes the experience carried out in the ULPGC between 2003 and 2007 to evaluate the methodology. This experience was called Management Memorandum Model (MMM) - see Fig. 1.

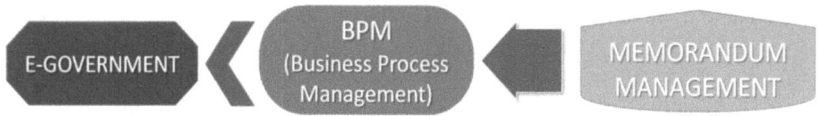

Fig. 1. Relationship among Management Memorandum Model (MM), Business Process Management (BPM) and e-Government (Source: Authors' own)

2 State of the Art: The Business Process Management (BPM)

BPM is a management system based on the use and development of organizational capabilities to manage processes and improve results thereof according to their strategies [5]. This management system has many benefits as shown in Table 1, but stresses the advantage of implementation for the deployment of electronic services and process automation.

Table 1. Advantages of BPM (Source: Authors' own, using information from several authors).

• Improve the competitiveness of organizations • Develop and continuously improve organizational strategies • Adequately predict and complete their objectives more effectively and efficiently • Streamline decision-making • Adapt quickly to changes in demand and a more complex environment with a growing number of international competitors • Improve production capacity, speeding up processes and reducing unnecessary costs and resources • Reduce errors in the production and timeouts • Transfer information between departments faster	• Maximize the grouping of activities to reduce stress • Geared toward generating customer value and even improve performance • Improve control of its results including financial • Innovation capacity • Integrating people and systems • Automate processes • Simulate contingencies without having an impact on ordinary activities • Manage and monitor staff performance • Beyond the compartmentalized departments in the organization • Improve customer communication and satisfaction to remain competitive • Implementing information technologies and communication technologies (ICT) • Establishing quality management systems

However, in most cases, BPM projects carried out in organizations have had a high failure rate [6]; this task may be even more complex in the public sector due to the functional culture and departmental thought, an aspect contrary to a process approach [7].

To ensure the implementation of BPM in an organization, it is necessary to ensure the proper development of a number of critical success factors (CSF), that is, those aspects that should be strengthened to successfully complete the project [6, 8–11]. Rosemann and vom Brocke [12] state six CSF for BPM: strategic alignment, governance, methods, ICT, people and culture. The work of these authors disaggregates these factors in other components called capabilities, which are referred to as *sub-factors* (s-CSF) in this work and are shown in Table 2. Several authors, such as Fettke et al. [13]; Niehaves et al. [14]; Santos et al. [15] and Lönn et al. [16], support these sub-factors as valid for the public sector.

Table 2. Critical success factors and sub-factors (Source: Rosemann and vom Brocke [12]).

Strategic alignment	ICT
• A.1. Process improvement plan	• D.1. ICT for design and process modelling
• A.2. Alignment between business strategy and processes	• D.2. ICT enabler for the implementation and execution of processes
• A.3. Business process architecture	• D.3. ICT for measurement and process control
• A.4. Key processes outputs and performance indicators (KPI)	• D.4. Tools for innovation and process improvement
• A.5. Priority of stakeholders	• D.5. ICT project management and program management
Governance	People
• B.1. Decision-making processes of BPM	• E.1. Skills and expertise in processes
• B.2. Roles and responsibilities process	• E.2. Knowledge of BPM
• B.3. Processes data collected	• E.3. Teaching and learning processes
• B.4. Standardized management processes	• E.4. Communication and collaboration in the processes
• B.5. Control of process management	• E.5. Leadership in management processes
Method	Culture
• C.1. Design and process modelling	• F.1. Responsiveness to shift to the process approach
• C.2. Processes implementation and execution	• F.2. Values and beliefs about the processes
• C.3. Process measurement and control	• F.3. Activities and behaviour to processes
• C.4. Innovation and process improvement	• F.4. Senior management leadership in process management
• C.5. Project and program management processes	• F.5. Social networking process management

Nevertheless, the deployment of CSF and s-CSF in an organization is not an automatic task, but on the contrary, it is very complex since it requires an adaptation of these components to the characteristics of the organization [6]. Either way, there are no described models that enable this adaptation, and even less in the public sector [17]. This being precisely what the study identified as the research problem.

3   The Research Method

The research methodology applied in this work has been deducted qualitatively [18] since, from the literature review, it was proposed a construction or model that was evaluated putting it into practice through the case of study [19]. Considering Fettke et al. [13], indicating the need for indirect ways to implement the critical success factors in BPM, and Santos et al. [15], pointing to the desirability of developing strategies with the same objective namely indirect methods, it was decided to design a model to launch a project or initiative that, including the implementation of the CSF and s-CSF as indirect finality or purpose, had the utility to solve a particular organizational problem as direct finality. The model was designed considering the CSF and s-CSF [12]. Likewise, to ensure effective implementation of the s-CSF in the organization, BPM maturity models were taken into account, such that each s-CSF improves its sophistication cyclically [6]. This was achieved by requiring the instrument to solve the direct purpose incorporating the criterion of continuous improvement cycle, closely associated with planning systems. Finally, a set of criteria (*design criteria*) were defined, matching the ten principles of BPM established by vom Brocke [20], which would ensure the successful implementation of BPM in an organization. Hence, to develop the CSF and s-CSF in a public organization, and therefore a successful implementation of BPM, this research proposes as a solution for the research problem the development of an initiative in the organization that solves a major problem and that relies on ten criteria or principles of vom Brocke.

Therefore, the organizational initiative is twofold: direct and indirect. Direct refers to an organizational problem solving and the second to implement BPM. The method used for the first purpose will depend on the problem to be solved; to ensure that the initiative answers the two purposes, the model states that the proposed tool to solve the organizational problem should be supported by BPM; at the same time, to achieve this support, the initiative must promote the development of the CSF. On the other hand, the method used for the second one will be the application of design criteria based on the ten principles of BPM. Table 3 shows the characteristics of the dual purpose of the organizational initiative that arises as a solution to successfully implement BPM.

Table 3.   Dual purpose of the organizational initiative (Source: Authors' own).

Organizational initiative		
Types of purpose	Direct	Indirect
Objectives	To solve an organizational problem	To implement BMP
Method	Organizational instrument (It must rely on BPM)	Criteria based on the Ten Principles of BPM
Results	Organizational problem solution	Development CSF and s-CSF

To evaluate the proposed model, this one should be applied to a specific public organization launching an organizational initiative. The level of implementation of the BPM will show the level of success of the method, so the expected result would be the development of different CSF and s-CSF, shown in Table 2. The results of the evaluation were qualitative conclusions about the validity of the initiative [21]. The data collection was done by direct observation techniques [22, 23], and based on experience because the researchers themselves were part of the senior management team that drove the innovation initiative.

4   The Management Memorandum Model: An Indirect Model to Implement BPM

To evaluate the designed model, the case of study was applied on an initiative called Management Memorandum Model (MMM), developed between 2003 and 2007 by the ULPGC, an institution with an annual budget of more than 130 million Euros.

4.1   Direct Purpose

The main purpose of MMM was to continuously improve their academic and administrative services. This was done to make its own staff identify, implement and evaluate performances to improve those services. The MMM model consisted mainly in implementing the following stages in the recurring cycle of one year:

(a) Identification of potential needs for improvement. Through different instruments for data collection, it pointed to service units with possible needs for improvement, which should be validated by the heads of the units with their teams and endorsed with the senior management of the University in a working group session during two days, that was engaged exclusively to this task.
(b) Solutions design. Multidisciplinary teams, made up of the unit heads, designed solutions to identify needs improvement. This work was done during the working group session and solutions measurements constituted the annual improvement plan.
(c) Implementation and monitoring. The unit heads coordinated the implementation of the measurements. They were put into operation in a collaborative working platform based on Moodle allowing tracking of the implementation of the plan and an adequate transfer of knowledge.
(d) End of cycle evaluation. At the end of the planning period a compliance report was produced from the received reporters. This report served as a working tool in the study days for the planning of the next period or cycle (Fig. 2).

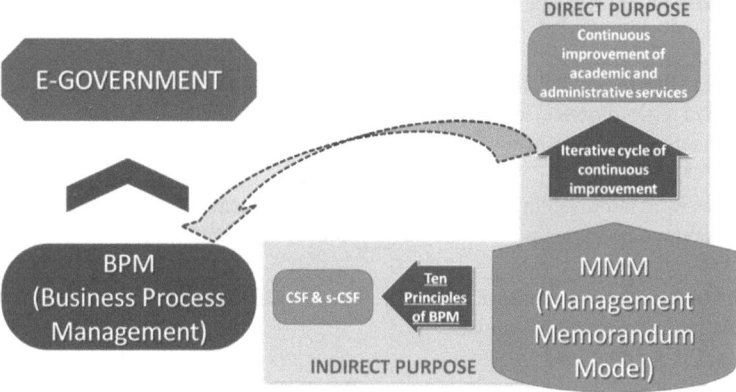

Fig. 2. Direct and indirect purposes of the Management Memorandum Model (Source: Authors' own)

The implementation of the MMM in ULPGC has provided the following information:

- Model execution duration. Since the improvement cycle referred to the model should be repeated several times to assess its validity, the project duration was three years.
- Improvement measures. During the three cycles, the MMM allowed to carry out 150 measures.
- The units involved. All administrative units of the organization were involved in the project, mainly by the exercise of leadership of senior management. In total, there were twenty units participating.
- Enhanced Services. The academic and administrative services that were subject to the improvements were about fifty.
- Implemented procedures. There were three hundred administrative procedures identified and homogenized.
- People involved. It should be noted that there are two types of people involved: the personnel who manage enhanced services and persons belonging to receptor group improvements. They were 400 working directly, 2,600 staff and 25,000 teachers and students as users of services.

To develop s-CSF, MMM required several conditions that made possible s-CSF during its four life cycles (therefore these conditions were needed to undertake the improvement of academic and administrative services). Thus, the MMM enabled the development of the s-CSF, and therefore the implementation of the BPM (see Table 4).

Table 4. Equivalence between conditions and s-CSF (Source: Authors' own).

Conditions	s-CSF
The services which should be improved were formulated in terms of processes, so that the annual plan referred to the MMM was a process improvement plan	A.1. Plan process improvement
The services were improved in concordance to the business strategy set out in the strategic plans of the organization	A.2. Alignment between business strategy and process
The criteria established to standardize processes and services were formulated according to these processes	A.3. Business process architecture
The persons responsible for each service were designated, and therefore, for each process	B.2. Roles and responsibilities of processes
Criteria homogenization process served to model the services	C.1. Design and process modelling
The services were executed according to the life cycle processes	C.2. Implementation and execution of processes
Own tool was used to model the processes	D.1. ICT for design and process modelling
Technologic workflow was launched to mechanize electronically the processes	D.2. ICT enabler for the implementation and execution of processes
Tool based on Moodle was pushed for collaborative work	E.3. Teaching and learning processes

4.2 Indirect Purpose

The MMM incorporated the design criteria set out in the strategy as follows:

- Criterion 1. Critical success sub-factors (see Table 4) should be applied only when they could be assumed by the characteristics of the organization.
- Criterion 2. Sub-factors should be incorporated gradually, as the organization could take over. To ensure the gradual incorporation of sub-factors, we worked at two levels. On the one hand, every sub-factor was launched the first year, but a deal for each cycle repeating pattern was scheduled. On the other hand, in each cycle, sub-factors that have already been built were increasing their level of development, as the organization was becoming more mature [24–26], applying to this the maturity model of Melenovsky and Gartner [27].
- Criterion 3. Organization personnel led the management model and therefore the sub-factors. Own staff, the management team ahead, not only managed the model, designing, planning and implementing the improvement actions, but established the coordination protocols that made the model work.
- Criterion 4. The scope of the model should cover every aspect of academic and administrative organization. The model was extended to all academic and administrative services and all the units in the organization.
- Criterion 5. The model should be integrated into the regular development of the organization and led by the management team. The unit heads for the operational

management of academic and administrative services would manage improvement measurements, which are planned and executed following the budget cycle, marking the pace of activity in the public organization. Thus, the MMM was part of the ordinary activities of the organization.

- Criterion 6. Every stakeholder in the organization should be involved in developing the model or perceive its effects. Over 50% of the staff participated in improving measurements arising from the application of the model and 100% appreciated the effect of these improvements in the performance of their activities on development.
- Criterion 7. The model should be formed by elements of the organization for the purpose it was perceived as friendly by all staff. The terminology used for the business process management was the same as the activity of the organization; in this way, nobody perceives the model strangely but as a different way to carry out their responsibilities.
- Criterion 8. The model must answer an important purpose and resolve any organizational problem. The model was launched to solve two problems: a) the lack of adaptation of service units to the needs of receptor groups thereof and b) the existence of multiple plans poorly aligned and with little effect on the improvement of services.
- Criterion 9. The model should be simple. The model consisted of a methodology incorporating developments in the management of the units, but did not involve an increase in the complexity of its business because these developments were improved in each cycle model.
- Criterion 10. The information and communications technology (ICT) plays an important role in the model. The improvements should have a technology component; in this way, everybody perceived improvements more palpable.

In addition to the successful implementation of BPM through the development of s-CSF, the MMM was really useful in order to incorporate the culture of continuous improvement in the teams that manage the academic and administrative services and the technological vision of such services, thus promoting the other two elements necessary for a successful implementation of e-Government [28].

4.3 Results

The direct evidences that corroborated the successful implementation of BPM and matched the critical success sub-factors were:

- The catalog of processes
- The improvement plans
- The planning system
- The tool for knowledge management
- The Information Systems Plan

Anyway, the main evidence of the effective implementation of BPM is the proper e-Government project, as it would not work without a deployed BPM.

5   Conclusion

The BPM is a needed element for the development of a variety of management systems, including the e-Government. Although many authors have highlighted the difficulties in implementing the BPM, especially in the public sector, this work has exposed that BMP solutions may be developed if it is used as a method consisting of launching an initiative that is to solve organizational problems through organizational tools that are based on the components of BPM, as the sub-factors (see Table 2). This method has been proven by its application in three public organizations: a university, case presented in this paper with the initiative called Management Memorandum Model, and two more departments of the Canary Islands Government that have been studied in a doctoral thesis.

The exposed model implies that the organizational tools have the direct purpose of solving a problem posed by the organization and, indirectly, implementing the BPM. It stands out from this that it has been able to compile practically powerful contributions made so far in terms of BPM as critical success factors, maturity models and fundamental principles to implement BPM. However, it arises for future works delving into different ways of assessing the degree of development of every sub-factor in any moment, so that the implementation of the components of BPM is more controllable.

References

1. Electronic Headquarters of the University of Las Palmas de Gran Canaria. https://sede.ulpgc.es/tramita/ulpgc/es/CatalogoServiciosAction!inicio.action
2. Spain: Ley 11/2007, de 22 de junio, de acceso electrónico de los ciudadanos a los Servicios Públicos. Published in n°. 150, 23 June 2007. https://www.boe.es/buscar/act.php?id=BOE-A-2007-12352
3. Janssen, M., Kuk, G.: E-government business models for public service networks. Int. J. Electron. Gov. Res. (IJEGR) 3(3), 54–71 (2007)
4. Corradini, F., Polini, A., Re, B.: Inter-organizational business process verification in public administration. Bus. Proc. Mgmt. J. 21(5), 1040–1065 (2015)
5. Benedict, T., Bilodeau, N., Vitkus, P., Powell, E., Morris, D., Scarsig, M., Lee, D., Field, G., Lohr, T., Saxena, R., Fuller, M., Furlan, J.: A Guide to the Business Process Management Common Body of Knowledge. In: 3rd edn. Association of Business Process Management Professionals (2013)
6. Trkman, P.: The critical success factors of business process management. Int. J. Inf. Manag. 30(2), 125–134 (2010)
7. Da Silva, L.A., Damian, I.P.M., de Pádua, S.I.D.: Process management tasks and barriers: functional to process approach. Bus. Proc. Manag. J. 18(5), 762–776 (2012). doi: 10.1108/14637151211270144
8. Ariyachandra, T.R., Frolick, M.N.: Critical success factors in business performance management – Striving for success. Inf. Syst. Manag. 25, 113–120 (2008). doi: 10.1080/10580530801941504
9. Bai, C., Sarkis, J.: A grey-based DEMATEL model for evaluating business process management critical success factors. Int. J. Prod. Econ. 146, 281–292 (2013)

10. Bandara, W., Alibabaei, A., Aghdasi, M.: Means of achieving business process management success factors. In: Ein-Dor, P., Poulymenakou, A., Amami, M. (eds.) Paper in 4th Mediterranean Conference on Information Systems. Athens: Athens University of Economics and Business (2009)
11. Karim, A., Arif-Uz-Zaman, K.: A methodology for effective implementation of lean strategies and its performance evaluation in manufacturing organizations. Bus. Proc. Manag. J. **19**(1), 169–196 (2013)
12. Rosemann, M., vom Brocke, J.: Six core elements of business process management. In vom Brocke, J., Rosemann, M. (eds.) Handbook on Business Process Management: Introduction, Methods, and Information Systems (International Handbooks on Information Systems), vol. 2(1), pp. 105–122. Springer, Berlin (2015)
13. Fettke, P., Zwicker, J., Loos, P.: Business process maturity in public administrations. In: vom Brocke, J., Rosemann, M. (eds.) Handbook on Business Process Management: Introduction, Methods, and Information Systems (International Handbooks on Information Systems), vol. 2(1), pp. 105–122. Springer, Berlin (2015)
14. Niehaves, C., Plattfaut, R., Becker, J.: Business process management capabilities in local governments: amulti-method study. Gov. Inf. Quart. **30**, 217–225 (2013)
15. Santos, H., Valença, G., Alves, C.: Strategies for managing critical success factors of BPM initiatives in brazilian public organizations: a qualitative empirical study. Revista Brasileira de Sistemas de Informaçao Rio de Janeiro **8**(1), 42–64 (2015)
16. Lönn, C.-M., Uppström, E.: Process management challenges in swedish public sector: a bottom up initiative. In: Wimmer, M.A., Janssen, M., Scholl, H.J. (eds.) EGOV 2013. LNCS, vol. 8074, pp. 212–223. Springer, Heidelberg (2013). doi:10.1007/978-3-642-40358-3_18
17. Škrinjar, R., Trkman, P.: Increasing process orientation with business process management: Critical practices. Int. J. Inf. Manag. **33**, 48–60 (2013)
18. Hyde, K.F.: Recognising deductive processes in qualitative research. Qual. Market Res. Int. J. **3**(2), 82–90 (2000)
19. Yin, R.: Case Study Research, Design and Methods. Sage Publications, Thousand Oaks (2003)
20. Brocke, V.: J., Schmiedel, T., Recker, J., Trkman, P., Mertens, W., Viaene, S.: Ten principles of good business process management. Bus. Proc. Manag. J. **20**(4), 530–548 (2014)
21. Keen, P.: Relevance and rigor in information systems research: improving quality, confidence, cohesion and impact. In: Nissen, H. E., Klein, H. K., Hirschheim, R. (eds.) Information System Research: Contemporary Approaches and Emergent Traditions, pp. 27–49. Elsevier (1991)
22. Bisquerra, R.: Metodología de la investigación educativa. La Muralla, San Sebastián (2012)
23. Flick, U.: Introducción a la investigación cualitativa. Madrid, España, Morata
24. Gottschalk, P.: Maturity levels for interoperability in digital government. Gov. Inf. Quart. **26**(1), 75–81 (2009)
25. Kazanjian, R.K., Drazin, R.: An empirical test of a stage of growth progression model. Manag. Sci. **35**(12), 1489–1503 (1989)
26. Van de Ven, A.H., Poole, M.: Explaining developments change in organizations. Acad. Manag. Rev. **20**(3), 510–540 (1995)
27. Melenovsky, M.J., Gartner, J.S.: BPM Maturity Model Identifies Six Phases for Successful BPM Adoption. Gartner Publication, 18 October 2006. ID Number: G00142643
28. Weerakkody, V., Baire, S., Choudrie, J.: E-Government: the need for effective process management in the public sector. In: Paper in the 39th Hawaii International Conference on System Sciences (2006)

Alternative Ways of Involving Stakeholders: The Rise of Entrepreneurism in Higher Education and the Case of a Learning Enterprise

Ana-Paula Correia[✉]

Educational Studies Department, The Ohio State University, Columbus, OH, USA
correia.12@osu.edu

Abstract. The education field has not traditionally stressed entrepreneurship; however, in light of current difficult economic scenarios and shrinking global job markets, a myriad of Educational Technology entrepreneurs is emerging across the world. Edupreneurs are here. They are self-motivated members of an enterprise who can recognize opportunities and take action on complex educational problems while aiming to create social value, financial value, and/or social benefits. Stakeholders hold a critical role when relating with edupreneurs. Stakeholders are the various individuals and groups who are directly invested in and may be affected (positively or negatively) by the entrepreneurial activities. The purpose of this chapter is to discuss the rise of entrepreneurism in higher education and explore the case of a learning enterprise that supports the preparation of educational technologists as up-and-coming entrepreneurs. The development of such a learning enterprise is connected to the concept of a civic-minded professional who is someone interested in using his or her knowledge and skills for the public good. The learning enterprise enhances its members' civic-minded agency, meaning the group's purposeful and reflective acts that aim to address community members' educational needs. Stakeholders are deeply involved in addressing needs and issues in collaboration with educational technologists.

Keywords: Entrepreneurism · Civic-minded professional · Educational technology · Stakeholders

1 The Rise of Entrepreneurism in Higher Education

Investments in Education Technology are on the rise with $2 billion deals closed last year in Educational Technology investments, which represents a 55% increase since the previous year [1]. Money is invested in a diverse group of products and services ranging from classroom-management apps to foreign language for adult learners. But an entrepreneurial mindset goes beyond starting a business, or making money. It is a way of life driven by the continuous impetus of looking at issues from a novel perspective with the intent to create solutions that people actually use. As Kao et al. [2, p. 41] explain, entrepreneurship meets the central human need to innovate and create. Entrepreneurship

© IFIP International Federation for Information Processing 2016
Published by Springer International Publishing AG 2016. All Rights Reserved
T. Brinda et al. (Eds.): SaITE 2016, IFIP AICT 493, pp. 124–129, 2016.
DOI: 10.1007/978-3-319-54687-2_12

consists "of doing something new (creation), and/or something different (innovation) for the purpose of creating wealth for the individual and adding value to the society".

Education, in general, and Educational Technology, in particular, have not been traditionally perceived as a proving ground for entrepreneurship initiatives; however, in light of current difficult economic scenario and shrinking global job markets it is imperative to ensure that students are adequately prepared to face the challenges ahead. As Wagner [3, p. 8] identifies, the gap between "what our best suburban, urban, and rural public schools are teaching and testing versus what all students will need to succeed as learners, workers, and citizens in today's global knowledge economy". Among seven survival skills for the 21st century, Wagner [3] highlights "initiative and entrepreneurialism" as ways to pursue new opportunities, ideas and strategies for improvement. Organizations are looking for highly adaptable employees who can produce creative solutions to complex problems. As social change takes over every dimension of people's lives, schools reveal themselves as too conservative and "lagging behind change" instead of helping students "understanding and living with social change" [4, p. 151]. As postgraduate programs in Educational Technology renew themselves to face the challenges ahead, they engage in educating the new generation of educational technologist – the edupreneurs.

1.1   The Edupreneur

Edupreneurs are "self-motivated learners/members of an enterprise who can recognize opportunities and take action on complex educational problems while aiming to create social value, financial value, and/or social benefits" [5, p. 115], [6].

Globalization and the digital revolution have allowed people to engage in low-risk start-ups. College and university postgraduates are no longer expected to put all their time and effort toward moving up the corporate ladder in a single company during the span of their entire career. Much to the contrary, they are experiencing different career paths in different organizations including, in all likelihood, a company of their own and embodying the true spirit of an edupreneur.

1.2   The Stakeholders

What do entrepreneurs do? They establish a network of relationships with their stakeholders. Stakeholders are the various individuals and groups who are directly invested in and may be affected (positively or negatively) by the entrepreneurial activities. This definition embodies Freeman's stakeholder theory and his wider definition of stakeholders that "includes any group or individual who can affect or is affected by the corporation" [7, p. 41].

In order to be successful, edupreneurs need to establish strong connections to anyone impacted by their work, such as, the people that they serve, their investors, suppliers and employees as well as other organizations and communities. If edupreneurs solve educational complex problems, then they need to engage with the people who are committed to address these problems and/or are impacted by them. The quality of stakeholder involvement results in more equitable and sustainable solutions to educational problems as more voices are heard and taken into consideration in the decision-making process. A high involvement of stakeholders leads to a more efficient management of resources (knowledge, people, money and technology) to solve problems and allows for a better understanding of complex operating environments, including market developments and cultural dynamics. Most importantly, it contributes to the development of trust-based and transparent educational technologist-stakeholder relationship.

As Freeman [7] points out the quickest manner to destroy a corporation is to ignore their stakeholders. When corporations operate with the consent of stakeholders and communities they not only display social responsibility but they also better identify opportunities and threats critical for strategic planning. According to Freeman's stakeholder theory, edupreneurs need to: (1) identify the stakeholders, (2) identify the relations they want with them, (3) identify the urgency/timing need for communicating with them, (4) identify their information needs, and (5) identify the best communication channels.

2   The Case of a Learning Enterprise

The following paragraphs describe a learning enterprise created under the School of Education at Iowa State University in the United States (U.S.). This enterprise supports the preparation of educational technologists as up-and-coming entrepreneurs. Iowa State University is a member of the Association of American Universities and ranked by U.S. News and World Report as one of the top public universities in the nation. Over 36,000 students are enrolled, and served by over 6,200 faculty and staff. The university is located in Ames, Iowa, a progressive community of 60,000, located approximately 30 min north of Des Moines, and considered one of the best most livable small cities in the U.S.

2.1   *Learning Design Solutions* Background

The learning enterprise, named *Learning Design Solutions*, grew out of an advanced instructional design course in which postgraduate students worked on real-world projects with clients from organizations in the community. The focal learning activity of the course was to be part of a multi-team instructional consulting company designed to simulate a small firm that provided professional-level services free of charge. Postgraduate students, taking on the roles of technology consultants, worked with both university clients and organizations within the community (e.g., government agencies, schools, and healthcare providers). However, the demand for instructional design work was greater than could be accommodated by the single advanced instructional design course offered only during a semester each year. In order to meet the needs of the community, the course instructor and a group of postgraduate students envisioned an organization that could provide instructional design services year round.

2.2 *Learning Design Solutions* Purpose and Operations

The primary purpose of *Learning Design Solutions* is to create a context within which postgraduate students can develop an entrepreneurial mindset and practice managing financial and business aspects of the enterprise. In addition, it hones their consulting skills and applies their instructional design expertise in ways that ultimately improve people's lives and add societal value. The students take responsibility for all roles within the organization, including project management, customer relations, advertising, and dissemination [5].

Learning Design Solutions members and collaborators weekly review and reflect on their processes and inquire how they can improve their services and make operations more effective. These learning experiences capitalize on students' practical strengths while testing the application of ideas, theories, and models learned in the classroom. These experiences happen in real time with real stakeholders, and the decision-making involved carries real implications. Examples of projects developed are needs analyses, evaluation of training solutions, design and development of e-learning solutions, just to mention a few. The length of the projects is also variable. They can last for 3 to 6 months to 4 to 6 weeks. Stakeholders belong to different communities ranging from the university to organizations outside the state of Iowa.

2.3 *Learning Design Solutions* Business Model

Learning Design Solutions offers educational technology consulting services to internal Iowa State University clients as well as external clients from business and industry, both within and outside of the local community. This organization is defined as a service center under the university structure and categorized as a non-profit organization that operates on a break-even basis. The per hour rate for services is calculated each year based on the anticipated number of projects that will be contracted and the anticipated costs to both keep the organization running and to complete the number of contracted projects anticipated. Any revenue generated is re-invested into the organization by, for example, offering competitive scholarships to postgraduate students in Educational Technology.

This learning enterprise was created in 2009 with start-up funds from the Iowa State University John Pappajohn Entrepreneurial Center, followed by a significant grant from the College of Human Sciences Entrepreneurship Initiative. *Learning Design Solutions* is a unique enterprise within the university and one of few that are self-sustaining. However, the first client project completed as part of this learning enterprise was a community-driven project with a significant social positive impact. Members in this organization strive to become civic-minded professionals.

2.4 Other Similar Learning Enterprises

Other similar learning enterprises have been reported in the U.S. For example, Indiana University at Bloomington has implemented a multitude of educational technology projects with real-world applications developed by the Instructional Systems

Technology department. Along the same lines, David Merrill's team at Utah State University has been working on educational materials targeting entrepreneurial education [e.g., 8]. Similar enterprises have also been identified across the U.S., mainly among students in business and management [e.g., 9] at Valdosta State University. Utah State University has started up a somewhat similar enterprise to *Learning Design Solutions*. It began as an educational technology consulting firm out of the department of Instructional Technology and Learning Sciences under David Merrill's supervision. It is currently a well-established venture in Logan, Utah, known as Letterpress Software, Inc. (www.lpsoftware.com).

2.5 A Civic-Minded Approach

Career-centric approaches to Educational Technology produce technocratic professionals more interested in economic gain than in using their knowledge and skills for the public good [10]. Based on the conceptualization of entrepreneurship presented above [2], one of the main purposes of entrepreneurship is to add value to society, which is the intent of many of creations and innovations in Educational Technology that aim to help people learn better and become responsible and active citizens. The term civic-minded agency is defined here as an individual's or group's purposeful and reflective acts that aim at addressing societal needs and issues [10]. In this line of reasoning, a civic-minded educational technologist (1) has the public interest and a sense of civic responsibility at the forefront of his or her work, (2) is attentive, responsible and responsive to the emergent educational needs of the members of the community, and (3) utilizes his or her knowledge and skills in Educational Technology to improve learning and performance of the community members. Civic-minded educational technologists are concerned with the well-being of all members of a society and utilize their knowledge and skills to improve people's lives and bring positive social change. Social change is at the heart of their work and contributing to an equal distribution of social goods (e.g., education and access to technology) is their drive [11]. Therefore, involvement from stakeholders at all the stages of the design and development process is critical.

3   Final Remarks

The rationale for creating a learning enterprise stemmed from the recognition of an opportunity to serve the many educational needs of the surrounding community. The drive came from the chance to offer postgraduate students different career venues in education and the invaluable opportunity to practice "live" what they were learning in their programs, especially skills and knowledge related to Educational Technology. Additional motivation derived from creating a self-sustaining unit that could provide resources and funds to support students' professional development and research.

Learning Design Solutions can enhance its members' civic-minded agency and relies on a quality stakeholder engagement to address educational needs and issues in collaboration with educational technologists.

Acknowledgments.   The author would like to thank Dr. Farrah Dina Yusop for her vision and relentless application of the civic-minded instructional designer framework. She also would like to thank *Learning Design Solutions* members and collaborators for their work and commitment to entrepreneurship in Educational Technology.

References

1. Singer, N.: Silicon Valley Turns Its Eye to Education. The New York Times. Accessed 12 Jan 2015. http://www.nytimes.com/2015/01/12/technology/silicon-valley-turns-its-eye-to-education.html?smid=pl-share&_r=3
2. Kao, R.W.Y., Kao, R., Kao, K.R.: Entrepreneurism: A Philosophy and a Sensible Alternative for the Market Economy. Imperial College Press, London (2002)
3. Wagner, T.: The Global Achievement Gap. Basic Books, New York (2008)
4. Ornstein, A.C., Hunkins, F.: Curriculum: Foundations, Principles, and Theory. Allyn and Bacon, Boston (2008)
5. Correia, A.-P.: Creating curriculum within the context of an enterprise. In: Gosper, M., Ifenthaler, D. (eds.) Curriculum Models for the 21st Century: Using Learning Technologies in Higher Education, pp. 113–134. Springer, New York (2013)
6. Kamenetz, A.: DIY U: Edupunks, Edupreneurs and the Coming Transformation of Higher Education. Chelsea Green, White River Junction (2010)
7. Freeman, R.E.,: Stakeholder theory of the modern corporation. In: Hartman, L.P. (ed.) Perspectives in Business Ethics, pp. 171–180. McGraw-Hill, New York (2001)
8. Mendenhall, A., Buhanan, C.W., Suhaka, M., Mills, G., Gibson, G.V., Merrill, M.D.: A task-centered approach to entrepreneurship. TechTrends **50**(4), 84–89 (2006)
9. Plumly, L.W., Marshall, L.L., Eastman, J., Iyer, R., Stanley, K.L., Boatwright, J.: Developing entrepreneurial competencies: a student business. J. Entrepreneurship Educ. **11**, 17–29 (2008)
10. Sullivan, W.M.: Work and integrity: the crisis and promise of professionalism in America. Jossey-Bass, San Francisco (2005)
11. Yusop, F., Correia, A.-P.: On becoming a civic-minded instructional designer: an ethnographic study of an instructional design experience. Br. J. Educ. Technol. **45**(5), 782–792 (2014)

Vingt Ans Après: Analysis of WG 3.7's Published Work on Information Technology in Educational Management (1994–2014)

Javier Osorio[✉] and Julia Nieves

Universidad de Las Palmas de Gran Canaria, Las Palmas, Spain
{javier.osorio,julia.nieves}@ulpgc.es

Abstract. In this paper, articles published in the proceedings of the IFIP Working Group 3.7 conferences during its twenty years of existence are reviewed. This work is a continuation of a previous one that classified the most relevant topics addressed by the Group in its first ten years and the major research methodologies adopted by the contributors to carry out their work. The paper has been structured to facilitate the comparison of the Group's first decade of activity with the second decade. The review shows that the topic of Assimilation and Integration of IT into Educational Management continues to be the leading theme in publications. The published work by IFIP Working Group 3.7, which accounts for some 213 papers, is a good indicator of the maturity of the research on information technology in educational management (ITEM).

Keywords: ITEM · Proceedings · Research topics · Research methodologies

1 Introduction

The first international conference on information technology in educational management (ITEM) took place in Jerusalem in 1994. Since then, the Working Group 3.7 of the International Federation for Information Processing (IFIP) has held a total of ten international meetings. During the conferences, researchers, academics and professionals have discussed and contributed to a better development and understanding of all the issues associated with the use of information technology (IT) in educational management. Most of these contributions, generally presented as papers, have been published, eventually becoming an important body of knowledge and experience.

ITEM studies have been considerably enriched by the varied profiles and backgrounds of the participants in these working conferences, to the point of acquiring certain characteristics of their own. This situation was described in 'ITEM: synthesis of experience, research and future perspectives on computer-assisted school information systems' [1]. ITEM analysis has been approached from very different perspectives that correspond to diverse academic disciplines, which is probably the underlying reason for the area's conceptual richness. After twenty years of uninterrupted periodic meetings

© IFIP International Federation for Information Processing 2016
Published by Springer International Publishing AG 2016. All Rights Reserved
T. Brinda et al. (Eds.): SaITE 2016, IFIP AICT 493, pp. 130–138, 2016.
DOI: 10.1007/978-3-319-54687-2_13

with outstanding academic results, it seems worthwhile to pause to reflect on what has been achieved during this period.

In the year 2006, during the conference that took place in Hamamatsu (Japan), a synthesis study was presented on the scientific production of Working Group 3.7 in its first ten years of existence [2]. The aim of the present paper is to study the literature resulting from the international ITEM conferences organised by the IFIP Working Group 3.7, comparing two periods, the first from 1994 to 2006, and the second from 2008 to 2014. The same structure will be followed as in the initial study in order to facilitate the comparison of the two periods.

2   Analysis Methodology

Since the WG 3.7 began its activity, a total of 11 conferences have been held on all the continents. The first, where the foundations of the group were established, took place in Jerusalem in 1994. All the conferences have been followed by publications comprising the most relevant papers presented. These publications have been edited by prestigious companies specialised in publishing scientific papers. Table 1 shows the city and country where the conference took place, the year, book title, publisher, year of publication, and the number of articles published in each book.

Table 1. International ITEM conferences and resulting publications.

Place	Year	Book title	Publisher	Year of publication	Number of papers published
Jerusalem (Israel)	1994	Information Technology in Educational Management [3]	Chapman & Hall	1995	31
Hong-Kong (China)	1996	Information Technology in Educational Management for the Schools of the Future [4]	Chapman & Hall	1997	26
Maine (USA)	1998	The Integration of Information for Educational Management [5]	Felicity Press	1998	17
Auckland (New Zealand)	2000	Pathways to Institutional Improvement with Information Technology in Educational Management [6]	Kluwer	2001	11
Helsinki (Finland)	2002	Management of Education in the Information Age: The Role of IT [7]	Kluwer	2003	14
Gran Canaria (Spain)	2004	Information Technology and Educational Management in the Knowledge Society [8]	Springer	2005	18
Hamamatsu (Japan)	2006	Knowledge Management for Educational Innovation [9]	Springer	2007	26
Darwin (Australia)	2008	Evolution of Information Technology in Educational Management [10]	Springer	2009	18
Kasane (Botswana)	2010	Information Technology and Managing Quality Education [11]	Springer	2011	20
Bremen (Germany)	2012	Next Generation of Information Technology in Educational Management [12]	Springer	2012	16
Potsdam (Germany)	2014	Key Competences in ICT and Informatics [13]	Springer	2014	16 (ITEM)

The publication corresponding to the 2014 Conference includes a total of 28 contributions, of which 16 are directly related to the ITEM field. This is due to the fact that the 2014 Conference joined two IFIP working groups, the WG 3.4 on Professional and Vocational Education in ICT, and the aforementioned WG 3.7 on Information Technology in Educational Management. Therefore, only the 16 papers corresponding to ITEM have been analysed.

The information resulting from papers' analysis has been classified into two groups: first, according to the topics addressed in each article; and second, considering the research methodology applied, in order to further group them considering the type of approach employed. This type of organization was chosen to maintain the format adopted in the publication corresponding to the review of the first 10 years of WG 3.7 (1994–2004). In the tables, the data have been added from the study of the next ten years of the work group, until the group's conference which took place in Potsdam (Germany) in 2014. Tables have been included with the data since the first publication to facilitate comparison of the two periods. In order to classify the articles under a specific topic and research methodology, the titles and abstracts of all 96 papers published during the 2006–2014 period were studied. In those cases where the classification was unclear the text was revised. In case the paper could be assigned to more than one topic or the research methodology was unclear, the two researchers that carried out the classification process confronted their opinions and jointly agreed the assignment to a specific category.

3   Data Analysis

Tables 2 and 3 show a set of general topics discussed at the international conferences of IFIP Working Group 3.7. Table 2 covers the 1994–2004 period, while Table 3 covers the 2006–2014 period. Both tables show the number of papers on each topic and the percentage they represent of the total number of papers per publication, as well as the accumulated total. The last column in Table 3 summarizes the total numbers for the whole period (twenty years).

The topics comprise rather large classification areas in an attempt to obtain significant results. Otherwise, a more detailed classification might have made the results excessively fragmented. For example, Grover et al. [14] suggests 20 IT related topics applicable to any study area, and authors such as Claver et al. [15] increase this number to 30. If it was considered each different type of educational management application as a research topic, this would probably result in an excessively large number of themes. In this case, it was decided to group all these applications in one single category, making no distinctions between the specific applications. This approach could offer a clearer vision of the attention given to this topic at the different conferences, which would be more difficult to perceive if the analysis was more fragmented. A total of 9 topics were identified, although some have an irregular appearance over time.

An initial comparison of Tables 2 and 3 shows a difference in the number of papers published between the two periods. This is due to the fact that in the first period 6 conferences were held, compared to 5 in the second period, yielding 117 and 96 publications, respectively. The last column in Table 2 shows that the most popular topics

Table 2. Papers classified by research subject (first period 1994–2004).

Topic	Conference						
	1994	1996	1998	2000	2002	2004	Total (first period)
	N. %	N. %	N. %	N. %	N. %	N. %	N. %
Strategies to integrate IT into educational management	2	1	2	1	1	2	9
	6.5	3.8	11.8	9.1	7.2	11	7.7
Assimilation and integration of IT into educational management	4	9	6	3	4	1	27
	12.9	34.6	35.2	27.3	28.6	5.5	23
ITEM state of the art. The discipline's present situation and trends	1	1	–	–	–	1	3
	3.2	3.8	–	–	–	5.5	2.7
Assessment of IT support for educational management	2	5	2	4	2	5	20
	6.5	19.2	11.8	6.3	14.3	27.9	17.1
National, regional and local experience in the use of IT for educational management	10	–	2	1	1	4	18
	32.3	–	11.8	9.1	7.1	22.3	15.4
IT applications in educational management	9	7	2	–	–	2	20
	29	27	11.8	–	–	11.1	17.1
Mathematical tools employed to create models for educational management	3	2	1	–	–	–	6
	9.6	7.8	5.8	–	–	–	5.1
IT applications for teaching	–	1	2	–	3	2	8
	–	3.8	11.8	–	21.4	11.1	6.8
Teacher and manager training in the use of IT for educational management	–	–	–	2	3	1	6
	–	–	–	18.2	21.4	5.5	5.1
Total	31	26	17	11	14	18	117
	100	100	100	100	100	100	100

during the first ten years were Assimilation and integration of IT into educational management (23%), followed by Assessment of IT support for educational management (17.1%), IT applications in educational management (17.1%), and National, regional and local experience in the use of IT for educational management (15.4%). Together, these topics represent 76.2% of all the papers published in that period. Interestingly, the most recurrent topic during the first 10 years of publications was Assessment of IT support for educational management, which has been repeatedly addressed because of the importance of analysing the results obtained after implementing new strategies, policies, techniques or tools. However, this topic has progressively lost importance in the second period, judging by the decreasing number of papers published about it.

In the 20 years of publications about ITEM, Assimilation and integration of IT into educational management is the topic that has received most attention (24.9%). In both periods, this topic has led the number of publications.

Table 3. Papers classified by research subject (second period 2006–2014).

Topic	Conference						
	2006	2008	2010	2012	2014	Total (second period)	Total (20 years)
	N. %	N. %	N. %	N. %	N. %	N. %	N. %
Strategies to integrate IT into educational management	–	2	5	–	–	7	16
	–	11.1	25	–	–	7.3	7.5
Assimilation and integration of IT into educational management	5	5	4	4	8	26	53
	19.2	27.8	20	25	50	27.1	24.9
ITEM state of the art. The discipline's present situation and trends	1	2	–	–	–	3	6
	3.8	11.1	–	–	–	3.1	2.8
Assessment of IT support for educational management	2	3	3	1	–	9	29
	7.7	16.7	15	6.3	–	9.4	13.6
National, regional and local experience in the use of IT for educational management	1	–	1	2	1	5	23
	3.8	–	5	12.5	6.3	5.2	10.8
IT applications in educational management	6	4	2	5	3	20	40
	23.1	22.2	10	31.3	18.8	20.8	18.8
Mathematical tools employed to create models for educational management	2	–	1	–	1	4	10
	7.7	–	5	–	6.3	4.2	4.7
IT applications for teaching	7	2	4	1	2	16	24
	26.9	11.1	20	6.3	12.5	16.7	11.7
Teacher and manager training in the use of IT for educational management	2	–	–	3	1	6	12
	7.7	–	–	18.8	6.3	6.3	5.6
Total	26	18	20	16	16	96	213
	100	100	100	100	100	100	100

The tables show that of the three topics with the greatest number of publications in the first ten years of WG 3.7 publications, two of them continue to figure among the three most frequent topics in the second period. These topics are: Assimilation and integration of IT into educational management, and IT applications in educational management. The topic Assessment of IT support for educational management was no longer among the most repeated topics in the second period, ceding its position to the topic of IT applications for teaching. Although the latter is not directly related to the scope of the WG 3.7, this theme gradually gained importance in the second period of analysis, doubling its former percentage and occupying the third position in the number of publications in the second period (16.7%). However, it is proposed that ITEM practitioners and researchers consider the reasons for this increase, given that this topic corresponds rather to other fields of study, such as IT use for educational purposes.

In both periods into which the analysis was divided, the following three topics produced fewer publications: ITEM state of the art, the discipline's present situation and trends; Mathematical tools employed to create models for educational management; and Teacher and manager training in the use of IT for educational management.

4   Research Methods

Regarding the research methodology, the papers that were reviewed can be divided into theoretical studies and empirical studies. The theoretical studies were grouped into conceptual and illustrative categories, and the empirical studies were classified as case studies and field studies. Each of these methods will be described briefly.

Theoretical studies are fundamentally based on ideas, structures and speculations, rather than a systematic observation of reality. Although non-empirical articles may contain some empirical observations or facts, they will be of secondary importance. In other words, the emphasis is on ideas rather than facts. Theoretical studies can have a conceptual and illustrative nature. Conceptual studies describe structures, models or theories, and they offer explanations and reasons. The illustrative ones, on the other hand, are designed to guide practice and make recommendations for action or establish stages for attending to certain circumstances. The emphasis is on what and how, rather than why.

The essence of the research carried out in empirical studies is to observe the reality being investigated. This is where case studies can be placed. These kinds of studies are becoming more numerous in the field of IS/IT, mostly for the following reasons [16]: (a) the researcher can study IS/IT in its natural environment, learn about the state of the art, and generate theories based on practice; (b) case studies allow researchers to answer questions about how and why and, therefore, understand the nature and complexity of the process that is taking place; and (c) they are appropriate for investigation in areas with few previous studies, and they are often the first stage of empirical research. However, case studies have often been criticised for their lack of scientific rigour, although this is not due to a problem in the method itself, but rather to the fact that often the label 'case study' has been given to what is merely a recounting of anecdotes [17].

Field study is another empirical research method that analyses one or several organisations commonly with regard to a set of variables. There is an experimental design, but no experimental control, which means that the researcher collects information about uncontrolled situations. The object of study operates in its usual fashion while the research is conducted. The aim is to relate results to certain explanatory variables. It is similar to the case study in that phenomena are analysed in their natural environment without introducing any variations in it. However, the methods differ in that field study is not interested in the whole phenomenon, but only specific aspects or variables. Moreover, the analysis of information in case studies is mostly qualitative, whereas field studies generally use quantitative methods.

Tables 4 and 5 show a classification of papers considering the research methodology employed. As in Tables 2 and 3, Tables 4 and 5 show the total number of papers per period, as well as the percentage of each according to the methodology used, and the progression of each method over time, expressed for each of the publications considered. The last column in Table 4 shows total values for the first period, while the last two columns in Table 5 summarize the total values for the second period and for the entire range of years.

In the 20-year period analysed, it can be observed that the proportion of publications based on theoretical studies is quite similar to the proportion based on empirical studies, being slightly more in the latter group.

An analysis of Table 4 shows that most of the articles published during the first period are empirical, exceeding the theoretical ones by more than ten percentage points. However, for the second period, Table 5 shows that the tendency of the first period was inverted, with the number of publications based on theoretical studies being greater than the number based on empirical studies. Among the theoretical studies, the illustrative type is the most frequent and doubles the conceptual type in each period and for the 20 years under study. By contrast, for publications based on empirical studies, the tendency was inverted, going from a greater percentage of publications based on case studies during the first ten years to a greater role of field studies during the second period. However, in the total calculation, there is still a predominance of empirical research based on case studies.

Table 4. Papers classified by research methodology (first period 1994–2004).

Research methodology	Conference						
	1994	1996	1998	2000	2002	2004	Total (first period)
	N. %	N. %	N. %	N. %	N. %	N. %	N. %
Theoretical studies	**15**	**15**	**4**	**5**	**4**	**7**	**50**
	48.4	**57.7**	**23.5**	**45.5**	**28.6**	**38.9**	**42.7**
Theoretical – conceptual	6	4	2	1	1	4	18
	19.4	15.4	11.8	9	7.2	22.2	15.4
Theoretical – illustrative	9	11	2	4	3	3	32
	29	42.3	11.8	36.4	21.4	16.7	27.3
Empirical studies	**16**	**11**	**13**	**6**	**10**	**11**	**67**
	51.6	**42.3**	**76.5**	**54.5**	**71.4**	**61.1**	**57.3**
Empirical – case studies	13	10	9	2	7	8	49
	41.9	38.5	52.9	18.2	50	44.4	41.9
Empirical – field studies	3	1	4	4	3	3	18
	9.7	3.8	23.5	36.4	21.4	16.7	15.4
Total	31	26	17	11	14	18	117
	100	100	100	100	100	100	100

Table 5. Papers classified by research methodology (second period 2006–2014).

Research methodology	Conference						
	2006	2008	2010	2012	2014	Total (second period)	Total (20 years)
	N. %	N. %	N. %	N. %	N. %	N. %	N. %
Theoretical studies	**15**	**13**	**10**	**6**	**6**	**50**	**100**
	57.7	**72.2**	**50**	**37.5**	**37.5**	**52.1**	**47**
Theoretical – conceptual	5	3	4	–	3	15	33
	19.2	16.7	20	–	18.8	15.6	15.5
Theoretical – illustrative	10	10	6	6	3	35	67
	38.5	55.6	30	37.5	18.8	36.5	31.5
Empirical studies	**11**	**5**	**10**	**10**	**10**	**46**	**113**
	42.3	**27.8**	**50**	**62.5**	**62.5**	**47.9**	**53**
Empirical – case studies	5	2	4	4	2	17	66
	19.2	11.1	20	25	12.5	17.7	31
Empirical – field studies	6	3	6	6	8	29	47
	23.1	16.7	30	37.5	50	30.2	22
Total	26	18	20	16	16	96	213
	100	100	100	100	100	100	100

5   Conclusions

The interest in overcoming problems derived from adapting a new and changing technology such as IT to educational management has set the standards for ITEM research during the 20-year existence of Working Group 3.7. In this period of time, eleven books have been published containing the main conclusions of the work conferences, which allows us to confirm that this area of study has reached maturity.

Nevertheless, ahead of us is the task of completing a compact body of knowledge consisting of theories that can help ITEM to acquire its own identity. This is not an easy task, due to its multidisciplinary nature and its strong dependence on a changing support like IT.

References

1. Visscher, A.J., Wild, P., Fung, A.C.W.: ITEM: Synthesis of Experience, Research and Future Perspectives on Computer-Assisted School Information Systems. Kluwer Academic Publishers, Dordrecht (2001)
2. Osorio, J., Bulchand, J.: Ten years of ITEM research. In: Tatnall, A., Okamoto, T., Visscher, A. (eds.) ITEM 2006. IIFIP, vol. 230, pp. 1–8. Springer, Heidelberg (2007). doi: 10.1007/978-0-387-69312-5_1
3. Barta, B., Telem, M., Gev, Y. (eds.): Information Technology in Educational Management. Chapman & Hall, London (1995)
4. Fung, A.C.W., Visscher, A.J., Barta, B., Teather, D. (eds.): Information Technology in Educational Management for the Schools of the Future. Chapman & Hall, London (1997)
5. Fulmer, C.L., Barta, B., Nolan, P. (eds.): The Integration of Information for Educational Management. Felicity Press, Whitefield (1998)
6. Nolan, C.J.P., Fung, A.C.W., Brown, M.A. (eds.): Pathways to Institutional Improvement with Information Technology in Educational Management. Kluwer, Boston (2001)
7. Selwood, I.D., Fung, A.C.W., O'Mahony, C.D. (eds.): Management of Education in the Information Age: The Role of IT. Kluwer, Boston (2003)
8. Tatnall, A., Osorio, J., Visscher, A. (eds.): ITEM 2004. IIFIP, vol. 170. Springer, Heidelberg (2005). doi:10.1007/b104289
9. Tatnall, A., Okamoto, T., Visscher, A. (eds.): ITEM 2006. IIFIP, vol. 230. Springer, Heidelberg (2007). doi:10.1007/978-0-387-69312-5
10. Tatnall, A., Visscher, A., Finegan, A., O'Mahony, C. (eds.): ITEM 2008. ITIFIP, vol. 292. Springer, Heidelberg (2009). doi:10.1007/978-0-387-93847-9
11. Tatnall, A., Kereteletswe, O.C., Visscher, A. (eds.): ITEM 2010. IAICT, vol. 348. Springer, Heidelberg (2011). doi:10.1007/978-3-642-19715-4
12. Passey, D., Breiter, A., Visscher, A. (eds.): ITEM 2012. IAICT, vol. 400. Springer, Heidelberg (2013). doi:10.1007/978-3-642-38411-0
13. Passey, D., Tatnall, A. (eds.): ITEM 2014. IAICT, vol. 444. Springer, Heidelberg (2014). doi: 10.1007/978-3-662-45770-2
14. Grover, V., Lee, C.C., Duran, D.: Analizing methodological rigor of MIS survey research from 1980–1989. Inf. Manage. 24(6), 305–317 (1993)
15. Claver, E., González, M.R., Llopis, J.: Estudio de la investigación en sistemas de información a través del análisis de dos revistas (1981–1997). Revista de Economía y Empresa. 36, 97–126 (1999)

16. Benbasat, I., Goldstein, D.K., Mead, M.: The case research strategy in studies of information systems. MIS Q. **11**(3), 369–386 (1987)
17. Lee, A.S.: A scientific methodology for MIS case studies. MIS Q. **13**(1), 33–50 (1989)

Information and Communication Technologies for Social and National Development

Digital Pedagogy for Enhanced Social Qualities, Collaborative Processes and Quality of Learning

Nicholas Mavengere[✉] and Mikko Ruohonen

University of Tampere, Tampere, Finland
{nicholas.mavengere,mikko.j.ruohonen}@uta.fi

Abstract. The best learning environment that enables excellence should always be sought. This research seeks to draw measures to promote virtual learning experience based on promotion of social interaction and collaborative processes. The research is based on a total virtual learning experience of a masters' level information and communication technology for development (ICT4D) class at the University of Tampere. A questionnaire was conducted at the end of the course to assess social qualities, collaborative processes and qualities of learning. The research seeks to promote quality learning by developing a social and collaborative learning environment. The results of this study included measures, such as, pedagogical techniques and technological tools that could foster such an environment.

Keywords: Digital pedagogy · Social qualities · Collaborative processes · Quality of learning

1 Introduction

There are increasing opportunities for information technology (IT) applications in education. Chou and Liu [1] noted the significant transformation in the learning and teaching process because of the web-based technology. Digital pedagogy involves the use of technology in enhancing the learning process. The value of digital pedagogy is derived from attempting to fully enjoy the benefits of technology in learning. The advantages of technology in adoption for learning could be summarized as "learning any time" and "learning anywhere" and thus self-control, independent thinking, diverse viewpoints and diffuse thinking models [1].

As much as we appreciate the advantages of technology in learning as presented above, there are also disadvantages that we should put efforts to minimize. Disadvantages, such as, possibility of students feeling isolated thus leading to anxiety and confusion thus reducing learning effectiveness [1]. Hence, as we adopt learning technologies we must try to maximize the benefits gained and reduce the negative impacts [2]. Digital pedagogy plays a crucial role in doing that. Spiro [3] defined digital pedagogy as "engaged and reflexive practice and scholarship of teaching and learning through digital technologies". Typical features of digital pedagogy include [3]:

T. Brinda et al. (Eds.): SaITE 2016, IFIP AICT 493, pp. 141–151, 2016.
DOI: 10.1007/978-3-319-54687-2_14

- Combining theory and practice, making and thinking
- Fostering creativity, play and problem solving
- Encouraging participation, collaboration and public engagement
- Aiming to increase critical understanding of digital environment

In this research, we seek to promote virtual learning by making use of digital pedagogy that enhance social qualities, collaborative processes and quality of learning. Kreijns et al. [4] advocated for sociability in virtual environments for enriched learning experience. Sociability is defined as the extent to which a virtual environment is "perceived to be able to facilitate the emergence of a sound social space with attributes as trust and belonging, a strong sense of community, and good working relationships" [4]. This would foster collaboration processes and qualities of learning. Thus, the research question is: how could digital pedagogy promote social qualities and collaborative processes for learning quality?

In the next section the theoretical background is elaborated. After that, the methodology is specified then the results are noted. The discussion section follows and finally conclusion.

2   Theoretical Background

Kreijns et al. [4] argue the need to consider and integrate social factors for successful virtual learning. Disregarding social psychological processes, such as, starting groups and sustainable social relationships could lead to failure of virtual learning. In fact, it is essential to promote social interaction in virtual learning environment, in that it reduces loneliness and isolation. As shown in Fig. 1, Kreijns et al. [4, p. 180] suggest that sociability influences social interaction, "the greater the sociability of an environment, the more likely it is that social interaction will take place and that it will result in the emergence of a sound social space". They defined social presence as "the perceived degree of illusion that the other in the communication appears to be a real physical person in either an immediate (i.e., real time or synchronous) or a delayed (i.e., time-deferred or asynchronous) communication episode". Pedagogical techniques depending on the contents of the course also promote social presence and interaction.

We should always strive for the best. There are fundamental aspects of learning, referred to as quality learning which we should always seek to achieve. These are the cornerstones which technology could aid to build upon to foster the learning process. The following qualities of learning are suggested [5, p. 293];

1. Active - Learners' role in learning process is active; they are engaged in mindful processing of information and they are responsible for the result.
2. Constructive - Learners construct new knowledge on the basis of their previous knowledge.
3. Collaborative - Learners work together in building new knowledge in co-operation with each other and exploiting each other's skills.
4. Intentional - Learners try actively and willingly to achieve a cognitive objective.

5. Contextual - Learning tasks are situated in a meaningful real world tasks or they are introduced through case-based or problem-based real life examples.
6. Transfer - Learners are able to transfer learning from the situations and contexts, where learning has taken place and use their knowledge in other situations.
7. Reflective - Learners articulate what they have learned and reflect on the processes and decisions entailed by the process.

These learning qualities were evaluated in the survey, which was conducted in the ICT4D course. This was done in order to adopt technological tools and pedagogical practices that promote the above-mentioned qualities of learning. Please see methodology section below for more information about the survey.

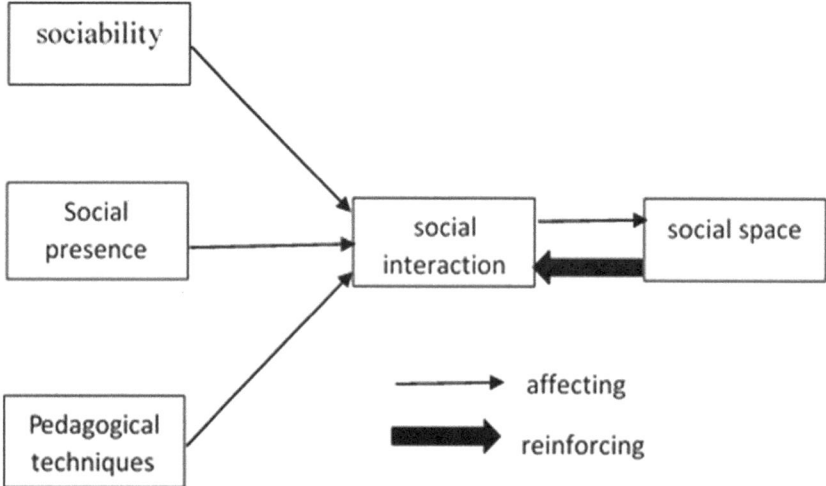

Fig. 1. Relationships between the variables sociability, social presence, pedagogical techniques, social interaction, and social space. Adapted from [4].

We suggest that digital pedagogy supported by social interaction and collaborative processes could create a learning environment that is conducive for enhancing qualities of learning as shown in Fig. 2. The qualities of learning reinforce the environment that is social and collaborative.

Illeris [6] suggested the three dimensions of learning and competence development as content, incentive and interaction as shown in Fig. 3.

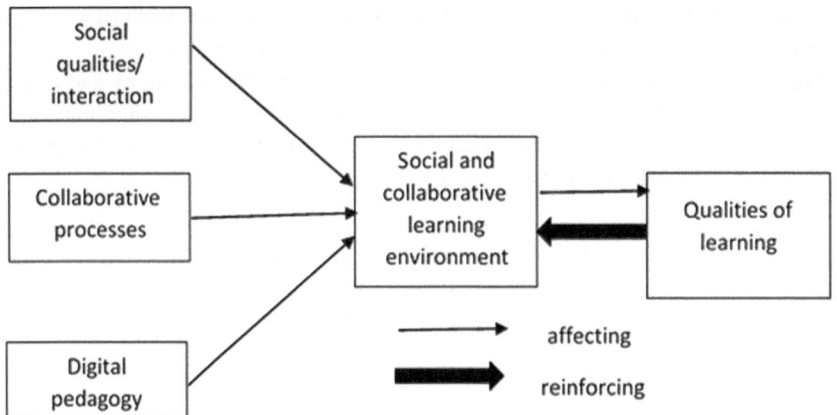

Fig. 2. Qualities of learning enabled in a social and collaborative learning environment tentative conceptual model

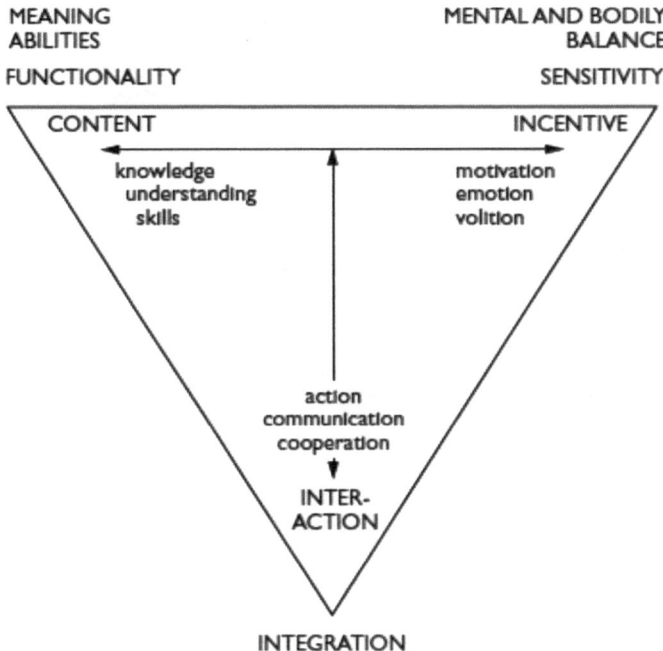

Fig. 3. The three dimensions of learning and competence development [6]

Content dimension is what is learned, for example, knowledge and skills. Incentive dimension is source of the mental energy that is essential for the learning process, such as, motivation and emotions. These two dimensions are initiated and cemented by the interaction process. These dimensions of learning are an elaboration of the social and collaborative learning environment shown in Fig. 2.

3   Methodology

The University of Tampere hosted an international virtual course with students from Finland, Germany, and South Africa. The course topic was Development 2.0, that is, Information Communications Technologies for Development 2.0. The course comprised of 33 participants who had diverse virtual learning experience as illustrated in Fig. 4. About 50% of the participants had 5 or more times of virtual learning experience.

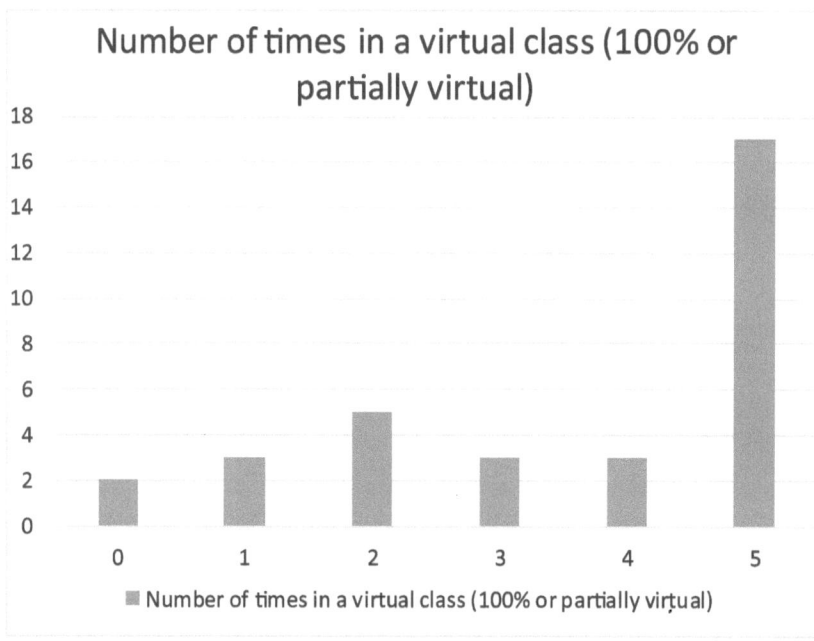

Fig. 4. Virtual learning experience

A survey was conducted at the middle and end of the course. The objectives in conducting the survey included assessing the virtual learning experience for the class and adopting measures, that is, pedagogical practices and technology tools to enhance virtual learning. This was done to improve the learning process the next time the course is offered.

4   Research Findings/Results

The study seeks to highlight how pedagogy in a virtual environment could be enforced to promote social qualities and collaborative processes for quality learning. In this section, we highlight results from the ICT4D course. These results are context dependent [7] in that the reflections of the participants could have been strongly influenced by factors, such as, study topic but nevertheless there are lessons that could be drawn that are useful for the wider audience interested in virtual learning.

4.1 Social Qualities

The measures of social qualities namely, loneliness, good impression of others and spontaneous informal conversation in the online course environment reflects a moderate satisfaction as shown in Fig. 5. Although a significant percentage of participants, 37.5% highlighted that they feel loneliness in the course environment.

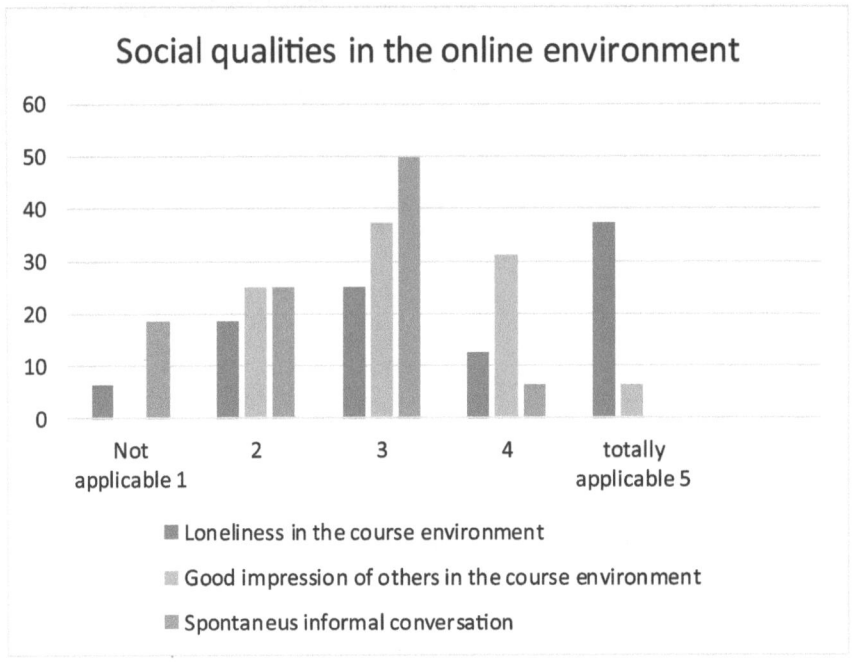

Fig. 5. Social qualities in the online environment

The interaction enabled by the course environment measures, these are, course environment enabled comfort, non-task related conversion and friendship development were deemed to be not applicable by the course participants as shown in Fig. 6. This is especially so for the perceived friendship development enabler by the course environment in which 68.8% of the course participants perceived it not applicable.

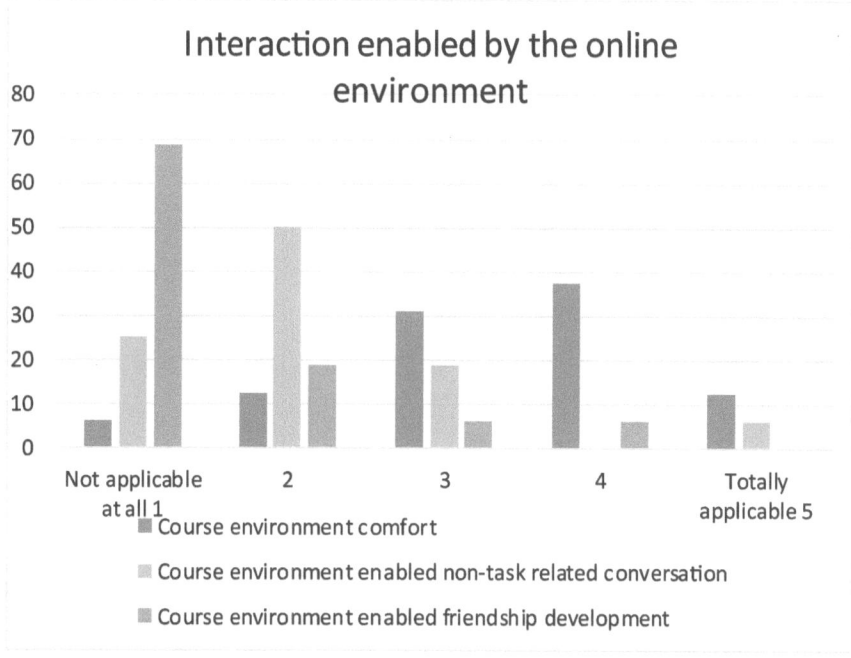

Fig. 6. Interaction enabled by the online environment

4.2   Collaborative Processes

Figure 7 shows that the collaborative processes were not well supported by the course environment. Collaborative processes measures, such as, course environment as enabler of team development and good work relationship among participants had 37.5% and 50% respectively which were the highest at second applicability.

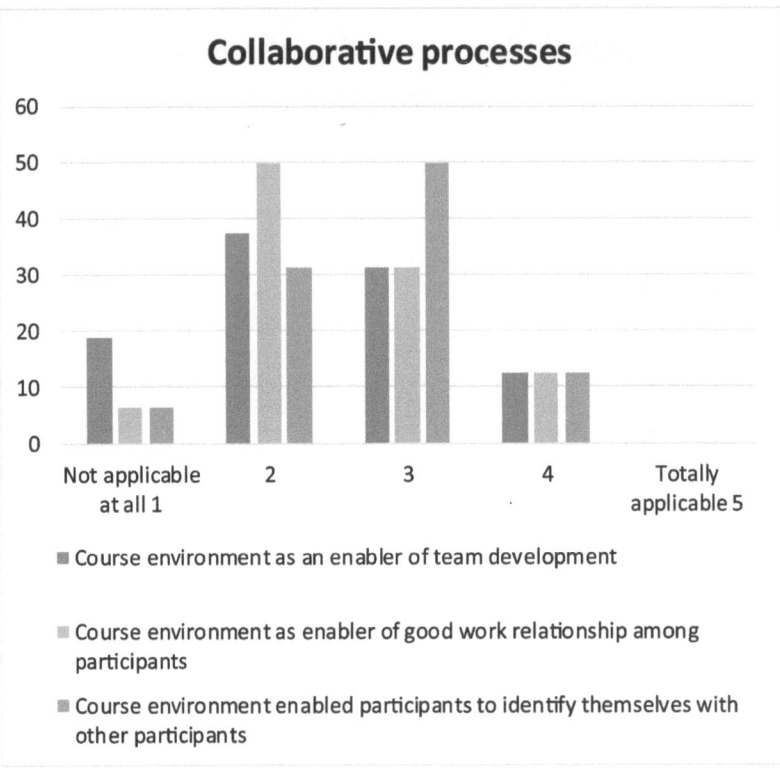

Fig. 7. Collaborative processes

4.3 Quality of Learning

The qualities of learning proposed by Ruokamo and Pohjolainen [5] were also evaluated at the middle and end of the course as shown in Fig. 8. Some qualities of learning were perceived to have increased from middle to end of course, such as, active, collaborative and reflective learning. However, some qualities, such as, collaborative, intentional, conversational, contextualized and transfer learning were perceived to have decreased.

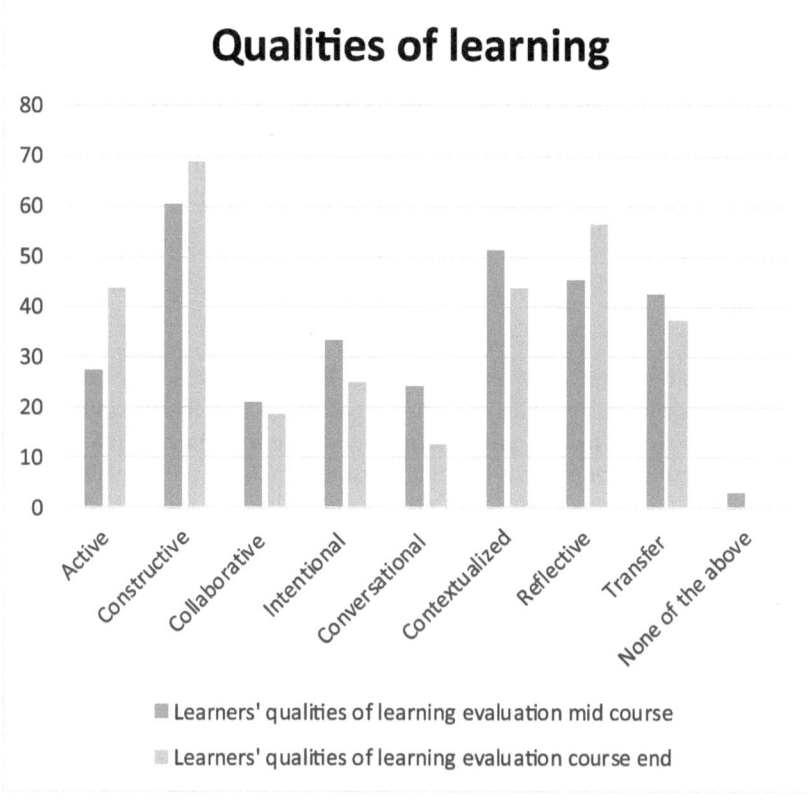

Fig. 8. Qualities of learning evaluation

5   Discussion

The use of technology to promote learning is not new, for example, in the 1990s Leidner and Jarvenpaa [8] advocated for technology inclusion to improve business management school. However, the advance in technology calls for constant research to improve how technology is incorporated in learning. Thus, this research seeks to highlight digital pedagogy that promote social qualities, collaborative processes and quality of learning in virtual learning. However, we would also bring to light the potential confliction between social qualities promotion and learning outcomes. That is to say, as we achieve social aspects this could limit or loose focus from the desired learning objectives. There-fore, there has to be an analysis of promoting social qualities that are in line with learning process and thus delivering positive learning outcomes.

Digital pedagogy, such as, embracing techniques that promote social qualities and collaboration like online open learning diaries could be used to create a social and collaborative learning environment. Open learning diary is a reflective essay, which students share with the rest of the participants in a virtual learning environment. This promotes interaction as students comment and discuss experiences. The value of interaction in learning is well emphasized, both in research and in practice [9]. In doing so, collaborative processes are enabled from this sharing of background knowledge of fellow participants. Technological tools, such as, wikis, blogs and discussion forums could also foster the desired social and collaborative learning environment. For example, in the development 2.0 course students were grouped into teams of 3 or 4 participants and each team wrote a page summary of a course book and together developed the book wiki. This wiki development fostered social interaction and collaborative processes with the aim of promoting qualities of learning.

6   Conclusion

Excellence should always be sought in learning. In this research, this excellence has been defined based on the qualities of learning, namely, active constructive, collaborative, intentional, contextual, transfer and reflective learning. In addition, technology advances offer another avenue in promoting learning. To do so, digital pedagogy has to be set to promote the desired factors that promote qualities of learning. In this research, a social and collaborative learning environment is proposed as the conducive environment to be fostered as a platform for quality learning promotion.

The research seeks to promote quality learning by developing a social and collaborative learning environment. A conceptual model is developed in this research to highlight how qualities of learning are enabled in a social and collaborative learning environment. In practice, in the case study conducted, there were diverse results (some positive and some negative) in the qualities of learning pointing to the fact that efforts need to be made to specifically try and improve each of the qualities of learning, namely, active constructive, collaborative, intentional, contextual, transfer and reflective learning.

References

1. Chou, S., Liu, C.: Learning effectiveness in a web-based virtual learning environment: a learner control perspective. J. Comput. Assist. Learn. **21**, 65–76 (2005)
2. Mavengere, N.B., Ruohonen, M.J.: Using open source software for improving dialog in computer science education – case Mozambique university. In: Tatnall, A., Kereteletswe, O.C., Visscher, A. (eds.) ITEM 2010. IAICT, vol. 348, pp. 52–61. Springer, Heidelberg (2011). doi: 10.1007/978-3-642-19715-4_6
3. Spiro, L.: Defining digital pedagogy (2013). https://digitalscholarship.files.wordpress.com/2013/03/gettysburgintrodigitalpedagogyfinal.pdf
4. Kreijns, K., Kirschner, P., Jochems, W.M., van Buuren, H.: Measuring perceived sociability of computer-supported collaborative learning environments. Comput. Educ. **49**, 176–192 (2015)
5. Ruokamo, H., Pohjolainen, S.: Pedagogical principles for evaluation of hypermedia-based learning environments in mathematics. JUCS – J. Univ. Comput. Sci. **4**(3), 292–307 (1998)
6. Illeris, K.: How We Learn: Learning and Non-learning in School and Beyond. Routledge, London (2005)

7. Mavengere, N.B., Ruohonen, M.J: Pursuit of quality learning: context and user needs in virtual learning. In: Think Cross-change Media Conference, 19–20 February 2016, Magdeburg, Germany (2016)
8. Leidner, D.E., Jarvenpaa, S.L.: The use of information technology to enhance management school education: a theoretical view. MIS Q. **19**(3), 265–291 (1995)
9. Beauchamp, G., Kennewell, S.: The influence of ICT on the interactivity of teaching. Educ. Inf. Technol. **13**(4), 305–315 (2008)

Exploring the Information and ICT Skills of Health Professionals in Low- and Middle-Income Countries

Annariina Koivu[1,2,3(✉)], Nicholas Mavengere[1], Mikko. J. Ruohonen[1],
Lucy Hederman[2], and Jane Grimson[2]

[1] School of Information Sciences, University of Tampere, Tampere, Finland
{nicholas.mavengere,mikko.j.ruohonen}@uta.fi
[2] School of Computer Science and Statistics, Trinity College, Dublin, Republic of Ireland
{koivua,lucy.hederman,jane.grimson}@tcd.ie
[3] Centre for Global Health, Trinity College, Dublin, Republic of Ireland

Abstract. Information is at the heart of healthcare because all stakeholders need fit-for-purpose information to make decisions. However, producing and utilizing information in the data-intensive and ever-changing health environment requires various skills. In the particular context of low- and middle-income countries, this study, consisting of a scoping review and a qualitative case study, explores the information and ICT skills of health professionals. Our review identifies challenges in several areas of health professionals' skills, including computer skills; skills required for using the routine health information system; data security skills; and data management and analysis skills. Our South African case study, based on interviews, adds a more nuanced understanding of the different types of training needs. This assessment shows that training and education aimed at improving the ICT and information skills of health professionals have to be versatile and cater to different groups with varying needs.

Keywords: ICT skills of health professionals · Low- and middle-income countries · Scoping review · South Africa · Case study · Training needs

1 Introduction

Health professionals in low- and middle-income countries (LMIC) in the 21st century are facing new challenges as a result of the increased need to be able to collect, capture, report and use data alongside the care delivery duties. Besides clinical skills, an ability to understand and analyze data and, increasingly, digital literacy and Information and Communication Technology (ICT) skills are in high demand. The significance of information in healthcare is by now well recognized in public and global health. For instance, the World Health Organization's (WHO) framework for strengthening health systems identifies six building blocks of a health system [1]. "Health information" is one of the building blocks, but "production, analysis, dissemination and use of reliable and timely information" also informs decision-making in each of the other building blocks, namely, health workforce; health services; health financing; governance and leadership; and

T. Brinda et al. (Eds.): SaITE 2016, IFIP AICT 493, pp. 152–162, 2016.
DOI: 10.1007/978-3-319-54687-2_15

medical products, vaccines and technologies [1, 2]. In other words, high-quality data is essential in health care because it is required basically at every corner of the health system from the clinical decision making in the case of individual patients to the monitoring and evaluating (M&E) of health programs, surveillance of diseases, planning of services and resources, informing policy-making, for global reporting purposes and ultimately, improving population health [3].

In the LMIC context, it is usually the doctors and nurses that are the source of such data, since they are often responsible for collecting and recording it [4]. Unfortunately, research suggests that in the developing world well-trained health professionals are unevenly distributed as well as insufficient in aggregate numbers, and there are serious challenges in their information and ICT skills [5]. This is no wonder, since even in high-income settings various cadres of health professionals struggle to keep up with technical developments in the ever-changing health environment.

The need for systematic assessments focusing on health information systems (HIS) with a view to identifying underlying factors affecting performance has been noted in the literature [6]. Addressing challenges in the health professionals' capacities related to information and ICT is vital for several reasons. First, issues related to human resources are a significant challenge for maintaining data quality in HIS, as has been found in many LMIC countries (e.g., [6, 7]). Second, it is important to understand and appreciate the rationale of health information systems (i.e., why the data is collected and reported) and the importance of the quality of data, because these are likely to affect the extent to which the collected data is used [4]. Health information should be utilized in various ways from health interventions to program evaluation, but a poor use of data in LMIC settings has often been reported (for instance, [8]). It is therefore critical to ensure the sufficient skill levels and understanding of those who provide the data and those who are supposed to use it in decision-making. Finally, health professionals' information and ICT skills have been linked to the utilization of ICT tools and eHealth [9] and the readiness to use electronic medical record systems (EMR) [10].

In order to identify the key issues regarding the information and ICT skills of health professionals we conducted a scoping review on the topic. A scoping review is a specific type of review which can provide a snapshot of the existing literature, as well as background information for further inquiry [11]. Specifically, we focused on limitations in health professionals' information and ICT skills, i.e., the skills required to collect, report, understand and utilize data required in the health systems in low- and middle-income countries (LMIC). In addition to the review, a qualitative case study was conducted in South Africa. For the case study we interviewed South African health professionals whose duties included working with health data.

For the purpose of this study, "health professional" refers to a range of people working with health information in the health system. In other words, it includes the frontline health workers, such as nurses and doctors, but also data capturers and clerks working in the clinics, and it refers to managers and other health officials at the different levels of the health system whose tasks require the utilization of health information for resource allocation and better services. As noted by previous LMIC research [6], the M&E and data management responsibilities are not always clearly assigned at field level in a low-resource context, and the responsibility for certain data may be assigned to an M&E officer in one place and a community health nurse or program officer in another place.

Over recent decades, the quality of healthcare has become increasingly connected to the systematic application of information processing; thus, a health worker needs to be skillful in the efficient use of the available information systems (IS), technologies and tools [12, 13]. Therefore, this study seeks to explore the skill levels of health professionals in relation to information and ICTs and to propose measures to address challenges related to this.

2   Methodology

In order to map the existing evidence base regarding our research topic, we conducted a scoping review. Such reviews are an increasingly accepted methodology for reviewing health research evidence [14], and they have been successfully applied in a variety of fields relevant to this study, such as assessing e-health programs in LMIC [15]. Additionally, further characteristics of scoping reviews support this approach: the scoping process benefits from an analytical reinterpretation of the literature, while it does not usually require assessing the quality of the studies included, and it may be especially relevant in disciplines with emerging evidence. Furthermore, scoping reviews allow the incorporation of a variety of evidence and study designs and may produce novel findings [14]. Two researchers (AK and NM) conducted searches of electronic databases in January and February 2016, including PubMed and Academic Search Complete (all databases) from the year 2000 to the present. Given the interconnected ways in which the terms "skills" or "information" are employed in health-related literature and their relationship to other multi-dimensional concepts, such as "data quality", "health system", "health workers" and so on, we kept the search terms broad to warrant a sufficiently wide coverage of the topic. These initial searches yielded many non-relevant papers, so an additional search string was included to increase the relevancy of the results, and this returned 519 articles that were reviewed by title or abstract. The database searches were complemented with additional searches on relevant organizational websites, reference lists of key papers and hand searching of journals online. We limited our search to full-text studies published in English and focusing on LMICs. Our review identified 18 studies that captured the key ideas relevant to the research question [16].

In addition to the scoping review, we interviewed a number of key informants involved with HIS in under-privileged settings in South Africa. This component of the study was conducted in 2012 by AK and was approved by the Trinity College Research Ethics Committee (in Dublin, Ireland) and the Western Cape Provincial Research Health Committee (in South Africa), as well as by the local health authorities. More specifically, the interview data was obtained from 28 informants, who worked in various roles at four levels (clinic, sub-district, district and provincial level) of the Western Cape public health system. Since each informant was in a role that involved collecting, producing, recording, reporting or using health data, they could inform us on how they perceive challenges in the HIS, including the human aspect of it. The semi-structured interviews were conducted face-to-face, predominantly at the place of work of each informant, as

18 individual interviews and 4 group interviews with 2 to 3 informants. The informants included females and males, as well as people of black, coloured and white origin. Not all informants were asked the same questions. Some of the informants did not focus primarily on the information skills of the health professionals, whereas others raised that as a key issue. Nevertheless, they all provided rich data relevant to the research question.

3   Information and ICT Skills of Health Professionals – Literature Review

Studies that have examined the health professionals' role in health information systems in an LMIC context have generally focused on the availability of human resources rather than on competence [17]. Furthermore, while the importance of human capacity building for the efficient functioning of various HIS in under-privileged settings is long acknowledged in academia [18], most studies merely mention the challenges in this area as a matter of course. In line with that notion, our review found a limited number of relevant articles on limitations in the information and ICT skills of health professionals.

3.1   Computer Skills

Despite the obvious benefits of ICTs to healthcare, their adoption has been problematic and the rates of use have been limited, particularly in many resource-restricted settings. Two large-scale surveys have been conducted in Ethiopia recently. In Addis Ababa hospitals, out of 270 participants, 91 (34%) showed an adequate knowledge of computers, while 108 (40%) had fair knowledge and 71(26%) inadequate knowledge [19]. In northwest Ethiopia, 356 (59%) of the 606 health professionals studied were computer literate [10]. A smaller-scale assessment in Kenya found that approximately half (58 out of 121) of the health workers had no knowledge on how to use computers, which contributes to further limitations in data analysis and utilization skills [20]. Studies in Iran [21], Nigeria [13] and India [22] have found variation in nurses' computer skills, the Iranian study reporting the mean of 43% of computer skills based on the International Computer Driving License (ICDL) [21]. In Nigeria, approximately one fifth of the 180 nurses studied rated themselves as "novices" in information technology and claimed to possess little or no skill in the use of computers, with 68 (38%) maintaining that they had never had formal training in information technology [13]. Similarly, an earlier Nigerian study [23] reports that approximately one fifth (22%) of the surveyed 148 health record officers, medical students and doctors showed poor knowledge of computers, while a majority (59%) had average knowledge and 19% demonstrated a good knowledge. Conversely, in Uganda, 82% of the 68 investigated self-reported being good or very good at using PCs, but reported significantly lower skill levels in using fax, printers or specific software, such as Microsoft Excel [9]. The authors suspect that the self-reported figures reflect the doctors' confidence and some understanding of ICT, but that the level of skills demonstrated in the study may nevertheless form a significant barrier to the use of ICT.

3.2   Skills and Understanding of the Routine Health Information System

While it is important to possess a set of basic skills to be able to use computers in general, sometimes it is a specific health information system that health professionals need to work with. These systems may be routine health information systems (RHIS) that "provide information at regular intervals of a year or less through mechanisms designed to meet predictable information needs" [24]. In Benin, a data quality assessment including a health worker survey (n = 116) noted that the health professionals were inadequately qualified, as few had been trained on RHIS and the training received had not always been fit for purpose [25]. Kenya established their RHIS in 1984; however, 55% (67) of health workers had no knowledge about it [20]. In South Africa, researchers call the lack of knowledge about the RHIS rationale "disturbing" [17]. Since the average knowledge of the RHIS rationale was 22%, this suggests a limited understanding of the significance of the health data collected. Correspondingly, more than half of the surveyed 161 health professionals claimed that they had not received RHIS training in the last six months prior to the study [17]. There is a need to allocate, train and support management and end users in RHIS use in South Africa [26].

3.3   Data Security Skills

A further category which is connected to the daily use of computers and the RHIS are data security skills. Confidentiality and data security, amongst other issues, are seen as an important part of any health record system both in the developed and the developing world, but literacy rates and cultural differences may influence the application and relevance of these concepts in LMIC [27]. A Botswanan [6] and an international study [28] report a lack of standard practices for backing-up the data, storing source documents and safeguarding confidentiality. Health data may not be backed up, and if it is, memory sticks are a customary method, which may result in the loss of data [6].

3.4   Data Management Skills and Analysis Skills

The ability to use a computer or a RHIS is closely connected to the ability to manage, manipulate, validate and analyze data. Hence, these overlapping categories are not distinguished as separate entities in all studies, though they may not necessarily be the same thing, either. Besides the health professionals' computer knowledge, the afore-mentioned Kenyan study [20] also evaluated the health workers' ability to perform basic information management functions. The study revealed that the majority were not able to perform such tasks: only 17% of the 121 health professionals could check for data accuracy, compute trends from bar charts or convert the collected data into meaningful information for use. This discovery is consistent with their finding that 91% had never received training for information management [20]. These figures show no progress compared to earlier evidence from a 15-country study: 13 out of 21 LMIC sites studied included personnel trained in data management or data quality control [28]. In South Africa, 64% of the 161 health professionals had poor numerical skills as regards being able to calculate percentages, amongst other things. Although the average confidence levels at performing routine tasks related to health information was 69%, only 22% actually displayed a competence above 50%. Furthermore, the average ability to check data quality was 36% [17]. Similar challenges have been experienced elsewhere [6, 29–31]. A study on the Kenyan HIV information system describes the staff's ability to check data quality, undertake basic data analysis and interpretation, and utilize the data for decision making as "limited" [29]. Likewise, in Botswana, most monitoring and evaluation (M&E) personnel at the national and district levels had received basic training in M&E, but their analytical skills were reported to be notably weak [6].

4   Empirical Findings

In addition to the scoping review, interview data was collected in South Africa in connection to a case study. There are ways to measure the actual skill and confidence levels of health professionals for information tasks, but such assessments were not made within this study. Rather, the empirical component of this study reports issues that are perceived as challenges by South African health professionals whose tasks include working with health data.

The first finding that was not revealed by the scoping review, but which feeds into all the further limitations in information and ICT skills is the issue of **language skills**. For a large proportion of the population in South Africa, the language barrier continues to compromise the quality of and access to healthcare [32]. The data of the current study suggests that such challenges may occur at every level, but the issue is particularly pressing at the facility level: a lot of time is spent "*getting information out of people*" (Informant, field level). In the clinic and sub-district investigated in the case study, most patients speak Xhosa as their first language and therefore recruitment at the facility and sub-district levels has been done locally. However, all the forms, registers and information systems that the staff is required to use, are in English.

A second finding, which did not emerge directly in the evidence reviewed but which is nevertheless consistent with the limitations reported in the literature, relates to the fact that a sizable number of South Africans still lack an adequate basic education. Amongst them are individuals who work in the health system or with a close connection to it (such as tuberculosis community workers). They may be providing lifesaving care, but still have rather **limited basic mathematical, reading and writing skills.** According to the informants, this may create challenges in understanding very basic concepts.

> "... a lot of people don't even have proper mathematical literacy skills. ... a lot of people are struggling with words ... so how can they interpret data?" (Informant, Province)

This reinforces the message from research from elsewhere in South Africa [17] and can be considered an underlying factor that contributes to further limitations in ICT and information skills.

Not surprisingly, several informants indicated that **poor computer literacy** prevails at the hospitals and clinics.

> "Most people who work in the hospitals are not computer literate when it comes to Microsoft Office ... ... Most of them can't work with pivot-tables, or most of them can't work well with Excel ..." (Informant, M&E position)

While the majority of the facility managers do have email, it was reported that they are not always confident about using it or other modes of electronic communication. Whilst most challenges were reported at the clinic level, it was also maintained that the higher-level health authorities have difficulties in understanding and utilizing technology.

Therefore, many agreed that while further computerization would be beneficial in terms of data quality and in reducing reporting duties, it should not be attempted until staff are a lot more information savvy. **Weaknesses in data security skills** were also reported. According to the informants, facility staff members use their own memory sticks on the computers, introducing viruses. Since many frontline health workers in under-privileged settings do not have computers at home, we assume that when they need to, they may be inclined to use the computer at work for non-work activities.

In the setting of our case study it was not possible to make a distinction between the skills and understanding of the RHIS and the overall data management and analysis skills. However, we did find challenges in this area. An informant argued that the utilization of data is limited by the lack of skills required to manipulate the data so as to make it easily usable for decision-making.

> *"[People cannot] ... do the manipulation to get whatever information you want. So, it is a headache in that sense and the managers are not prioritizing this dataset ... ... because they can't get anything out."* (Informant, M&E position)

We also found that **concepts that help in interpreting data might be unfamiliar**. This is consistent with the South African studies reviewed [17, 30]. In our case study setting, shortcomings in this area became particularly evident in the context of the feed-back loop. Informants described how, after attending meetings, coordinators feedback the key messages from the printouts in such a way that the lowest-level staff and community workers can understand the trends. This requires that the concepts that communicate the information in ratios or visually are also explained. For instance, a field-level informant reported: "*Sometimes they don't understand this percentage thing. So, I have to explain to them*". Or: "*Graphs gotta be very basic, bar graphs, you can't go for pies or anything just bar graphs, just plain and simple*" (Another informant) and even the bars need to be fully explained: "*This bar means this. This bar means that. What we are looking for is to see this bar going up*".

Finally, we also identified **a lack of epidemiological or clinical understanding of the data elements and indicators required**. Those whose role was within a single health program (such as management of the antiretroviral medication (ART) program for HIV) were keen to point out a difference to those who mainly work with general health information:

> *"they don't pick up the errors, so they are not Program people; they're just punching numbers... because for us from Programs you can very easily spot something that looks funny...... whereas someone who's just punching number; if they punch 1, 2, 3 ... 1, 2, 3, 48 they won't necessarily think about the 48, whereas you would immediately realize that, that 48 can't be."* (Informant in Program Management)

This is consistent with the results from another South African case study [33]. The researchers assessed the degree to which general health service (horizontal) managers exercise authority over the HIV program's M&E function, namely, HIV data collection, collation, analysis and use. They found that compared to vertical managers, i.e., managers working in a disease-specific (HIV) position, horizontal managers had lower HIV M&E knowledge, and were more likely to produce HIV data but less likely to use it [33].

5   Discussion

Our study illustrates that there are various weaknesses in health workers' skills in an LMIC context and it is vital to address them, whether they relate to the ability to use computers in general or to the RHIS concerned or to capabilities to convert that data into meaningful information. Therefore, our study reinforces earlier evidence of a need to identify effective solutions and simple interventions to address the human competence and other underlying factors in order to improve data quality and to strengthen the health systems [6].

How to address the weaknesses identified? A global vision to develop informatics has been proposed by the American Medical Informatics Association. It recommends a system-wide approach where education and training should be offered at the leader/ policy level (for instance, in the form of seminars); to health professionals (degree and certificate programs; short courses); and ICT technology and support level (degree and certificate programs; short courses) [5], thus echoing other studies that have highlighted the importance of educational strategies, curricula development and tertiary training programs to improve the level of informatics knowledge, skills, and attitudes in both formally and informally trained health professionals [6, 18].

However, this approach should be complemented with a decentralization of mentoring and training initiatives from the national to the district levels for the health work force delivering care at the facility level [6]. On-the-job training and mentoring and short interventions have yielded positive results in LMICs [34].

6   Conclusions

Healthcare is an ever-evolving and profoundly information-based discipline. It is vital that health professionals have sufficient capabilities to respond to the increasingly complex information needs. These needs may be particularly pressing in settings where the resources are already thinly spread. Our findings reinforce the message from previous research [5]: a basic-level information/ICT training is essential for all practicing health professionals, and more effort should be invested in it, especially at the field level, but also at other levels of the health system. What our study adds is a more nuanced understanding of the different types of training needs that exist. Moreover, it highlights the challenges related to language and basic literacy skills that undermine any improvement efforts, unless addressed first. Therefore, the training and education aimed at improving the ICT and information skills of the health professionals have to be versatile and cater to varying groups with differing needs, and approaches should be adapted to the local context. It is only then that the benefits of the information collected can be utilized to strengthen the health system.

References

1. World Health Organization: Everybody's business: strengthening health systems to improve health outcomes: WHO's framework for action. Geneva: World Health Organization (2007)
2. Nutley, T.: Improving Data Use in Decision Making: An Intervention to Strengthen Health Systems. MEASURE Evaluation, Carolina Population Center, Chapel Hill (2012)
3. HIQA - Health Information and Quality Authority.: Guiding Principles for National Health and Social Care Data Collections. Dublin: Health Information and Quality Authority (2013)
4. Koivu, A.: Key Challenges in the Current TB and HIV Information System in South Africa. A Case Study in Khayelitsha, Western Cape. (Doctoral Dissertation). Trinity College, Dublin (2015)
5. Detmer, D.E.: Capacity building in e-health and health informatics: A review of the global vision and informatics educational initiatives of the american medical informatics association. Yearb. Med. Inform. **2010**, 101–105 (2010)
6. Ledikwe, J.H., Grignon, J., Lebelonyane, R., Ludick, S., Matshediso, E., Sento, B., Sharma, A., Semo, B.W.: Improving the quality of health information: a qualitative assessment of data management and reporting systems in Botswana. Health Res. Policy Syst. **12**, 7 (2014)
7. Makombe, S.D., Hochgesang, M., Jahn, A., Tweya, H., Hedt, B., Chuka, S., Yu, J.K., Aberle-Grasse, J., Pasulani, O., Bailey, C., Kamoto, K., Schouten, E.J., Harries, A.D.: Assessing the quality of data aggregated by the antiretroviral treatment clinics in Malawi. Bull. World Health Organ. **86**(4), 310–314 (2008)
8. Braa, J., Heywood, A., Sahay, S.: Improving quality and use of data through data-use workshops: Zanzibar, United Republic of Tanzania. Bull. World Health Organ. **90**, 379–384 (2012)
9. Olok, G.T., Yagos, W.O., Ovuga, E.: Knowledge and attitudes of doctors towards e-health use in healthcare delivery in government and private hospitals in Northern Uganda: A cross-sectional study. BMC Med. Inform. Decis. Mak. **15**, 87 (2015)
10. Biruk, S., Yilma, T., Andualem, M., Tilahun, B.: Health professionals' readiness to implement electronic medical record system at three hospitals in Ethiopia: a cross sectional study. BMC Med. Inform. Decis. Mak. **14**, 115 (2014)
11. Armstrong, R., Hall, B.J., Doyle, J., Waters, E.: Cochrane update 'Scoping the scope' of a cochrane review. J. Public Health **33**(1), 147–150 (2011)
12. Haux, R., Swinkels, W., Ball, M., Knaup, P., Lun, K.C.: Transformation of health care through innovative use of information technology: Challenges for health and medical informatics education. Int. J. Med. Inform. **50**(1–3), 1–6 (1998)
13. Irinoye, O.O., Ayandiran, E.O., Fakunle, I., Mtshali, N.: Nurses' perception and barriers to use of information communication technology in a teaching hospital in Nigeria. Comput. Inform. Nurs. **31**(8), 394–400 (2013)
14. Levac, D., Colquhoun, H., O'Brien, K.: Scoping studies: advancing the methodology. Implementation Sci. 5(69) (2010)
15. Piette, J., Lun, K.C., Moura Jr., L., Fraser, H., Mechael, P., Powell, J., Khoja, S.: Impacts of e-health on the outcomes of care in low- and middle-income countries: where do we go from here? Bull. World Health Organ. **90**, 365–372 (2012)
16. McDougall, R.: Reviewing literature in bioethics research increasing rigour in non-systematic reviews. Bioethics **29**(7), 523–528 (2015)
17. Nicol, E., Bradshaw, D., Phillips, T., Dudley, L.: Human factors affecting the quality of routinely collected data in South Africa. Stud. Health Technol. Inform. **192**, 788–792 (2013)

18. Luna, D., Almerares, A., Mayan, J.C., de Quirós, F.G.B., Otero, C.: Health informatics in developing countries: going beyond pilot practices to sustainable implementations: A review of the current challenges. Healthc. Inf. Res. **20**(1), 3–10 (2014)

19. Mohammed, E., Andargie, G., Meseret, S., Girma, E.: Knowledge and utilization of computer among health workers in Addis Ababa hospitals, Ethiopia: Computer literacy in the health sector. BMC Res. Notes 6(106) (2013)

20. Kiilu, E.M., Okero, D.C., Muiruri, L., Owuondo, P.A.: Human resource capacity for information management in selected public healthcare facilities in Meru County, Kenya. Pan Afr. Med. J. **20**, 334 (2015)

21. Habibi-Koolaee, M., Safdari, R., Bouraghi, H.: Nurses readiness and electronic health records. Acta Inform. Med. **23**(2), 105–107 (2015)

22. Raja, E.E., Mahal, R., Masih, V.B.: An exploratory study to assess the computer knowledge, attitude and skill among nurses in health care setting of a selected hospital in Ludhiana, Punjab, India. Stud. Health Technol. Inform. **107**(Pt2), 1304–1307 (2004)

23. Bello, I.S., Arogundade, F.A., Sanusi, A.A., Ezeoma, I.T., Abioye-Kuteyi, E.A., Akinsola, A.: Knowledge and utilization of Information Technology among health care professionals and students in Ile-Ife, Nigeria: a case study of a university teaching hospital. J. Med. Internet Res. **6**(4), e45 (2004)

24. Hotchkiss, D., Diana, M., Foreit, K. How can routine health information systems improve health systems functioning in low-resource settings? Assessing the evidence base. Chapel Hill: MEASURE Evaluation, Carolina Population Center (2012)

25. Ahanhanzo, Y.G., Ouedraogo, L.T., Kpozèhouen, A., Coppieters, Y., Makoutodé, M., Wilmet-Dramaix, M.: Factors associated with data quality in the routine health information system of Benin. Arch Public Health **72**(1), 25 (2014)

26. Nicol, E., Hanmer, L.: Routine health information systems in South Africa - opportunities for improvement. In: Sarkar et al. (eds.) MEDINFO 2015: eHealth-enabled Health (2015)

27. Were, M.C., Meslin, E.M.: Ethics of implementing electronic health records in developing countries: points to consider. In: 2011 AMIA Annual Symposium Proceedings, pp. 1499–1505 (2011)

28. Forster, M., Bailey, C., Brinkhof, M., Graber, C., Boulle, A., Spohr, M., Balestre, E., May, M., Keiser, O., Jahn, A., Egger, M.: ART-linc collaboration of the international epidemiological databases to evaluate AIDS: Electronic medical record systems, data quality and loss to follow-up: survey of antiretroviral therapy programmes in resource-limited settings. Bull. World Health Organ. 86, 939–947 (2008)

29. Mbondo, M., Scherer, J., Aluoch, G.O., Sundsmo, A., Mwaura, N.: Organizational HIV monitoring and evaluation capacity rapid needs assessment: the case of Kenya. Pan Afr. Med. J. **3**(14), 129 (2013)

30. Garrib, A., Stoops, N., McKenzie, A., Dlamini, L., Govender, T., Rohde, J., Herbst, K.: An evaluation of the district health information system in rural South Africa. S. Afr. Med. J. **98**(7), 549–552 (2008)

31. Kintu, P., Nanjynja, N., Nzabanita, A., Magoola, R.: Development of HMIS in poor countries: Uganda as a case study. Health Policy Dev. **3**(1), 46–53 (2005)

32. Hussay, N.: The language barrier: The overlooked challenge to equitable healthcare. In: Padarath, A., English, R. (eds.) South African Health Review 2012/13. Health Systems Trust, Durban (2013)

33. Kawonga, M., Fonn, S., Blaauw, D.: Administrative integration of vertical HIV monitoring and evaluation into health systems: a case study from South Africa. Glob Health Action, 6 (2013)

34. Ledikwe, J.H., Reason, L.L., Burnett, S.M., Busang, L., Bodika, S., Lebelonyane, R., et al.: Establishing a health information workforce: innovation for low- and middle-income countries. Hum. Resour. Health **11**, 35 (2013)

An ICT Model to Enhance Teaching and Learning in a Resource Constrained Setting: A Case of Malawi

Richard Pankomera[✉] and Darelle Van Greunen

School of ICT, Nelson Mandela Metropolitan University,
P.O Box 77000, Port Elizabeth 6035, South Africa
rpankomera@gmail.com, darelle.vangreunen@nmmu.ac.za

Abstract. Information and Communication Technologies (ICTs) play a pivotal role in enhancing learning and teaching at all levels of education across the globe. Many developed countries appreciate that the use of ICTs has improved the quality of education. Developing countries such as Malawi have also incorporated ICTs in various curricula of programmes at all levels of education. Unfortunately, these resource constrained countries face a number of challenges in gleaning the maximum benefits of ICT in education sector.

This paper discusses the fundamental challenges underlying ICT development in the education system in Malawi. Some recommendations have also been made on how to mitigate the challenges that are encountered in the education sector in Malawi. The paper further advances the notion that the ICT intervention in education can be meaningful and effective if all stakeholders such as government, private sector, policy and decision makers, communities, students, teachers and international agencies are engaged at all levels of the education system. An attempt has also been made to compare different models of implementing ICT in the education system in a resource constrained environment. The paper finally proposes an inclusive model for the ICT intervention in education system in Malawi.

Keywords: Model · Resource constrained · Malawi · Holistic approach

1 Introduction

Information and Communication Technologies (ICTs) are indispensable tools in enhancing learning and teaching at all levels of education across the globe. Many developed countries appreciate that the use of ICTs has improved the quality of education. Developing countries such as Malawi have also strived to incorporate the usage of ICT tools in various curricula of courses at all levels of education. Unfortunately, these resource constrained countries face a number of challenges in gleaning the maximum benefits of ICT in education sector. This paper therefore endeavours to highlight the emerging challenges of the usage of ICT in the education system of Malawi. It then gives some recommendations to address these challenges. The paper finally proposes an ICT model to enhance teaching and learning in the education system in Malawi.

© IFIP International Federation for Information Processing 2016
Published by Springer International Publishing AG 2016. All Rights Reserved
T. Brinda et al. (Eds.): SaITE 2016, IFIP AICT 493, pp. 163–173, 2016.
DOI: 10.1007/978-3-319-54687-2_16

Section 2 gives the objectives of the study which is followed by Sect. 3 on methodology. Section 4 provides the background of the study. Section 5 outlines the challenges underlying ICT development in education in Malawi. This is followed by Sect. 6 which discusses a holistic model to ICT interventions in education system. Recommendations are succinctly explained in Sect. 7 which is followed by a conclusion of the paper in Sect. 8.

2 Objectives of the Study

The aim of conducting the study is to propose a model that will be used by various stakeholders including teachers, policy makers, decision makers and others in implementing ICT in the education sector at all levels in Malawi. The following specific research questions are addressed during the study:

(i)   What is the status of ICT interventions in the education sector in Malawi?
(ii) What are the challenges that are encountered in implementing ICT interventions in the education sector in Malawi?
(iii) What model can be used to implement sustainable ICT interventions in Malawi?

3 Methodology

The study embraced the systematic review of different journal articles, peer reviewed conference papers and books with an aim of answering specific research questions. This involved the formulation of research questions; searching of relevant work from multiple sources; describing study characteristics; summarising the evidence and finally interpreting the findings [1]. A number of articles by various researchers were accessed from electronic databases such as Science Direct, Google Scholar, web of science, ERIC and EBSCOhost. Most of the journals that have been analysed are from 2002 to 2016. The study also endeavoured to examine other documents such as Malawi ICT National Policy, Global Information Technology Report, E-learning Africa report and books.

A combination of keywords such as *model, framework, guideline, ICT, computer, education, developing, underdeveloped, poor setting, implementation, challenges, barriers, ICT interventions, resource constrained* and *Malawi* were used to select appropriate articles. This resulted in displaying more than 10,000 articles. Special Boolean operators like *AND, OR* and *NOT* were employed in order to alter the scope of the search. These articles were further filtered by year and title of the publication with their relevance to the implementation of ICT in education and learning in a resource constrained setting such as Malawi.

4 Background

4.1 Context Setting

Malawi follows an 8-4-4 education system which is composed of primary schools, secondary schools and University. This means that primary school, secondary school and university education takes 8 years, 4 years and another 4 years to complete respectively [2]. With a population of approximately 16 million, Malawi has a total of 4,449,000 pupils enrolled in primary and secondary education. 83% of them are enrolled in primary education [3]. It is also interesting to note on average 62% of 15 to 24 year olds do not complete primary education in Malawi. However, the literacy rate is 72% among the youth population; this is higher than the average youth literacy rate in other low income countries [3]. For the purpose of this paper, literacy rate is the ability to read and write with understanding a simple statement related to one's daily life. With regards to ICT literacy, most public primary schools do not offer computer lessons. It is only in the isolated few private primary schools where pupils can learn the basics about computers. At the secondary school level, very few isolated schools offer computer studies as a subject due to a number of challenges. As for public institutions of higher learning, only Mzuzu University, the University of Malawi and Malawi University of Science and Technology offer degree programmes in either computer science or ICT.

4.2 ICT Interventions in Education

Many ICT interventions have been put in place in an effort to circumvent some of the aforementioned challenges. The major goal of these interventions is to improve the quality and quantity of learning and teaching at all levels of the education system since ICT has proven to provide opportunities for teachers and students to collaborate within the schools and the rest of the world [4].

The government of Malawi adopted a National ICT Policy in December 2005 which aimed at developing the ICT industry and at the same time promoting the development and use of ICTs in all sectors including the education sector [5]. It was therefore envisaged that the use of ICT in education sector would assist in improving the management of education systems in Malawi, thereby transforming Malawi into an information and knowledge driven ICT literate nation [5]. This would consequently enable the improvement of ICT literacy levels by both students and teachers. To achieve these objectives, many strategies were developed such as ensuring that primary, secondary schools and colleges have adequate and reliable computers; building facilities to promote ICT training and education in schools and colleges; promoting e-learning, e-teaching and e-distance learning; and developing user-friendly electronic management information systems to improve the quality of management of educational institution [6]. Institutions were therefore formed to facilitate the implementation of the National ICT policies. In collaboration with the Department of E-Government, the responsibility of the Ministry of Education is to promote and facilitate the development and utilization of ICT skills in the education sector. On the other hand, Malawi Regulatory Authority is an ICT regulator that promotes the development of the ICT sector through investment, monitoring, research and training to professionally deliver reliable and affordable communication services throughout Malawi [7].

There are a number of projects that assist to bridge the digital gap in Malawi. For instance, Computer for African Schools (CFAS) is a scheme that was administered by British council in collaboration with SchoolNet Malawi Trust. This enabled the introduction of computer lessons in some of the secondary schools in Malawi in 2003. The scheme provides computers to schools that have the right facilities and security to house the equipment. Erach and Roshan Sadri Foundation (ERSF) is another charity organization which has managed to donate a number of ICT equipment including desktop computers, wireless access points, laser printers and internet access to various schools. The secondary school beneficiaries are Blantyre, Chichiri, Zingwangwa and Chipasula secondary school. For instance, in appreciation of this ICT intervention, the headmistress of Blantyre secondary school said, "The lab has increased the enrolment ratio of students pursuing computer studies. It has also simplified teaching and learning for the teachers and the students" [8]. This is one of the scenarios that substantiates how ICT can transform the teaching and learning environment in schools. Table 1 summarises some of the projects in education in Malawi. It must be known that most of these projects are donor funded and therefore they are not centrally run by the government.

Table 1. Some ICT Project interventions in education in Malawi

No.	Project	Focus	Beneficiaries
1	MAREN	Internet connectivity for the tertiary education and research sectors in Malawi [9].	Institutions of higher learning in Malawi: Mzuzu University and Chancellor college, College of Medicine.
2	FAIR Denmark	Bridging the digital divide between developed and developing countries by providing refurbished ICT equipment [10].	Secondary Schools in the northern and central regions which received over 1000 desktop and laptops.
3	ITSchoolsAfrica - Computers for Malawian Schools	Creating e-learning centres for students and training of teachers [11].	Secondary Schools such as Blantyre, Chichiri, Chipasula, Zingwangwa.

5   Challenges in ICT in Education in Malawi

Malawi is rated as one of the poorest countries in the world owing to a number of factors. For instance, its infrastructure is underdeveloped. There is poor road network infrastructure, poor and few number of school facilities. There are few schools with limited number of classrooms. As a result of this, most pupils learn under the tree. Therefore increasing number of schools remains a priority over the acquisition of computers in an effort to introduce computer lessons at all levels of education. The power supply in Malawi remains unreliable. There is intermittent power supply across the country. In some instances, black out may even last for days. World Bank states that 8% of the population in Malawi has access to electricity. In addition to this, 84% of the population lives in the rural areas where there is no electricity [12]. This means that the national electrical energy system is accessible to less than 1% of the rural population [13]. It is an undeniable fact that computers need regular supply of power for them to operate. This poses a number of difficulties even in primary, secondary and let alone university where computers lessons have been introduced.

High cost of telecommunications aggravates the feasibility of introducing computer education at all levels of education too. Malawi remains a country where the cost of internet access is still high [14]. Unfortunately, some computer lessons at all levels of education require access to the internet in order to obtain current and updated study materials. Internet access may be necessary when students and teachers need to communicate in real time over a long distance. As if these problems are not enough, cellular network coverage still remains limited. Even though, better cellular network is found in the urban areas, over 80% of the population live in the rural areas. Introducing ICT at all levels of education still remains a hassle in Malawi because most pupils cannot afford to acquire even the basic ICT gadgets. The penetration of mobile and fixed phones too is one of the lowest in Malawi as compared with other countries across the African continent. 45% of the households in Malawi use a mobile phone while 1% use fixed phones [7, 15]. It is therefore not surprising that Global Information Technology Report ranked Malawi as among the countries that is below the average Network Read Index (NRI) [16].

The quality of education in Malawi is very low with high student/teacher ratio of 63:1 at primary level. The absence of teaching and learning materials, adoption of pedagogical learning and deployment of untrained teachers especially at primary level contribute to the dwindling quality of education in Malawi [17]. Most teachers in the primary, secondary and even at the university level are computer illiterate due to negative attitude towards technology change. No wonder there is a proliferation of sub-standard ICT syllabi and poor ICT service delivery in the schools. This presents difficulties in offering computer lessons to pupils or students at all levels of education in Malawi. Besides this, most qualified trained ICT teachers opt to go for greener pasture. They either migrate from Malawi to other countries especially within SADC region or they may opt to move to a private sector rendering the public schools still in dire need of ICT competent teachers. Due to high levels of ICT illiteracy in schools, teachers have problems in appreciating the introduction of ICT in education. To this end, most teachers who are used to traditional ways of teaching may not have enough confidence in embracing the ICT interventions.

As one of the poorest countries in the word, Malawi still depends upon donors for financial support across all sectors. In fact, approximately 40% of the national budget for Malawi comes from donors. Since ICT is taken as an enabler to the implementations of core services, it is not given enough financial allocation.

With the dynamic advancement of internet technology, most researchers can easily collaborate and even easily share research publications. However, this is not the case where there are high levels of ICT illiteracy. As a result, current best practices of teaching and learning are not being incorporated in the curriculum.

In conclusion, Malawi being part of Africa, it shares the some problems with the other countries in the adoption of ICT in education system as stipulated in the E-learning Africa 2015 Report. Generally, common obstacles that prevent greater use of ICTs are: high cost of ICT services, unavailability of ICT equipment, poor electricity or energy, lack of awareness of how best to use ICT in education, lack of government investment or support, lack of private investment, lack of relevant content and lack of confidence in embracing ICT [18].

6   Approaches in Implementing ICT in Resource Constrained Setting

There are a number of models that have been used to implement ICT in the education system in resourced constrained settings such as developing countries. Hawkridge stipulated six rationales for adoption of ICT in schools especially in the developing countries [19]. First, the preparative rationale ensures that students use ICT so that they are equipped with skills for their social and vocational functioning. Second, the pedagogical rationale uses ICT as an enabler to improve student learning, understanding and retention. Third, catalytic rationale employs ICT as a catalyst to stimulate educational change. Fourth, the accessibility rationale ensures ubiquitous access to education by every student. It is noteworthy that mobile learning technology seems to be a promising solution in enhancing accessibility in remote and resource constrained setting. Fifth, the motivational rationale entails that ICT motivates students to engage in learning activities. Sixth, the administrative rationale uses ICT to monitor students and manage educational processes and components in institutions [19]. It is not surprising that most models and approaches in implementing ICT interventions evolve around these rationales.

Mishra and Koehler proposed a generic Technological Pedagogical Content Knowledge (TPACK) framework that facilitates technology integration in the teaching and learning environment. It is envisaged that this framework requires that teachers have technological pedagogical content knowledge to competently embrace ICT in the classroom environment [23, 24]. On the other hand, the Substitution Augmentation Modification Redefinition Model (SAMR) emphasizes different levels of ICT integration; from enhancement to transformation of lessons. At the enhancement level, technology acts as a direct tool to be used firstly with no functional change but secondly with an improvement change. At the transformation level, technology allows for the redesign of significant task and also it allows for the creation of new tasks which were inconceivable before [25]. SAMR model has been used to evaluate the deployment of ICT intervention in the mobile learning environment. On the other hand, Donnor and Kentaro recommends the model of ICT integration in education that focuses on processes and outcomes rather than the supply of hardware and equipment [26]. This is related to Hamel's human development approach that employs the technology to enable people to collaborate, network and learn beyond national borders [27].

Another promising approach in resource constrained environment is mobile learning technology intervention. The benefits of mobile learning are: (i) It is flexible for learners as they can use their mobile devices anywhere and at any time with different forms of data such as video, text and audio. (ii) Content in mobile platform is concise which contributes to better completion rate by learners (iii) Online communities enhance collaborative learning. (iv) It enables learners to assimilate concepts at their own pace as it facilitates an increasing personalised learning. Despite all these benefits, implementation of ICT in the education sector in resource constrained environment has not been rosy. Table 2 endeavours to compare some of the different approaches in deploying ICT interventions in the education sector in some of the resource constrained environments.

Table 2. Approaches in implementing ICT intervention in some of the resource constrained environments.

No.	Country	Framework/Approaches	Focus/Components
1	South Africa	A Pragmatic framework for integrating ICT into education in South Africa [20]	Mobile instant messaging service
			Mobile tutoring platform
			Mobile teaching platform
			Learning content by content providers
			Learning management systems
			Various learning activities
			Multiple learning models
2	Nigeria	ICT integration in education [21].	Establishment of computer laboratories in university and some institutions with support from external sources
			Computers and blended learning being used in the distance learning programmes of some teacher raining institutions
			Radio and television in distance learning
			Establishment of ICT laboratories and cyber cafés
3	Tanzania	An approach to ICT based school education in Tanzania [22]	Introduction of mobile computing laboratory facilities
			Computer assisted instruction-learning/web based learning
			Computer supported teaching
			Institutions of higher education adopting the nearby schools

Much as the ICT has been appreciated in advancing the quality of education at all levels, it is of paramount importance not all ICT solutions that have worked in developed countries can also be successfully implemented in a resource constrained setting such as Malawi. These solutions need to be customised in response to the local knowledge and cultural beliefs. The relevant and appropriate solutions must meet the needs of the developing country such as Malawi. In this context of argument, a simplistic model is proposed that must be followed when implementing ICT interventions in a resource constrained setting such as Malawi. With reference to Fig. 1, the model has three major phases: planning; implementation; monitoring and evaluation. Figure 1 depicts these phases as explained in the following [26]:

(i) *Planning*

This may involve establishing institutional goals at district, regional and national levels. Malawi had three administrative regions which are further divided in 28 districts. Stakeholders and necessary resources need to be identified to meet the formulated visions, goals, and objectives. Planning teams need to be formulated for the acquisition, deployment and disposition of resources. Technological, social, cultural, financial and political requirements that are necessary for the deployment of ICT interventions must succinctly be explored. Staffing and training needs must be considered during the

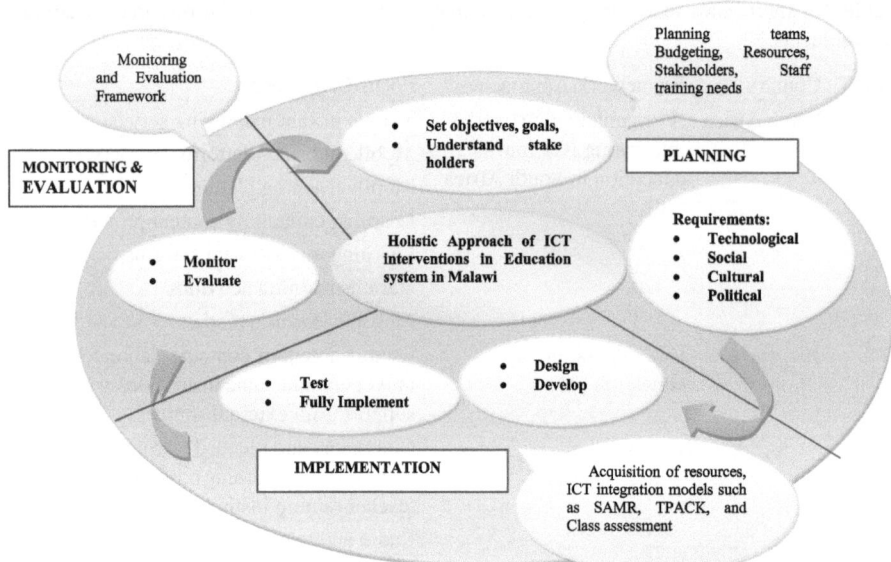

Fig. 1. A model to ICT interventions in Education system in Malawi

budgeting process during this phase. It is important that all stakeholders such as teachers, parents, policy makers and even students are involved at an early stage as possible.

(ii) *Implementation*

At this phase an action plan must be designed and fully implemented. This may involve the actual acquisition of the necessary resources as well as the planning of their integration in the classroom to meet the institutional goals. Other activities may include the design and implementation of course content; design an approach to classroom assessment; design professional development activities for teachers; and the design of monitoring and evaluation framework.

(iii) *Monitoring and evaluation*

Once the ICT interventions are fully operationalised, the monitoring and evaluation framework assists the management and other stakeholders to determine whether the objectives have been accomplished.

7   Recommendations

This paper therefore endeavours to provide a number of recommendations. Since mobile technology has an advantage of being accessed ubiquitously, it is a promising technology for resource constrained settings especially where road network infrastructure is bad. With the proliferation of basic mobile phones in Malawi, an investment of mobile application in education by both the public and private sector stake holders is highly recommended. Strides must be made so that applications that are used in education sector must be developed in a language and cultural context of the learner. This may eventually reduce the learning curve when ICT interventions are introduced. This will also motivate the leaner to accept the new technology. The major problem of internet connectivity in the education sector needs to be addressed if ICT is to reap adequate benefits. Private-public partnerships can be set up in order to improve poor ICT infrastructure and limited cellular network coverage. Policies must be formulated in order to assist rural areas to have an access to affordable ICT gadgets and services.

As it has been noted that most teachers and instructors at all levels of education are ICT illiterate, deliberate policies must be put in place to ensure the acquisition and development of ICT skills. This can be done by incorporating ICT in the curriculum at all levels. Through e-learning, e-teaching and e-distance learning, students and teachers must be encouraged to adventure various ways of improving their ICT skills. It is argued that channelling resources towards empowering teachers in ICT skills and profession-alism will have a longer-term and sustainable impact on the education of the students [28]. Being one of the poorest countries, Malawi lacks a number of resources including computers and network equipment. It is therefore recommended that collaborative effort must be made among government, international agencies and private sector to ensure the availability of computer hardware and software in primary schools, secondary schools and colleges. There is a need for ICT policies to be formulated so that they are in tandem with promoting ICT education. This will facilitate the adoption of ICT as a tool for research and e-learning. There must be a political will by the government to promote the implementation and utilization of ICT in the education sector. To circum-vent the lack of electric power, solar energy can be used to power mobile devices. Teachers need to be involved in the creation of content of course content for mobile technology learning as early as possible. Finally, monitoring and evaluation mechanisms must be put in place in collaboration with the public and private sector to ensure the sustainability of ICT policies and projects in education. This is why a model is proposed in introducing ICT interventions in the education system in Malawi. This model can be sustainable only if there is fiscal discipline and political will by the government in collaboration with other stakeholders.

8   Conclusion

This paper has highlighted the ICT interventions that have been put in place by various stakeholders in order to improve the quality of education at all levels. It has also endeav-oured to outline the challenges that are encountered in a resource constrained environment such as Malawi. This paper has also highlighted that, even though there are workable ICT solutions in the developed countries, not all of them can successfully be implemented in a resource setting. This is because of disparities in terms of cultural, technological and social differences in this setting. Recommendations have been therefore made to address these challenges in a resource constrained environment. It is also recommended that a model be adopted to assist in the planning, implementing, monitoring and evaluating of ICT inter-ventions at all levels of the education system in Malawi. Emphasis is therefore made that this model can be sustainable only if there is fiscal discipline and political will by the government in collaboration with other stakeholders. It is envisaged that the implementation of the model will ensure the availability, accessibility, acceptability and adaptability of ICT solutions in the education sector while enhancing teaching and learning especially in the resource constrained environment.

References

1. Gough, D., Oliver, S., Thomas, J.: An introduction to systematic reviews. Sage (2012)
2. Maluwa-Banda, D.: Gender sensitive educational policy and practice: the case of Malawi. Prospects **34**(1), 71–84 (2004)
3. World Bank: National Education Profile (2014). cited 29 Febrauary 2016 Available from 2016
4. Davis, N., Tearle, P.: A core curriculum for telematics in teacher training. In: Teleteaching 98 Conference, Vienna (1999)
5. Ministry of Information and Tourism: Malawi National ICT Policy for Development (2006). Cited 28 February 2016. http://unpan1.un.org/intradoc/groups/public/documents/unpan/unpan033688.pdf
6. Malawi National ICT Policy: Malawi National ICT Policy (2006). Cited 28 February 2016. http://unpan1.un.org/intradoc/groups/public/documents/unpan/unpan033688.pdf
7. MACRA: MACRA, Protecting ICT universal Access (1998). Cited 2016. http://www.macra.org.mw/?page_id=170
8. Gwauya, H.: Erach and Roshan Sadri Foundation, Itschoolsafrica (2014). Cited 28 February 2016. http://www.itschoolsafrica.org/blantyre-secondary-school.html
9. MAREN: Malawi Research and Education Network (2016). Cited February 28 2016. http://www.maren.ac.mw/
10. Denmark, F.: 2016. Cited 28 February 2016. https://www.fairdanmark.dk/en/
11. Samaritan's Trust Compound: Computers for Malawian Schools (2014). http://www.itschoolsafrica.org/malawi.html
12. The United States Agency for International Development: USAID Malawi health systems strengthening fact sheet (2012). Cited 8 may 2015. http://www.usaid.gov/malawi/fact-sheets/usaid-malawi-health-systems-strengthening-fact-sheet-2012-13
13. Gamula, G.E., Hui, L., Peng, W.: An Overview of the Energy Sector in Malawi (2013)
14. BuddeComm: Malawi - Telecoms, Mobile and Broadband - Statistics and Analyses - See more at: http://www.budde.com.au/Research/Malawi-Telecoms-Mobile-and-Broadband-Statistics-and-Analyses.html#sthash.IOBbdYfy.dpuf (2015). cited 28 February 2016; http://www.budde.com.au/Research/Malawi-Telecoms-Mobile-and-Broadband-Statistics-and-Analyses.html
15. Vega-Mana, T.: Lilongwe, Nyasatimes (2016). http://www.nyasatimes.com/2016/02/19/addressing-ict-gap-via-telecentres-in-malawi/
16. World Economic Forum: The Global Information Technology Report 2015. Insight Report (2015). Cited 3 July 2016. http://www3.weforum.org/docs/WEF_Global_IT_Report_2015.pdf
17. Maluwa-Banda, D., Lunguzi, J.M.: Basline Survey Report on Meeting Development and Participation Rights of Adolescent Girls in Malawi: Final Report for UNFPA, UNICEF, Department of Youth & National Youth Council of Malawi: Project MLW/01 (2002)
18. Elletson, H., Burgess, A.: The eLearning Africa Report 2015 (2015), ICWE: Germany
19. Hawkridge, D.: Machine-Mediated Learning in Third-World Schools? Mach. Mediated Learn. **3**(4), 319–328 (1989)
20. Ford, M., Botha, A.: A pragmatic framework for integrating ICT into education in South Africa. In: IST-Africa (2010)

21. Agyeman, O.T.: ICT for Education in Nigeria. Survey of ICT and education (2007)
22. Senzige, J., Sarukesi, K.: An approach to ICT-based school education in Tanzania. Afr. J. Finance Manag. **12**(2), 88–97 (2004)
23. Mishra, P., Koehler, M.J.: Technological pedagogical content knowledge: A framework for teacher knowledge. Teachers Coll. Rec. **108**(6), 1017 (2006)
24. Chai, C.S., et al.: Modeling primary school pre-service teachers' Technological Pedagogical Content Knowledge (TPACK) for meaningful learning with information and communication technology (ICT). Comput. Educ. **57**(1), 1184–1193 (2011)
25. Puentedura, R.: The SAMR model: Background and exemplars (2012) Cited July 3 2016; 2013. http://wiki.milaca.k12.mn.us/sandbox/groups/samr/wiki/welcome/attachments/9dbda/SAMR%20Geography%20Examples.pdf
26. Donner, J., Toyama, K.: Persistent themes in ICT4D Research: priorities for inter-methodological exchange. In: 57th Session of the International Statistics Institute, Durban, South Africa, pp. 17–21 (2009)
27. Hamel, J.-Y.: ICT4D and the human development and capabilities approach: The potentials of information and communication technology (2010)
28. Punya, M., Anurag, B.: ICTs in Schools: Why Focusing Policy and Resources on Educators, Not Children, Will Improve Educational Outcomes. In: The Global Information Technology Report 2015, USA, p. 73 (2015)

The Project Case: A West African Digital University

Adewunmi Obafemi Ogunbase[✉] and Roope Raisamo

Tampere Unit for Computer-Human Interaction (TAUCHI),
School of Information Sciences, University of Tampere, Tampere, Finland
femiogunbasea@hotmail.com, roope.raisamo@sis.uta.fi

Abstract. This paper is a project case report of a proposed West African Digital University that started based on the outcome of several research findings that focused on three West African countries mainly on export e-education through e-learning environments, which has been discussed as a way to improve African students' learning culture, designs and usability of web-based learning. The main aim and objective of this digital higher education institution are to contribute to the possible solutions to problems of higher education in developing countries, in particular the sub-Saharan West African countries by providing export e-education to West Africa citizens. The West African Digital University, put in practice, would develop students' minds and raise awareness for peace and tolerance as a way of integrating the West African region.

Keywords: West Africa (W/A) · Digital university · Higher education institution (HE) · Export e-education · e-learning environment/web-based learning environment

1 Introduction

The Economic Community of West African States (ECOWAS) in its education sector has increased the importance of export education through e-learning for higher education across the boundaries of ECOWAS in order to diversify member states' education systems and attract more international students [1].

To achieve this aim of ECOWAS, West African countries are facing challenges in the attempt to adopt export e-education due to the issues of educational policies in West African States' infrastructure, acceptance, accessibility and willingness of member states' governments, students and teachers or/and the perceived acceptability of e-learning methods [2, 3].

This project case for the West African Digital University report will focus on the processes and practice of achieving this ECOWAS aim through e-learning environments has been discussed as a way to improve African students' learning culture, designs and usability of web-based learning environments. Web-based environments/e-learning through a digital higher education institution have also been discussed to contribute to the possible solutions to problems of higher education in developing countries, in particular the sub-Saharan West African countries by providing export e-education to West Africa citizens. This is in order to develop students' minds and raise awareness for peace

© IFIP International Federation for Information Processing 2016
Published by Springer International Publishing AG 2016. All Rights Reserved
T. Brinda et al. (Eds.): SaITE 2016, IFIP AICT 493, pp. 174–181, 2016.
DOI: 10.1007/978-3-319-54687-2_17

and tolerance as a way of integrating the West African region [1], which is the main aim and objective of the West African Digital University.

This project case report will be based mainly on three parts in respect to the context of a case for the West African Digital University (an on-going project) as a medium of regional integration in West Africa. These parts are:

(1) The description of the electronic site of the Digital University and its infrastructures.
(2) The description of the traditional or physical site of the Digital University and its operational structures.
(3) The study contents and contexts, such as, university affiliations or partnerships, degree certifications, and the three educational actors' win-lose situations in West Africa focusing on education and export e-education as a way of promoting a culture of peace and tolerance.

Essentially, the practical and operational results of the West African Digital University would provide meaningful students' acceptance, accessibility and willingness of adopting export e-education (in higher education) through a smart digital higher education institution in West African developing countries. It would in practice and process showcase the solutions to questions that reflect on these areas of students' acceptance, accessibility and willingness of adopting export e-education (in higher education) through a smart digital higher education institution in West African developing countries.

2   Literature Review and Theoretical Background to the Region of West African States

The idea and motivation for the project for a West African Digital University reflects on the findings and outcomes of several research studies in respect to the followings:

- The benefits of e-learning, web-based learning and virtual learning that has been anticipated for more than a decade since governments and university educators and researchers have been discussing the change from the traditional teaching and learning methods based on the revolutionary adoption of technology and technology-supported approaches through use of computers [4].
- ECOWAS education sector's commentaries on the digital divide in education institutions among member states ready for e-learning and wed-based learning environments use show that less than 35% of higher education institutions in Gambia, Ghana and Nigeria had the infrastructures and equipments to effectively implement e-learning in their teaching and learning processes [4–6]. Despite these infrastructure and implementation problems, the West African governments through ECOWAS's education wing have been very active to develop educational technology policies to promote the use of technology in HE institutions in the region [1].
- Additional problems that seem to hinder development and adoption of online learning seem to include lack of motivation to adopt e-learning, lack of financial support, and lack of a clear-cut education development policy from the governments of these West African states in respect to their higher education systems [7].

- African learners' collective learning values as one of the key requirements to e-learning environment designs and usability in an African context, while learning through online, VLE, MOOCs and etcetera is learner centered. In this perspective, the study on cultural influences in the designs and usability of web-based learning environments from Africa and Europe points out that pedagogical designs for African learners should be based on learners' motivation and self-regulation among students as well as the higher reliance on group learning because the learning culture of the West African is influenced by strong values of collectivism and respect for authority [8].

It is based on these foregoing that the West African Digital University will implement and put into practice and process as a medium of promoting culture of peace and tolerance as a way of integrating the West African region through export e-education.

According to the United Nations [9], Western Africa includes the following sixteen countries: Cape Verde, Senegal, Gambia, Guinea, Guinea-Bissau, Sierra Leone, Liberia, Mali, Burkina Faso, Mauritania, Niger, Cote d'Ivoire, Ghana, Togo, Benin and Nigeria. These Western Africa countries formed the Economic Commission of West African States (ECOWAS) in 1975. Its mission is to promote economic integration in "all fields of economic activity, particularly industry, transport, telecommunications, energy, agriculture, natural resources, commerce, monetary and financial questions, social and cultural matters" [1]. Figure 1 shows the geographical locations of the sixteen member states of ECOWAS. These sixteen West African countries consist of former British, French and Portuguese colonies, and the West African Digital University will be focusing on these sixteen countries of ECOWAS, which will be referred to as West

Fig. 1. Geographical locations of the sixteen member states of ECOWAS Source: http://www.mfwa.org/wp-content/uploads/2015/11/ecowas_map.jpg

Africa in this project case report. Although the initial startup project of the West African Digital University will focus on the Anglo-phone West African countries of ECOWAS and later as it succeeds moves to the Franco-phone West African countries.

The practice and processes of the West African Digital University are going to be based on e-learning design and evaluating courses, designing e-modules, technical usability support, and project management for learning HE institutions in West Africa. It will enable less privileged ambitious West African youths to learn in different areas of academic excellences in different prominent universities within West African countries and especially, in Western European countries where about 75% of African students are presently studying either directly or indirectly [4]. This West African Digital University, as earlier stated, will serve as a way of integrating the West African region through the power of (higher) education in a flexible learning digital world.

3   The Project Case Report of the West African Digital University

The idea of the project case is to implement preceding research of this project case as possible solutions to these problems of higher education in West Africa. These previous research works are [4, 7, 10].

This section of the project report focuses mainly on three parts in respect to the context of a case for the West African Digital University (an on-going project) as a medium of regional integration in West Africa. These parts, processes and practice, are:

- The description of the electronic site of the West African Digital University and its infrastructures.
- The description of the traditional or physical site of the West African Digital University and its operational structures.

3.1   The Electronic Site and Its Infrastructures

The West African Digital University though is going to be a blended learning higher education institution with in-house real-time course programme activities. The blended approach will mainly be based on the idea of core technology and complementary technology [11]. The e-site features will mainly be based on core technology of WWW-based systems including information, communication, dissemination, collaboration and learning resources. This will be supported with a complementary approach of prints and real-time session learning activities, that is, complementary technology.

The West African Digital University will have its own specially developed tools, such as, 'tablet-computers', 'cloud-computing' internet server and tuition export e-education from the parenting HE institutions. The West African Digital University's web-based learning environment (e-site) will be linked with password to the partnerships/parents' module (VLE) sites for an effective e-learning system.

Project tools and manpower assistance and academic partnerships are anticipated from Nokia, Microsoft and Huawei for prototype tablet-computers and HE institutions from Finland, Netherlands and other prominent European and West African countries' universities.

The West African Digital University will be a 'wall-less' (education without border) HE institution with absolute contact via the World Wide Web (WWW). It will consist among others, of the followings:

(1) E-learning platform (i.e. e-books, e-classrooms, work activities, assessments and submissions, group discussion and feedbacks).
(2) Partnerships (i.e. collaborating foreign universities in W/A and Western European countries).
(3) E-learning degrees and courses that mainly based on HE such as Bachelor, Master, Doctorate and Doctoral degrees/courses in sciences (minor non-practical based sciences like mathematics and statistics), social sciences and education.
(4) The partnerships' e-learning modules (VLEs links).

Figure 2 below shows the proposed World Wide Web (WWW) layout of the anticipated West African Digital University's WBLE.

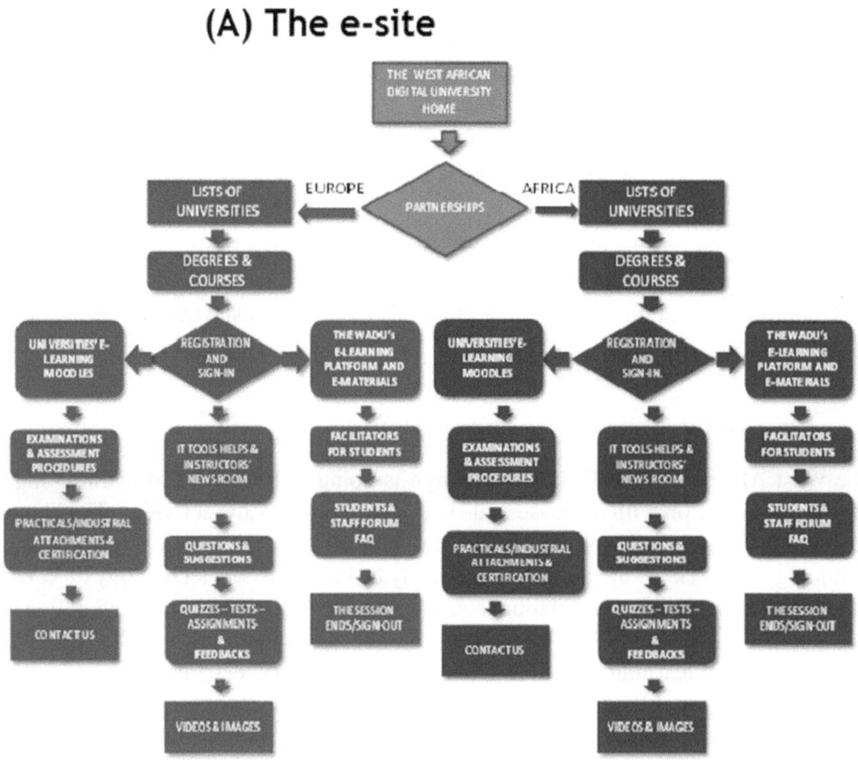

The proposed online layout of the West African Digital University's WBLE

Fig. 2. The E-site of the West African Digital University.

The study contents and contexts, such as, university affiliations or/and partnerships, degree certifications, and the three educational actors' win-lose situations focusing on education and export e-education as way of promoting a culture of peace and tolerance in W/A countries would be practically experienced in the project.

3.2   The Traditional/Physical Site and Its Operational Structures

The West African Digital University will have locations (traditional site) in three West African countries with a total of eight highly IT competent academic staff who will serve as facilitators supporting the students online via the e-site and from these different locations in the West African region.

The physical site structure will be the same in these three African countries and serves as a complementary approach to the core approach of learning activities of the West African Digital University. It is connected and run along with the e-site where students or/and visiting lecturers and researchers stay over, especially when different time zones are involved while learning with the parents' universities. And students and lecturers can also use the work or study rooms for real-time teaching and learning activities while on site. The physical site will also consist of studio or computer display rooms that will be used for live tele conferencing, live learning streams, on-site real time examinations, and other live real time teaching and learning activities. The physical site is shown in Figs. 3 and 4 below as floor layout drawing and building layout drawing respectively.

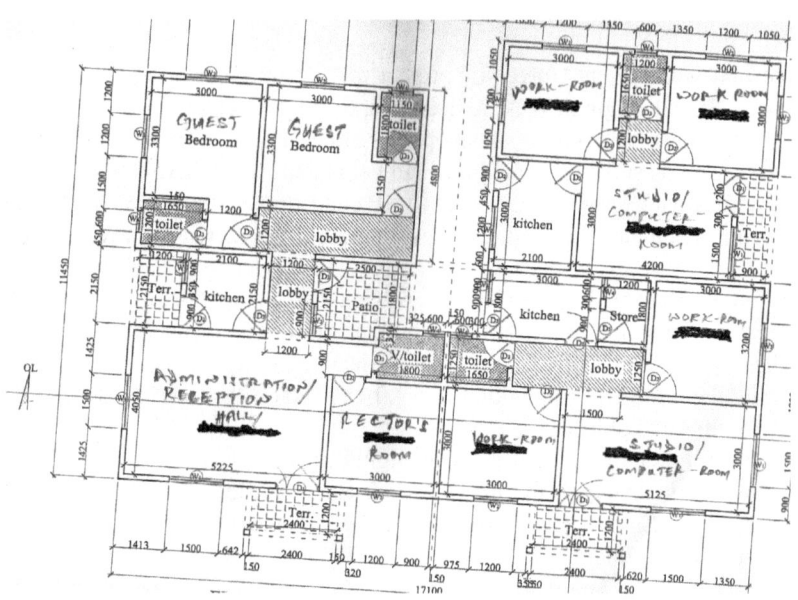

Fig. 3. The physical site - floor layout drawing

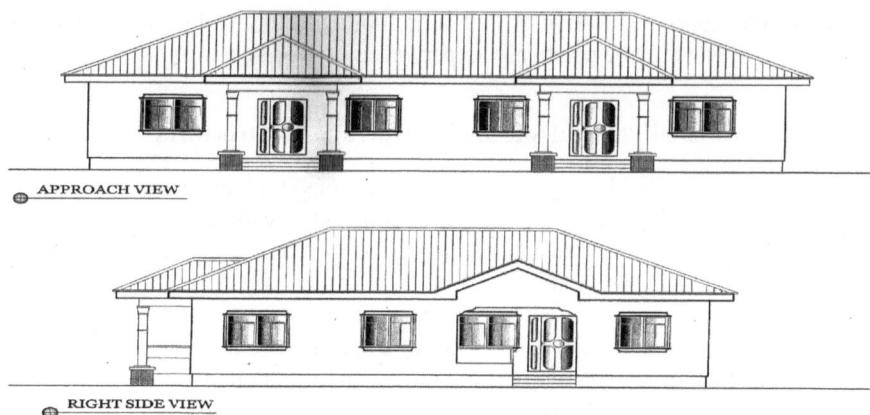

Fig. 4. The physical site - building layout drawing

The traditional/physical site will have its private owned electricity power supply, such as, owned electricity transformer and diesel powered generator, to solve the problem of distribution of public electricity supply.

4   Conclusion

The West African Digital University project will aim to contribute to the solutions to problem of HE education in West African countries by providing export e-education to West African citizens in order to develop their minds and raise awareness for peace and tolerance in the West African region. It will help tackle qualitative HE education challenges, such as, lack of universal access to HE education; poor quality of HE education and poor management of the education system; and the increasing irrelevance of the current West African HE education system in the knowledge society. It will help find possible solutions to the socio-economic problems, such as, gender aspect for e-learning (particularly well suited for female learners), armed conflicts resolution, cyber crimes and other socio-political ills facing West African countries. It will serve as a way of integrating the educated youths of West African region towards the development of ECOWAS aims and objectives.

The construction of the West African Digital University is in its development/start-up stage with initial start up in three West African countries (The Gambia, Ghana and Nigeria) and two European countries (Finland and Netherlands), already used as case study in the author's doctoral research study. Tuition, in form of export e-education, would be provided by partnership universities in West Africa and Western Europe notably, those European countries also used as case study in the author's doctoral research study [8].

The project would confirm students' supports, consents and willingness to access export e-education through an electronic higher education institution and applications of information communication technology in teaching and learning processes. It will confirm students' responses, accessibilities and willingness to use and acquire e-education at a higher education institution in West African countries. The West African Digital University will continue to promote the West African students' use of several forms of technologies in their learning process that also has implications for the design and usability of e-learning environments.

Many West African students have extensive experiences using computers connected to network applications and information communication technology use in e-learning, however, they need to be informed in the use of other collaborative learning tools embedded in a digital higher education institution. This major obstacle in this region of Africa would be minimised through the approach of a West African Digital University.

References

1. Ogunbase, A.: The West African Digital University: a case for reconstructing education/e-education and seizing the peace premium towards promoting a culture of peace and tolerance in post-conflict situations in West Africa. In: Proceedings of E-Learn: World Conference on E-Learning in Corporate, Government, Healthcare, and Higher Education 2015, pp. 1264–1273. AACE, Chesapeake, VA (2015)
2. Adams, J.: Understanding the factors that limit the acceptability of online courses and degrees. Int. J. E-Learn. 7(4), 573–587 (2008)
3. Siritongthaworn, S., Krairit, D., Dimmitt, N.J., Paul, H.: The study of e-learning technology implementation: a preliminary investigation of universities in Thailand. Educ. Inf. Technol. 11(2), 137–160 (2006). doi:10.1007/s11134-006-7363-8
4. Ogunbase, A.: Pedagogical design and pedagogical usability of web-based learning environments: comparative cultural implications between Africa and Europe. In: Proceedings of World Conference on Educational Multimedia, Hypermedia and Telecommunications, pp. 840–849. AACE, Chesapeake, VA (2014
5. Afoakwa, E.O.: Promoting a culture of peace – some useful thoughts. In: Paper Presented at the UNESCO 2003 Pre-conference on the Ways of Promoting a Culture of Peace, Pallervo Institute, Helsinki, Finland, 13–15 June (2003)
6. Oye, N.D., Salleh, M., Iahad, N.A.: Holistic e-learning in nigerian higher education institutions. J. Comput. 2(11), 20–26 (2010)
7. Ogunbase, A.: Acceptance and use of web-based learning environments/e-learning environments in higher education: West African learners experience. In: Proceedings of World Conference on E-Learning in Corporate, Government, Healthcare, and Higher Education 2014, pp. 1467–1475. AACE, Chesapeake, VA (2014)
8. Ogunbase, A.: Pedagogical design and pedagogical usability of web-based learning environments: comparative cultural implications from Africa and Europe. Doctoral dissertations in Interactive Technology, vol. 23. University of Tampere, Tampere (2016). ISBN 978-951-44-9756-8, ISSN 1795-9489
9. West Africa – Wikipedia article. http://en.wikipedia.org/wiki/West_Africa#Culture
10. Ogunbase, A.: Investigating the acceptability and accessibility of a smart digital university in West Africa (2016)
11. Collis, B., Moonen, J.: Flexible Learning in a Digital World: Experiences and Expectations. Stylus Publishing Inc., Sterling (2002). 22883 Quicksilver Drive, VA, 20166-2012, USA

Author Index